Early Colonial Religious Drama in Mexico:

FROM TZOMPANTLI TO GOLGOTHA

Early Colonial Religious Drama in Mexico:

FROM TZOMPANTLI TO GOLGOTHA

by
Marilyn Ekdahl Ravicz

The Catholic University of America
Press, Inc.

Washington, D.C. 20017

1970

Copyright © 1970 by
The Catholic University of America Press, Inc.
All Rights Reserved

Library of Congress Catalog No.: 77-76157
SBN 8132-0495-X

TABLE OF CONTENTS

PROLOGUE

ACKNOWLEDGMENT

PREFACE

I	The Prehispanic Background For The Study Of Colonial Drama	1
II	Colonial Religious Drama: Education And Culture Change	27

EXAMPLES OF EARLY RELIGIOUS DRAMA: TEXTS AND COMMENTARY

III	The Sacrifice of Isaac	83
IV	The Merchant	99
V	The Adoration of the Kings	119
VI	The Final Judgment	141
VII	How The Blessed St. Helen Found the Holy Cross	159
VIII	The Destruction of Jerusalem	181
IX	Souls and Testamentary Executors	211
X	Epilogue	235
	Notes	237
	Bibliography	255
	Index	261

prologue

The Prehispanic Background for the Study of Colonial Drama

WE EXIST—HERE!

Do men have roots; do men possess truths?
No one will truly understand
What your richness is, what your flowers are,
You—oh creator of yourself!¹

Men leave things imperfect.
Because of this I weep,
I am afflicted.

Here I entwine carefully my flowers
Of dignity and friends.
Let us rejoice!

Our common home is the earth.
Any beyond is the Place of Mystery.
But is it also here?
Oh, truly it is not the same!

Here upon the earth are flowers and song.
And here we men exist!

Acknowledgment

The author wishes to dispense with many of the formalities included in preface and prologue except those of acknowledgment. Since this study did not spring forth as a *fait accompli,* the author would like to extend her sincere gratitude for valuable assistance received from several other persons: to Robert Ravicz, *mi compañero,* for his personal aid and encouragement; to Byron McAfee, for the generous sharing of his unpublished manuscripts and the extension of editing privileges; to Miguel León-Portilla, for sharing answers to many questions; to Howard F. Cline, Director of the Hispanic Foundation of the Library of Congress; to the staff of the Latin American Library at the University of Texas; and to the many cataloguers, archivists, conversation-friends, Mexican *nanas,* and family members who made this study possible and pleasant in the doing.

PREFACE

I

The Prehispanic Background for the Study of Colonial Drama

The plan of this study is briefly this: to investigate one phase of the process of acculturation in the early Colonial period of Mexican history, that is, the use of religious drama as a didactic device directed toward the Indians of Mexico.

To accomplish this, certain phases of Prehispanic ritual life are described and related to the teaching techniques later chosen by the sixteenth-century Spanish colonizers. Individual plays for which we have sound historical references are discussed, as well as the legal status of religious drama, the mechanics of the general educating procedure, and the actual literary-didactic techniques of the early Spanish Christianizers.

Finally, seven plays, *each originally translated from Nahuatl*, are included as exemplary of the method and tradition under discussion. Three of these have never previously been published. The remaining four were published in Spanish during the late nineteenth century, however in booklet form and in such limited editions as to make it nearly impossible to consult them. None has been published in English.

The change from the value system which supported the *tzompantli* to that involved in what *golgotha* symbolizes was, and is, so complex that a comprehensive structural study of it has not yet been accomplished. Anthropologists are still doing research on this acculturation process. It is important to remember that when one studies a phase or aspect of cultural processes, one has mechanically isolated a part of an organic whole and therefore gives a limited picture. The author has chosen culturally limited symbols to represent an organic whole. The *tzompantli* was the skull-rack constructed adjacent to principal temples. These racks held the skulls of sacrificial victims as an everpresent mnemonic tribute to the gods and men that blood had been shed—as it always must be—to support the ongoing process of all being. The *tzompantli* is thus a powerful symbol of an ultimate goal of Prehispanic religious ritual, supported by the myths and cosmologies of the oral tradition. *Golgotha*, literally "place of the skull," is the name of the hill on which Christ was crucified. So it too is a symbol that blood has been shed so that there might be life more abundantly. Yet between these two similar symbols stands a vast expanse of different meanings, values, and metaphysical theories; the mental journey from one to another is difficult. Examples such as those which follow help to make it possible.

THE WISE MAN

The wise man: a light, a torch—a stout torch which does not smoke.
A pierced mirror, a mirror which is pierced on both sides.
His are the red and black colors,
His are the codices.
His are the books of pictures.[2]
Writing and wisdom these are the same.
They are as a road, a true guide for others.
This path leads men to know.
It is a guide in human affairs.
The truly wise man is careful like a physician,
And cherishes tradition.
He *is* the wisdom which is transmitted.
It is he who teaches and who follows truth.
A teacher of truth, he fails not to correct.
He makes wise the unwise,
And incites others to shape their persons.
He opens their ears. He illuminates them.
He is a teacher of ways, and gives men their proper road.
Upon him one depends;
He places a mirror before others.
He makes them prudent, careful.
He acts so that others might be transformed into complete persons.[3]

He is steadfast in life.
He regulates his road; he orders and arranges it.
He gives his light to the world.
He knows what is superior to us, and of the Region of the Dead.
The wise man is serious.
Whatever is invigorating to him is wisely learned.
Thanks to him the people humanize their desires,
And receive a strict indoctrination.
He comforts the heart; he comforts the people.
He aids; he meditates.
He cures all![4]

These are some of the poetic and philosophically sophisticated sentiments of the Aztecs of the fifteenth century, before a handful of zealous Spaniards and their mystifying horses managed completely to subjugate these warlike yet accomplished people. In 1521 with the arrival of the Spaniards, already predicted by ill omens to the Aztec priests, commenced the drama of historical interludes, catastrophes, and struggles which produced the present culture of Mexico. The unique quality of Mexican culture derives from an amalgam of indigenous and European-Christian elements. Basic to this cultural amalgam, and to the value system which supports it, is Mexican Roman Catholicism. Many of the reasons for the peculiarities of Mexican Catholicism lie in the methods of acculturation adopted by the early missionaries, whose most ardent desires were to replace paganism with Christianity, and indigenous ideas with a Spanish-inspired culture. Pyramid-temples were reduced to rubble, and Christian churches were built over their ruins. Prehispanic codices and the precious histories they depicted were destroyed; heavy tributes were exacted from the Indians, and thousands of them sickened and died through enforced slavery or new diseases. A complex culture which had produced notable scientific and esthetic creations, as well as a highly evolved social system, was laid low and virtually destroyed.

Yet the persistent survival of indigenous traits and cultural values endured to stamp the Christianizing process with an essentially unique flavor. This was possible principally because the missionaries used pre-existing religious patterns as often as possible in their evangelistic labors, and because many of them recognized the extreme importance of certain religious symbols and ritual trappings and employed these elements to their own ends.

One of the important ways in which the first missionaries used pre-existing religious patterns to reshape them to Christian specifications was the didactic device of a liturgical theatre created primarily for an indigenous audience.

Historians invariably describe the Aztec culture as having been theocratic and completely priest-ridden. While the degree to which these descriptions are true is debatable, from all that we do know about these people it can be said that extreme *religiosity* earmarked their culture. There is scarcely an artifact found, or a text or codex translated, which fails to attest the fact that the daily lives of the Aztecs were imbued with a preoccupation for ritual and things religious. These were a colorful and dramatic people, guided by a driving sense of their own religious destiny.[5] They were a people with a mission: to conquer but not to destroy; to conquer as a means to feed and sustain the gods; and constantly to replenish the ontological structure of the universe. They lived a drama with metaphysical implications of great purport.

The Aztecs, as latecomers into the valley of Mexico, developed a way of looking at the world which could be called a warrior mystique. This cult they developed largely independently of their Toltec precursors.[6] During the fifteenth century, and largely under the aegis of strong political leadership, there developed a vision of history in which the Aztecs truly saw themselves as the "people of the sun" or of Huitzilopochtli. Their mission was to subdue all the peoples of the world so that the life of the Sun might be preserved. Huitzilopochtli thus conserved the life of the fifth age or "sun" (in which the Aztecs lived at the moment of the conquest) by inspiring warfare for the purpose of capturing victims.[7] Thus it can be understood that the Wars of Flowers *("guerras floridas")* in which they engaged their neighbors were ritual wars with human sacrifice as the ultimate objective. This evaluation does not mean to ignore the usual socio-economic causes of warfare, but seeks merely to define the structural elements of the popular ideology which supported them.

The Nahuatl conception of the universe was based upon mathematical insights. Their conception of time as based upon numbers had been developed into remarkably correct calendar systems, both solar and lunar. The Toltecs, Nahuatl-speaking precursors of the Aztecs, were largely responsible for the creation of these calendrical systems, as they also were for the esthetic view of the universe later inherited and developed by the Aztecs.[8] The Aztecs used two calendars, the *Xiuhpohualli* or "count of the years", and the *Tonalpohualli,* or "count of the days or destinies". The *Xiuhpohualli* had eighteen groups or "months" of twenty days each, plus the five "useless" days or *nemontemi,* all equalling 365 days. The *Tonalpohualli* had twenty groups of thirteen days each, totalling 260 days, and revolved again and again. The *Xiuhpohualli* was therefore like a larger cog of 365 days which meshed with the smaller *Tonalpohualli* of 260 days. They were both part of a longer time division of fifty-two years, which for lack of a better name can be designated as the Aztec "century". The Aztecs had this to say about the Toltecs, their creative culture-ancestors:

> These Toltecs were most wise,
> > they customarily held dialogue with
> > > their own hearts.
>
> They gave origin
> > to the count of the year, *Xiuhpo-*
> > > *hualli,*
> > to the count of the days and des-
> > > tinies, *Tonalpohualli.*
>
> They determined how the day and the
> night gave auguries,
> > which signs of the days are good
> > > and profitable,

and which are not good;
And further which ones are called the
wild signs.
They created a system,
    the book of visions.
Those Toltecs were wise,
    they had an experienced knowledge
        of the stars in the sky.
They gave them names.
They knew their influence.
They knew well how the heaven moves,
    how it turns around.
This they saw in the stars.[9]

The Toltecs also developed the idea—which the Aztecs later held—of the temporal progression of the universe through ages or "suns". The Nahuatls had a cosmological sense of history and space. The earth was distributed into four large areas, each with its unique characteristics. Some conceived the west to be the region of the red; the south as the region of the blue; the east of the white; and the north of the black. Diverse gods influenced each of these quadrants which were also the seats of the four elements, earth, air, fire, and water. In the first four ages or "suns", the elements (earth, air, fire, and water) had each in its turn exercised an absolute dominance or autonomous influence over the ages. It was the opposition between these elemental forces, symbolized by deities, which caused the cataclysmic end of each age.

To explain the termination of cosmological struggle and destruction, and the possibility of subsequent harmony, a new view was developed. The fifth age, the *Ollintonatiuh* or "sun of Movement," was interpreted in a revolutionary way. Instead of defining the absolute and peculiar domination of each of the cosmic elements and their locations as had been formerly done, for each "sun" the idea of successive domination within the same age was introduced. The time of the fifth "sun" was therefore to be submitted to the successive influences of each of the four regions of the universe. In this "sun", time was to undergo a spatializing, so that there would be a reoccurence of the "year of the east", the "year of the west", of the north, south, and so on. This successive spatial domination included the implicated parallel domination of elements as well.

The frequent use of the symbolism of the number four is a complex and philosophic problem. The source of the importance of this number is uncertain, but the reason for its enduring conceptual importance to the indigenous Prehispanic cultures of Mesoamerica are apparent. Intersects of the number four were basic to their interpretations of the relationship of space and time. These ideas in turn influenced numerous cultural elements, such as the correct direction for architecture, the calendrical system, and the vigesimal counting system.[10]

The Nahuatl thinkers and poets were aware of the old myths about the ages or "suns" which succeeded each other in somber sequence and always terminated in cataclysms. This was reflected in poetry as the idea of the transitoriness of human existence. Personal experience clearly showed that man is on earth "for only a moment." They tried in their esthetic creations to absolutize this brief span with creations of ontological significance, that is with offerings in poetry of "flowers and song" which captured a moment of truth with metaphysical implications. They searched for truth, for that which would remain. The Nahuatl concept of truth or *neltiliztli* is derived from the syllable *nel*, whose connotation is that which is solid, firm, with roots, upright and constant.[11]

A number of extant Nahuatl poems deal with the fleetingness of life, and with the subsequent human resolution of this predicament: that is, either resignation and despair, or the "live for today, for tomorrow we die" attitude. The following is in the form of a dialogue with a god who is usually believed to be the Creator of Life, and deals with the possibility of speaking true words on earth:

> Can we perhaps say something true
> here, oh Giver of Life?

>   We are only dreaming, we are as if
>   awakening from sleep.
>   It is only as a dream . . .
>   No one here speaks the truth. . . .[12]

Or again:
>   Are men perhaps the truth?
>   Then therefore our song is not true.
>   What is there which is permanent?
>   What is there which comes out well?[13]

It is usually thought that the pantheon of the Aztecs was extensive and difficult to analyze. While its extensiveness is undeniable, it is clear from our extant texts that behind the many individual manifestations of deities the idea of one basic divine force as a dual principle had been developed. It had two faces, the one feminine and the other masculine; but it existed as one single god, the *Tloque Nahuaque,* Lord of the Near and the Far. The *Tloque Nahuaque* is the giver of life, who is always creating himself *(Moyocoyani).*[14]

The following poem from the *Informantes de Sahagún* refers to this conception:

>   The Toltecs knew that the heavens are
>   many.
>   They said that there are twelve divi-
>   sions superimposed.
>   There he exists;
>   There lives the true god and his con-
>   sort (alter-being).
>   The celestial god is called Lord of
>   Duality.
>   His counterpart is called Lady of
>   Duality, Celestial Woman.
>   This means that he is Lord over the
>   twelve heavens.
>   From there we receive life,
>   do we the men, the *macehuales.*
>   From there springs our destiny

Prehispanic Background of Colonial Drama

> as it is placed when the little child
> is born.
> From there comes his being and his
> destiny.
> They are placed within him
> as the Lord of Duality ordains it.[15]

It is clear that the Nahuatl speakers had evolved a highly sophisticated concept of god and cosmology.

The ritual cycle of the Aztecs exemplified dramatic elements. The ritual year *was* the calendrical year imbued with negative and positive values ascertained through astronomical calculations. For the people, the unfolding of the seasons became a narration, the content of which was ultimately controlled by the gods; but it was the sacred duty of man to fill the roles dedicated to placation, thanksgiving, or avoidance of undesirable events.

In this fashion, each ritual became a dramatic enactment of the relationship of the Aztecs to their gods, and through them to the universe itself. In order that the people might share in and empathize with the realization of this relationship and be taught the religious content of their culture in a dramatic fashion, the role of the particular god whose ritual was being celebrated was literally enacted by a chosen member of the celebrants themselves; the ritual was commemorated in the manner of a passion play.

Each of these religious rituals can be analyzed as containing the following dramatic elements: they represented narrative content; they incorporated music; they utilized the dance; they involved rudimentary plots in which action involved or was precipitated by the protagonist; they included elaborate costuming of their dramatic personages; they used staging and sound effects; they utilized monologues, dialogues, or colloquies to support the dramatic action of the ritual; and, lastly, they were performed as spectacles involving both the audience and the performers. They did not involve western or Aristotelian concepts of tragedy or comedy, proper divisions of action into beginning, middle, and end; nor was the dramatic action divided into acts and scenes in the manner with which the Western world is familiar.

The narrative content of each religious ritual or *fiesta* defined the significance of the celebration concerned; often it centered upon the thematic homily of man's reoccuring duties to the gods. Foremost among these duties was man's sacred obligation to maintain or "feed" the gods; thus they culminated in ritual sacrifice often involving human victims. Descriptions of many of these ceremonies are presented in the chronicles of the sixteenth-century Spanish *conquistadores* and missionaries.

Since the Aztecs did not have a written language before the conquest, we are dependent for our knowledge of these religious practices upon these sixteenth-century chroniclers, and upon available archeological evidence. Since Nahuatl, the spoken language of the Aztecs, contained only twenty-seven phonemes, the first priests found it an easy task to transcribe the phonetic system of the Aztecs into the Roman alphabet. Consequently, they were able to transmit and preserve some of the texts of these celebrations through the use of educated indigenous informants who had knowledge of the extensive ceremonial oral tradition of their people.[16]

The following descriptions of important Aztec calendrical rituals are from Book II of the *Florentine Codex* by Fray Bernardino de Sahagún; the dramatic elements they exemplify are notable.[17]

> In the fifth month, the *fiesta* in honor of Tezcatlipoca:
> This *fiesta* was the most important of the feasts. It was like Easter, and fell near Easter Sunday—a few days after . . . .
> When, on this feast, they slew the young man who had been reared for (the role), they at once produced another, who was to die after one year. He walked everywhere in the town finely arrayed, with flowers in his hand, and with people who accompanied him. He greeted with good grace those whom he met. All knew that this one was the likeness of Tezcatlipoca, and they bowed before him and worshipped him whenever they met him.

In the seventh month was the *fiesta* in honor of Uixtociuatl:

> They said that she was the elder sister of the Tlaloc gods. In honor of this goddess they slew a woman decked in the ornaments with which they represented the same goddess. . . . Among them went the woman who was to die arrayed in rich ornaments. . . . Thus dancing, they took many captives to the pyramid of Tlaloc, and, with them, the woman who was to die, who was the likeness of the goddess Uixtociuatl. They slew first the captives and then her.[18]

There was yet another type of calendrical religious celebration:

> (In the (1) second month feasts when all the captives taken in war died . . . there were mock and real gladiatorial contests.
>
> . . . Then all four (acted as if) fighting. They raised their shields and war clubs (as offerings) to the sun . . . . And therefore Youallauan came forth, garbed like Totec; only he came last, after the others, behind the four great eagle and ocelot (warriors); they lifted up their shields and war clubs, offering them and dedicating them to the sun. Then all the impersonators, the proxies, of all the gods emerged in order, ahead of all. They were called the lieutenants, the delegates, the images. They . . . came in order . . . . They came hence, from Iopico, from the very top of the pyramid temple of Iopitli.[19]

Many other examples from the same detailed description of the rituals celebrating the calendrical year could be quoted, but these are representative enough to be exemplary of this kind of dramatic enactment.

In Prehispanic Nahuatl culture, it was the aristocratic class of *señores* (or lords) and the priests in charge of maintaining the ceremonial traditions of the culture who kept the history alive. The priestly class accomplished this by controlling the body of knowledge available to the people and by dominating the educational systems of all the social classes. The *señores* or lords maintained and furthered the traditions in time of war by fighting, and in time of peace by acting as patrons and fostering the composition of songs or poetry which defined the glorious history and military prowess of the Aztecs. These compositions were almost invariably of both a religious and historical nature.

It has been conjectured that the early forms of some of the myths or cultic hero stories contained elements clearly dramatic in nature. For example, the famous poem entitled *Hymn of Netzahualcoyotl* appears to have vestiges of original dialogue, and the first portion of the poem can be considered to contain notations tantamount to stage directions.[20]

Angel Garibay, in his *Historia de la Literatura Nahuatl*, describes the process and development of such Nahuatl poetry which he designates as "dramatic poetry"; briefly, the lords of a given region would meet together by invitation of one of their number and would present songs in honor of a chosen historical event or of their collective deeds of valor. These symposia were called *cohuayotl icniuhyotl*, that is, "collaborations," or "reunions of friends."[21]

In the manuscript entitled *Cantares Mexicanos* from the area of Huexotzinco are several examples of these poems. For example, during the first decades of the sixteenth century, there was a king named Tecayehuatzin, who invited the princes of his area to a literary symposium. According to custom, they all met in the patio of his residence which had been decorated with flowers and the branches of blossoming trees.[22] Some of the names mentioned can be identified through other historical references. While the various members of the group presented their poetic offerings, the remainder acted as audience. Each lord brought with him his singer and/or chorus, as well as the necessary musicians for his presentation. There was a division of labor among the acting participants: there was the "singer" or one who actually *composed* the poem; the ones who actually *enacted* the verbal portion of the poetic composition; and the various musicians who furnished the orchestration and *played* the instruments which provided the accompanying music.

In the *Cantares Mexicanos* are included some "stage" directions which help us to understand some of the dramatic elements of this poetry. Some of the poems have included at their beginnings such signs as: *"ti qui to co"* in various permutations; these serve as rhythmic directions for the percussion accompaniment, that is, the drums were to create like rhythmic patterns to those specified. Many of the dramatic poems contain further instructions that both music and dance should accompany them. Here are a few examples from the *Cantares Mexicanos* to clarify the references given.

NICAN OMPEHUA TEPONAZCUICATL
 (The songs start here with the *teponaztli*.) [23]
TICO TOCO TOCO TOCO
IC ON TLANTIUH CUICATL
 (Here the song is rhytmically diminished.)
 (Folio 2).

TICO TOCO TOCO
TIQUITI QUITI QUITI QUITI
ZAN IC MOCUEPTIUH
 (With this annotation is given the rhythmic pattern serving as the cue for the dancers' steps.)
 (Folio 27).

TOTO TINOCO YANICA
 (Same as *crescendo agitato*.)
 TLAXCATECAYOTL IC ON HUEHUETL
 (Tlaxcaltecan song; the *huehuetl* makes a *diminuendo*.) [24]
 (Folio 54).

The texts and general tenor of the poems indicate both the change of persons and situations for the presentation. There may be several interlocutors involved, some announcing themselves with, *"Soy fulano . . . ,"* "I am such a one."[25]

That costumes were often used during the course of the poetic symposia is attested by Sahagún in the *Florentine Codex*, where the following description is noted:

If the song were to be intoned after the manner of Huexotzinco, they (the singers) were adorned like men of Huexotzinco, and they spoke even as they did; they were imitated with the song and in their adornment and in their equipment. Likewise, if the song were to be intoned after the manner of Anahuac, the speech of the men of Anahuac was imitated, and their adornment as well as their equipment.[26]

No stage annotations or character part names are contained in the margins of the manuscripts of these dramatic poems as are customarily included in plays today. Since these works were really conceived as dramatic songs to be presented with music, in Garibay's opinion they might best be categorized as melodrama.[27] Actually, they are comprised of a series of dramatic situations, interludes, and scenes, sometimes with diverse characters reciting what would properly fall within one strophe. The poems include monologues, dialogues, and colloquies; scholars of Nahuatl claim that they are of high literary quality.[28]

The following is an example of a melodramatic poem in the Prehispanic Nahuatl literary tradition. It is written with three interconnected parts. The first fragmentatary portion deals with the well-known theme of the departure of the beloved culture hero Quetzalcóatl from Tula. One singer commences and sets the scene:

SINGER: He had a home in Tula made of woodly things.
          Today only the serpent-form columns remain standing in rows.
          He fled! He left all orphaned, did our prince Nácxitl.[29]
          a chorus of singers chant the refrain.
CHORUS: With trumpet shells our princes are mourned.
          Ah, truly he has fled! He will lose himself thither in Tlapala![30]
SINGER: Thither we shall journey to Cholula
          Hard by the mountain of subtle mists,
          To the place of the rain, to the place of the boats.
CHORUS: With trumpet shells our princes are mourned.
          Ah, truly he has fled! He will lose himself thither in Tlapala!

There follows an interlude of dance and song without words, but during which the exclamations "HUAY AYAY OYAHO" are often used. These appear to be rhythmic devices without semantic content. This interlude is of uncertain duration. Next follows a brief dialogue between the nobles or princes *Ihuiquecholli* and *Matlacxochitl,* the latter of whom is the king successor to Quetzalcóatl.

IHUIQ: I come from Nonoalco, I Ihuiquecholli,
       I the prince Mamalli, whom he left desolate.
MATLAC: I am sick at heart. My king is gone.
        Ihuitimalli (Quetzalcóatl) has left me orphaned,
        Alone am I, Matlacxochitl!
IHUIQ: Cleft asunder are the mountains.
       Because of this I weep!
       The shining sands are rebellious.
       Because of this I weep!

There follows an enumeration of the various places to which the king has fled; and the second part concludes with another song of pure exclamations. There follows the third and final part comprised of alternating songs between the singer and the chorus.

SINGER: In the place of the mist, he is not there.
        In the place of the mist, he is not there.
CHORUS: How can you leave desolate all your homes?
        How can you leave empty all your palaces?
        Oh, you have left them orphaned in Tula, thence
           in Nonoalco!
SINGER: Even you yourself weep, prince Timal.
        Even you yourself weep, prince Timal.
CHORUS: How can you leave desolate all your homes?
        How can you leave empty all your palaces?
        Oh, you have left them orphaned in Tula,
           thence in Nonoalco!

There follows a section of music and dance without words, and then a new and final set of recitatives.

SINGER: You have left them painted in wood and in stone
thither in Tula.
Let us cry out!
CHORUS: Oh, Nácxitl, our prince,
Never shall your reknown be quenched.
Your vassals shall weep for it.
SINGER: Only the house of turquoise remains upright,
The house of serpents which you left standing,
thither in Tula.
Let us cry out!
CHORUS: Oh, Nácxitl, our prince,
Never shall your reknown be quenched.
Your vassals shall weep for it.

Without a knowledge of the meanings of the names and symbols mentioned in the body of the text, the sense of the poem may remain obscure; however, the above example serves to give some idea of the form and body of the Prehispanic dramatic poem.

This poem concludes with a final song and dance. The scene changes, and the characters appear to go farther and farther away, rather in the style of a fadeout. Quetzalcóatl (or Nácxitl) is accompanied by the Toltec princes. We can only imagine their costumes and demeanor.[31]

During the frequent and complex Aztec ritual celebrations, in addition to the representational elements of those who played the roles of the gods and goddesses, other dramatic components were present such as the ritual enactment of stories and myths in dances, mock battles and gladiatorial combats, and many satirical or farcical interludes.

The extant sources of information pertaining to these dramatic enactments are three: primarily the aforementioned sixteenth-century descriptions of the chroniclers; secondly, the pictorial references in the codices which are genuinely related to Prehispanic times; and finally, archeological investigations, which have revealed architectural details as well as Prehispanic murals and vases which depict dancing figures, groups of musi-

Prehispanic Background of Colonial Drama

cians, and processions of priests with sacrificial victims carefully costumed for the roles which they are enacting.[32]

We know from existing manuscripts that the Aztecs also had travelling troubadours called *tlaquetzqui,* who circuited the villages and seignorial estates, singing the myths and the traditional historical and religious stories in a dramatic fashion. Their theatrical abilities were highly prized, and they were described as those of the *"boca florida"* (flowery mouth or speech). Some *tlaquetzqui* specialized in dramatic poetry of a decidedly obscene or farcical nature. For example, there are extant but untranslated several manuscripts with bits of dramatic interludes dealing with lively conversations between prostitutes and clowns, as well as the more serious dramatic elaborations on mythical themes. These little farcical interludes tell us much about the social problems and daily life of the Pre-Conquest Aztecs.

We have one Nahuatl[33] manuscript of a dramatic interlude among some prostitutes entitled "Song of the Little Women."[34] Some of the meanings and allusions in this play are obscure; however, it is clear that the plot revolves around a main character whose name is NANOTZIN. She is a prostitute who seems to be having love problems as prostitutes so often have in the history of drama. She, Nanotzin, is talking to a few of her fellow workers and also to her mother. The dialogue is interesting mainly because it expresses the philosophy of these women who played such an important role in the society of the time.

As the scene opens, a friend says to Nanotzin, who is apparently downcast:

CHALCHIUHNENE: Have I perhaps wounded you somehow, my sister Nanotzin?

NANOTZIN: Oh friend, actually I don't even know. Let us go to my house. My mother is there.

CHALCHIUHNENE: Nanotzin, where did he go then?

NANOTZIN: Oh, that I might die, my companion!

Truly, he didn't even understand! Come, my friend, there is my mother.

(The MOTHER *asks the girls to enter, and then bids her daughter to remain with her; in this way perhaps she would find a little peace.)*

MOTHER: Oh come! Enter in with me a little while. If you do this, perhaps you'll find a little peace.

(Two new characters appear. They are also prostitutes, but clearly disillusioned ones. They are designated as being reformed women. The first one speaks to NANOTZIN's *mother.)*

QUETZALMIYAHUAXOCHITL: Oh, my mother, my heart detests itself! Oh, many are those who have lived for pleasure and for happiness—and perhaps some have passed by here—and yet you censure me for the same idea. My man lived in pleasure, my mother! These were my visage and thoughts; but what did I understand in those days? Oh, and now I weep, do I, a woman of pleasure! But others have gone on before me like this, and I shall die in the same way.

(The action and references go back to NANOTZIN, *who is suffering some kind of love sickness. The prostitute friend, who has also suffered, tries to laugh at herself. She gives the following counsel):*

QUETZALMIYAHUAXOCHITL: I, well I simply try to laugh at myself! How, you ask? Well—you laugh with me, my friend! 'Though I weep because I shall die in the same state, yet I—well, I shall simply laugh at myself!

(The reformed prostitute points to the dissolute life lived by most other prostitutes; concluding, she says that it would be

much better to be in love with oneself than to go about getting involved with others. She says:)

QUETZALXOCHITL: I am Quetzalxóchitl. I am in love with myself—a beautiful woman! I blame my companions Cozcamalintzin and Xiuhtlamiyahuatzin because they live so dissolutely! So carefully do they wash and care for their heads! (make their toilette). My mother! You, oh my mother, you too blame my friends Cozcamalintzin and Xiuhtlamiyahuatzin because they live so dissolutely, and so carefully do they wash and care for their heads.

(At this point as an interlude, a young man, AHUIZOTL, *appears and pronounces a poem full of vain ideas elevated to philosophic stature. Perhaps influenced by* AHUIZOTL's *ideas, they again turn to hear* NANOTZIN's *words. She sums up her personal views about pleasure and states that she doubts that she will survive personal unhappiness.)*

NANOTZIN: What then shall I have? My man values me simply as a red woodland flower. But when I have become withered in his hands, he will but abandon me!

Apparently the Aztecs had a high appreciation of little farces and comedies of a secular nature which were often presented in the marketplaces as well as in the private patios of the *señores*. Mendieta describes the posturing of clowns as:

These as I have said are buffoons and they go about ready to perform, making many gestures and saying many amusing and witty things, which make everyone watching and hearing them laugh. Some go about as old women, and others as fools.[35]

Both Sahagún and Bernal Diaz mention the presence and appreciation of court jesters, that is, of dwarfs, hunchbacks, and other malformed individuals who furnished entertainment for the king and for his royal court of nobles. They sang, tumbled, gave poetic readings, and enacted little farces or brief interludes.

In the *Informantes de Sahagún* is mentioned a kind of entertainer named the *teuquiquixti,* that is, "he who brings forth and makes move the gods." The *teuquiquixti* was a kind of puppeteer who carried about with him a bag of little figures primarily of the gods and goddesses. He would present his performances in the marketplaces, in private patios, or wherever he could command a paying and interested audience. A brief description of his activities as included in the *Informantes de Sahagún* follows:

(He would take out of his bag those [puppets] which he had with him.) They would come out, some as little children. Some are women and their costumes are very well done, for example, their skirts and blouses. In the same manner, the young men were very well costumed; that is, their breechclouts, their capes, and their collars were of precious stones. They dance, sing, and represent whatever his (the puppeteer's) heart desires. When they are finished, he puts them into the bag again until the next performance. For this they (the audience) give recompense to the one who "brings out, and moves or makes representations with the god-figures."[36]

Again, the same text alludes to the popularity of magicians who performed in the marketplaces or in the patios of fine houses, and who accomplished such remarkable tricks as: creating the illusion of cutting off their hands and feet, only to have them reappear as unblemished; or of seeming to set fire to the surrounding houses so that they actually appeared to be burning. For this too these prestidigitators were amply reimbursed.[37]

Because of the great importance of music and dance in the culture of the Aztecs, the priests as educators maintained special schools for the training and preparation of composers, musicians, singers and dancers. These schools were called *cuicacalli,* and were constructed usually within temple compounds and adjacent to the principal temples.[38] That there was a highly inflected division of labor in the production of song and dance is evident from the following quotation from Sahagún:

Prehispanic Background of Colonial Drama

There were also then prizes. . . . They gave presents to all the singers: singers of the dance; composers of songs; directors of the song. This was also true for the musicians: those who played the drum; to those who had the *huehuetls* and who played them; to those who spoke the words of the poet; to those who composed the melody; to those who arranged and produced it; and to those who whistled or clapped their hands (in imitation of battle noises); to those who directed the others; to those who danced representing something; to those who danced in groups; to those who initiated the dance steps; to those who enacted the farcical songs; to those who chanted the funeral dirges; and to those who did acrobatic dances.

The following description from the *Codex Ramirez* gives us a sixteenth-century account of both the place and kind of performance which was popular among the Nahuatl speakers. This excerpt refers to the temple and worship of the god Quetzalcóatl in Cholula:

This temple had a moderate [sized] patio, where, on the day of his *fiesta* [that of Quetzalcóatl] were performed great dances, with much merriment, and very amusing farces. For the purpose of these, there was a small theater which was about thirty feet square, and quaintly decorated, in the middle of this patio. The people covered this with boughs of flowers and adorned it with all neatness possible for that day, encircling it entirely with arches made of a variety of flowers and feathers. And they suspended at intervals many birds and rabbits and other meek things. After having eaten, all the people gathered there and the actors [*representantes*] came out and performed farces. They pretended to be deaf, seized with colds, limping, blind, and maimed, all coming to ask health of the idol. The deaf were acting ridiculously, those with colds (were) coughing and wheezing, and the lame were limping and listing their many miseries and complaints. All this made the people laugh greatly. Then others representing little creatures entered, some dressed as beetles, some as toads, and others as lizards. . . . Gathered together there, each announced his role; and in turn each told certain stories which greatly pleased the audience, for they were most ingenious.

In the same manner, they imitated many birds and butterflies of diverse colors. And the [temple boys] also donned various of these costumes, and climbed up into a tree planted there. The priests of the temple fired upon them with peashooters, and made witty sayings in defense of some and as offence to others, with which they entertained the audience. This concluded, there was a great *mitote* or dance by all these personages, and this terminated the celebration. This they were accustomed to do on their most important feasts.[39]

Fray Diego Durán includes the following description pertinent to the dramatic elements present in Aztec ritual celebrations:

Many other kinds of dances and amusements did the Indians have for the solemn celebrations of their gods. They composed a different song for each idol according to his merit and magnitude; and even many days before the arrival of the celebration they held great rehearsals of the songs and dances for that day. For the new songs they brought out different costumes and ornaments of fabric and feathers; headdresses and masks were styled according to the themes of the songs which were composed, thus conforming them to the solemnity of the commemorations. And so they disguised themselves sometimes as eagles, other times as tigers and lions, or as soldiers, or as people of the *Huazteca* [inhabitants of an area to the north and east,] or as hunters, or as savages, or as cunning dogs, or as a thousand other semblances.

The dance which pleased them most was that for which they wrapped themselves around and crowned themselves with adornments of blossoms. For this dance they made a house of flowers in the principal *momoztli*[40] of the temple of their great god Huitzilopochtli; and with their hands they fashioned trees there, full of fragrant flowers. There they placed the goddess Xochiquetzalli, while young men dressed as birds and butterflies—all beautifully adorned with feathers of rich greens, blues, reds, and yellows—climbed up into the trees and went about from bough to bough as if sucking up the dew from the roses. Then the gods came out, each dressed as the Indians saw them on their altars, that is, in the same manner, and with their particular symbols in their hands. They walked about and fired upon the birds climbing in the trees.[41] Then the goddess of the flowers, who was Xochiquetzalli, came out and received them and took their hands; she seated them all together with much honor and respect as such gods indeed merit. Next she gave them flowers and pipes (to smoke) to give the gods—or their representatives—rest (pleasure).[42]

Durán also refers to the presentation of farces and little comical interludes:

> They have another dance of the old men in which they dance with bent backs and with the masks of old men; this is not a little amusing or entertaining. In the same comical vein, they have a dance and song of the buffoons in which they introduce a fool who pretends to understand what his master orders and then changes the words and meanings all about.[43]

All of the known references to dramatic presentations of either large or small proportions define these events as taking place out-of-doors. For the literary symposia, the private patios or courtyards of residences were used. For religious celebrations, mock battles, and other presentations or dances of a larger scope, courtyards or other special areas within temple compounds were used. In a collection of letters sent by Cortés to Charles V is contained the first post-Conquest reference to "theaters" as they undoubtedly existed before as well as immediately after the arrival of the Spaniards. In the third letter is the following brief allusion to a theater in Tlaltelolco:

> ... in something like a theater which was in the middle of it (the plaza), made of lime and stone, square, and of two and a half yards in height, and of thirty paces from corner to corner. They (the Aztecs) used this when they held religious celebrations and games which their actors *(representadores)*

presented there; so that all the people who were in the market as well as those who were below and beside the portals were able to see what they were doing.⁴⁴

Archeological excavation and restoration of areas within temple compounds of considerable scope reveal that such raised diases were often constructed in front of one or more of the principal temples of a ritual center. These are similar in appearance to the one described by Cortés, and most likely were used for the same purposes as those mentioned in the quotation. These would seem to have furnished settings *par excellence* for dramatic enactments of a ritual nature. That they were used as dance platforms is also likely; and that they were used as oratories for sacrifices is certain.

Each temple was constructed on the pattern of a pyramid, the actual temple housing being on the peak or top of the pyramid, and the entire lower portion consisting primarily of stairways and superimposed platforms of succeedingly smaller dimensions. The priests and whoever else were concerned in any particular ritual situation enacted their roles both within the temple housings on the great stairways and stepped platforms, or in the courtyards around the temples concerned.⁴⁵ Since the processions, dances, and pageantry culminating in the ritual sacrifice comprised the content of these celebrations, and since the use of much music and many elaborate and colorful costumes were also standardized components of these events, the general effect upon the audience as well as upon the actors themselves must have been very great.

In addition to the few surviving mauscripts in Nahuatl which contain dramatic poems, myths, or other theatrical interludes, a text survives from a Prehispanic dramatic ballet or drama from the May-Quiche culture which was centered to the south and east of the main Aztec culture stream. At the time of the conquest, however, the Mayans were under the military and occupational jurisdiction of the more warlike Aztecs. This drama, entitled the *Rabinal Achi*, delineates the capture, interrogation, and death of a warrior who has committed certain reprehensible acts. Each speech is initiated with a salutation and ends with a pat phrase. There are many standardized forms of courtesy used as well as much repetition and a montonous reiteration of questions and answers.[46] The action is slow and deliberate, and the dialogue enlarged by the pattern of formality represented; the play includes the use of both dance and musical interludes. That this drama is an accurate reflection of the customary ritualization and formalization of almost every daily event in the Mayan culture is probably true. Every phrase seems permeated with religiosity and didacticism.

We know from the literature and descriptions preserved by the chroniclers that Aztec culture likewise exhibited strongly ritualized and didactic mannerisms, and that religion formalized most daily events and personal relationships. In this analogy one departs from fact, and we can only imagine that if a complete Nahuatl drama of the same type were extant it might well be similar in style to the *Rabinal Achi* of the Maya-Quiche.

The presence of genuine theater in the Yucatan has been attested to by Bishop Diego Landa and Pedro Sánchez de Aguilar. Scholars have written about the presence of early theater in South America, especially in Cuzco, where the drama entitled the *"Ollantay"* is believed by many to have been presented in the Prehispanic era. Sánchez de Aguilar states the following about the theater in the Yucatan:

> They had and they have many farces which represent stories and histories. The speeches and jokes which they recite are most amusing . . . and in order to understand them and to know whom they are ridiculing, one must know their language very well, both the phrases and modes of speaking which they have in their dialect, and the conversations which are both witty and amusing.[47]

All of the excerpts quoted are reminiscent of one another; that is, from any one of them one could abstract one or more ideas about Prehispanic theater in general and probably be correct.

II

Colonial Religious Drama: Education and Culture Change

Before turning to the section of this study which deals with the kind of theater presented in central Mexico during the early colonial period, especially the sixteenth century, a few ideas should be clarified about the theater in Spain, which influenced the particular form of drama later used in Mexico; for it will become clear that Mexican theater is a blending of Spanish elements with some of the indigenous traditions to which we have already referred.

Italy was the first Christian country to celebrate widely the religious drama. At first, this drama consisted principally of mysteries and farces; the latter purported to serve as controlled and censored versions of the popular, more bawdy farces of a secular nature. By the time that Pope Innocent III had forbidden the clergy to take part in these farces, they had already spread to other countries.

Farces and mysteries had reached Spain by the eleventh century. The Spanish form came to represent a blending of the mystery, the morality, and the allegory drama.[48]

The oldest extant example of Spanish religious drama was composed for presentation on the Epiphany, that is, the sixth of January. It is entitled *"Auto de los Reyes Magos," ("Auto of the Magi")*, and dates from the first part of the thirteenth century.[49] It probably came first from France, and was then translated into fairly rude Spanish of the epoch. One hundred and forty-seven verses of this drama are extant; they contain the monologues of the Kings on their way to Bethlehem.[50]

At first, liturgical dramas were simply presented either before the altar and/or below the choir of the church. Priests both wrote and enacted these dramas, and children's choruses of music were often included. The purpose of presentation was clearly that of instruction with an adjunct of entertainment. A simple row of chairs could represent heaven or hell; but paradise was usually carefully situated in the altar itself. As liturgical dramas became more popular and larger areas were required for presentation, they were moved to the *atrium* of the church, and perhaps then to the space immediately outside the church; and finally they moved to the public plazas or to little *carros* or wagons which were used as movable stages.[51] The scenario and costuming for the religious drama became increasingly complex until large ornate staging devices were commonly used, and a desire for extreme realism in settings dictated the pattern of presentation.

Before the thirteenth century, *Corpus Christi* was celebrated in particular churches. In 1264 Pope Urban IV extended this celebration to all Christians by the papal bull entitled *Transiturus*. This celebration was always to be held on Thursday after Trinity Sunday and "everlastingly to commemorate the institution of the Holy Eucharist." [52]

At first, *Corpus Christi* was commemorated with a certain amount of merriment and accompanied by a few religious scenes or interludes. During the fourteenth century the allegorical elements of the morality plays become associated with the historical and dogmatic elements of the mysteries. From this union came a new genre of religious drama, theological in nature and with elements of both the biblical and the scholastic. This form, known as the *auto sacramentale,* is a Spanish aberration of a more general liturgical drama.

In the beginning, the feast of *Corpus Christi* was the usual occasion for the presentation of the *autos,* but ultimately the *autos* themselves became the most essential element of the *Corpus Christi* celebration.[53] Because of their theological flavor, they were peculiarly suited to the commemoration of the feast in which was instituted the greatest Christian theological mystery, the Eucharist.[54]

In the *autos,* the Eucharist was not usually directly treated, but rather referred to by intermediaries such as one or two people discoursing upon the subject. Later, a new genre of allegory grew out of this subject, utilizing materials from the Old and the New Testaments; this kind of allegory became the core of the *auto sacramentale*. As the *auto* form became more complex, *loas* or introductory salutations of praise and bids for the attention of the audience were added to them, and they often ended with a *villancico* or carol.[55]

This was the general state of the development of the religious drama in Spain at the time of the Spanish conquest in the New World.

The *autos* which were originally designed for *Corpus Christi* were later used for other church *fiestas* such as: Christmas, Epiphany, Easter, and the most important saints' days. The *coloquio*, a simpler literary dramatic form, also became very popular in Mexico. The *coloquio* is most often written in dialogue form; it can be written in either prose or verse, and has very little plot. The above distinctions are literary and analytic in their reference, and oftentimes have been incorrectly incorporated as nomenclature in the titles of dramatic pieces. Consequently, *autos* are not always *autos* as defined, nor are *coloquios* what they are often analyzed to be. The distinctions have been included here as they remain helpful both in classifying and in understanding the various plays which will subsequently be discussed.

Neither European medieval drama nor Mexican drama was forceful in the sense of exemplifying a structural dramatic conflict or inner plot. The usual pattern of presentation in Spain consisted of a procession followed by the recitation of an introductory *loa*, after which the drama itself was presented. The dramatic interlude was often punctuated by musical interludes and often terminated with a verbal recapitulation of the entire program.

Mexican religious dramatic presentations usually followed the same pattern, but the missionary drama most often lacked the nicety of the *loa*. They were of mediocre literary quality and usually simply narrative or didactic. Vestiges of introductory passages or *loas* are sometimes found, but they simply summarize in homiletic terms the purpose of the presentation.

The use of music in Europe was continued with great success in Mexico. As well as providing a linkage between scenes and unifying otherwise unrelated narrative elements, in Mexico music served to offer emotional and esthetic satisfaction to members of a culture which had been accustomed to this kind of empathy and catharsis. Many Mexican *autos* were virtually oratorios and used music as a structural necessity.

The language of Mexican missionary drama in Nahuatl remained richly poetic. Its imagery-patterns were always rhythmically repetitious; the accepted metaphors often reflected their origins in sacred myths. On the contrary, the language of the ordinary religious drama of medieval Europe reflected the intrusion of the daily and "realistic" elements of life into the dramatic form.[56] The repeated use of patterned interrogations, of hyperbolic statements, of hortatory subjunctives, of human descriptions in terms of rich and valued objects and of natural beauty was distinctly Nahuatl.

The Spanish conquest of the Meso American culture was primarily military and economic in its inception and goal. However, along with the more mundane preoccupations with power, there invariably coexisted a genuinely religious fervor to christianize every indigenous group with whom the Spanish came into contact. A quotation from Bernal Diaz, the famous soldier-chronicler who accompanied Cortés, epitomizes this religious zeal and sets the tempo with which the priests worked to eradicate the "pagan" religions and to replace them with Roman Catholic Christianity.

> Cortés . . . said to Padre de la Merced, who was present: "It is a good opportunity, Father, as we have good material at hand, to explain through our interpreters matters touching our holy faith." And then he delivered a discourse to the Caciques so fitting to the occasion that no theologian could have bettered it . . . . Cortés also told them that one of the objects for which our great Emperor had sent us to their countries was to abolish human sacrifices, and the other evil rites which they practiced and to see that they did not rob one another, or worship those cursed images. And Cortés

prayed them to set up in their city, in their temples where they kept the idols which they believed to be gods, a cross like the one which they saw before them, and to set up in the same place an image of Our Lady, which he would give them, with her precious son in her arms, and they would see how well is would go with them, and what our God would do for them.[57]

On April 5, 1521, Pope Leo X issued a papal bull granting to Cortés his request for missionaries. Within two years of this request, a band of twelve Franciscan missionaries arrived in Mexico. They were the friars Martín de Valencia, Francisco de Soto, Martín de la Coruna, Antonio de Cuidad Rodrigo, García de Cisneros, Juan de Rivas, Francisco Jiménez, Juan Suárez, Luis de Fuensalida, Toribio Motolinía, Juan de Palos, and Andrés de Córdoba.[58]

The Franciscans became well established in five provinces: Mexico; Michoacan; Guatemala; Nicaragua and the Yucatan. They were followed shortly by the Dominicans, the Augustinians, the Jesuits, and the Carmelites. Since the Franciscans were established earliest in the missionary era, and because of their peculiar interest and ability in teaching the Indians on a rudimentary level, the case is strong for their having first and perhaps most consistently used the drama for didactic missionary purposes in Mexico.

The missionaries labored zealously to convert the Indians from their polytheistic convictions to what they conceived to be the one true religion, Roman Catholic Christianity. The barriers which they faced in this activity were tremendous. First of all, they had to learn the various Indian languages in order to communicate even the minimal amount of necessary information. Even after this could be accomplished, the existing differences in both the material and ideological content of their two cultures were so great as to seem insurmountable even in retrospect. It is among the didactic methods first utilized by many of these pioneer missionaries that the drama played such an important role. The choices and method of teaching selected by the missionaries set an educational pattern which has had profound and enduring effects upon subsequent Mexican Roman Catholicism in both its ritual and ideological aspects.

The first missionaries were often men of considerable learning and awareness of their own culture. They seemed to have been apt students of indigenous languages and life, and to have utilized their observations in an astute and productive manner. They correctly observed that dramatic ritual comprised a large portion of the social life of the Aztecs for example, and that religiosity was the guiding principle of their culture. They seemed to have understood the need for color and pageantry which had to be satisfied in any substitution of a new religion for an old. They sought not simply to destroy these needs and patterns but rather to *adapt, utilize, and emulate* them.

There is a brief description in Torquemada[59] of the probable manner in which the first lessons in Christianity were presented to the Indians:

> These things were taught by the holy religious men in pantomime, and only in signs; in signalling to the sky and saying that they ought to believe that the only God was there; and turning their eyes to the earth, they signified that there was hell, wherein walked (were) the likeness of toads and serpents. These were the demons tormenting the condemned souls.[60]

As the first missionaries worked to master the indigenous languages, they also struggled to establish a general system of education in each province. Many churches and monasteries were constructed with the assistance and labor of the Indians. Education was a prerogative of the Church, and classes were held in rooms or in the patio adjacent to the cathedral or monastery compounds. In the same manner as before the conquest, the priests had charge of the education of the people, and this process was carried out in the religious centers themselves. Education in general, however, was accomplished in a much more limited fashion than it had been before the conquest; the Aztecs had managed to create an amazingly efficient system of education extended to the children of nobles and commoners alike, as well as to male and female students.[61]

By the end of the sixteenth century, several colleges had been established: the College of San Francisco in Mexico, founded by Pedro de Gante; the College of Santa Cruz in Tlaltelolco, founded by Juan de Zumárraga in 1556; the House of Studies founded by the Augustinians in Tiripitio in 1540; the College of Santa Maria de Todos los Santos in 1573; and the University of Mexico in Mexico City in 1553, by royal letters patent dated in 1551.[62]

The basic goal of the educational system being established was to prepare the Mexican to aid the Spanish in their economic endeavors such as farming, mining, and the construction of new cities. To insure the highest degree of cooperation, the conquerors found it necessary to imbue the Indians with a new set of values, those which the European Spaniard of the sixteenth century understood and accepted.

Adults as well as children had to be educated at the same time; there were still too few missionary-teachers, and fewer still who had an adequate grasp of the Indian languages. Religion and education in general were integrated into one and the same pattern. The early colonial architecture of the schools and churches was clearly adapted to the basic needs and problems of the expedited acculturation process. The majority of church-school compounds were constructed on the same physical pattern. The church was oriented from the east to the west, and forming a square to it toward the north were the school and dormitories for the resident students. In this area also, a chapel was often constructed especially for the use of the indigenous peoples. This chapel was often larger than the principal cathedral of the compound. Such a chapel was often constructed with many naves and open on the two extreme ends with a view to a large atrium which completed the square of the entire compound.[63] Minor buildings such as cells for the resident priests and their trainee;-helpers and storerooms were scattered in a variety of places in this typical pattern. The market place was adjacent to the church compound, usually to the front of the portals of the main church gate.[64]

This large and open patio area served as a place to teach

both the children and the adults of the lower socio-economic group among the Indians. Regular daily school training for resident pupils was largely reserved for the children of the noble or wealthy class of Indian. This was by no means a hard and fast practiced rule, and the exceptions were notable and many. It is true, however, that the Spanish felt that since the *macehuales* or commoners had no active political or public obligations it was necessary for them to learn only the basic doctrines of the Church and its practices. The niceties of reading, writing, Latin, history, theology, etc., were reserved for those indigenes designated to help the Spanish in their governing.

The early missionary-teachers coaxed, exhorted, and finally demanded that the *señores* among the Indians send their sons to these schools. Through fear, or simple refusal to do so, sometimes the noble Indian fathers would send their servants' sons in place of their own children; thus the commoners would inadvertently profit by the system.[65]

The school buildings were usually of one story in height and with the dormitory buildings contiguous. In the principal convents or religious compounds, 800 to 1,000 children were taught at one time.

The first and largest compound of this kind was the famous San José de Belén de los Naturales in Mexico City. Fray Pedro de Gante was in charge of this church, which was so large that it had seven naves open to an immense atrium. Since Gante was very well-known and respected for his work, a brief account of his method will serve as a clue to the generalized Franciscan procedure.

Gante was in charge of teaching 1,000 children. A typical workday consisted of the following schedule: in the morning, Gante lectured on reading, writing, and song; in the afternoon, he taught doctrine and preached. Furthermore, on prescribed days, he assisted in *fiestas* and sang Masses. His resident students were not allowed to communicate with their families, to avoid possible contamination by any anti-Christian ideas the older generation might still have entertained.

Gante then chose about fifty of the best and oldest students and taught them catechism privately. These students later preached by his order on Sundays. Gante sent them by twos out to the outlying *barrios* or areas of Mexico City to preach on Sunday mornings. They were sent out each twenty days or only for *fiestas* if the distance was over fifteen or twenty leagues. If Gante and his group heard about any idolatrous celebrations being held, members of this select group were sent out to disturb them. They destroyed temples and/or any idols which they learned about.[66]

It is clear that each of these schools was at the same time a strong center of religious propaganda. They were also influential in the formation of a group of political workers. Here they trained corps of religious judges, mayors, and petty officials to be sent to the surrounding villages.

Gante emphasized the value of celebrating the church holidays with color and pomp so that the Indians would not feel a lack of emotional satisfaction in Christianity as compared to their Prehispanic religion. He emphasized the importance of drama, song, and dance in ritual situations.[67]

Gante also expedited the construction of four other churches, in addition to San José de Belén, to serve each of the four *barrios* into which the indigenous population of Mexico City was divided. These were Santa Maria, San Juan, San Pablo, and San Sebastian. During this period he probably had charge of the construction of approximately one hundred chapels.

Pedro de Gante taught a few of his students Latin. The Indians learned well and rapidly, and he composed special masses for them to perform. Gante knew that the Spaniards had fewer images to replace the plethora of idols which the Indians had used; therefore, he founded a department of art where the Indians could learn to paint and carve according to the esthetic canons of the Western European visual arts. They already knew the technique of painting, had excellent color dyes, and so carefully aped the Flemish and Spanish paintings which they were given to use as models. This trained corps of artisans also made images, vases, crosses, altars, and such articles. Gante arranged that the Indians be taught embroidery and encouraged them to continue with their featherwork.[68] Gante also initiated carpentry shops, smithies, tailor shops, and shoes shops, all in connection with the monastery or church compound.

These schools were very difficult to support financially, and only the *frailes* themselves seemed to understand the immediate and constant need for funds. Gante even petitioned corn and money from the king during occasions of special need.

Although the degree of Gante's activity, success, and his specific interest in advancing craftsmanship and education among the Indians was greater than those of the majority of his peers, his goals and methods were typical of those of the early colonial period. Educating and missionizing were united *and* pushed forward at a fever pitch. In a letter which Gante sent to brothers of his order in Flanders in 1529, he noted that he himself had baptized from ten to fourteen thousand people in one day.[69]

The teaching of the catechism itself was similarly accomplished by the Augustinians, the Franciscans, and the Dominicans. The Jesuits, while utilizing the same basic techniques in preliminary matters, tended to focus on abstract and theological niceties, and to cater to the advanced student who was often able to read and write both Spanish and Latin.

The catechism was translated as quickly and efficiently as possible into the various Indian languages. The Church Council of 1555 placed an interdict upon the baptizing of adults who were either insufficiently instructed or illegally married.[70] Exactly what comprised this preliminary instruction is impossible to know. Our best source on the subject is the *Platicas de los Doce,* which although incomplete concerns the sermons presented by the first twelve missionaries to their indigenous audiences.[71] The preliminary discourse attributed to the Twelve is enlightening:

> Do not believe, the missionaries said to the Lords of Mexico, that we are gods. Fear not; we are men even as you. We are merely messengers, only envoys of the Great Lord the Holy

Father. He is the spiritual Lord of the Universe, and the state of your souls fills him with suffering and sadness. We desire nothing else. Toward this end, we shall teach you of the book of Holy Scripture which contains the words about the only true God—Lord of the heaven and earth—whom you have not yet known. This, then, is why we have come. We wish neither gold, nor silver, nor precious stones; we only desire your well-being.[72] . . . You have a god whose worship your king and your ancestors have taught you. No, you have a crowd of gods; and each has his name and each his character. You yourselves can recognize your errors in this! You harm them when you are displeased and call them stupid. What these gods demand of you in sacrifice is your blood and your heart! . . . The true and universal God, our Lord, Creator and Sustainer of being and life, of whom we have come to preach, is not of the same essence as your gods. He does not make mistakes. He does not lie. He neither detests nor mocks any person. There is nothing of evil in him. He has a profound horror of all that is evil and forbids it. He is perfectly good. He is the abyss of all goods; He is the fountainhead of compassion, of love, and *misericordia*. He has taught us why and how He demonstrated his infinite compassion most clearly; that is why He became as Man here below in this world—humble and poor even as we are. He died for us. He spilled his blood for our salvation, and to deliver us from the power of the demons. . . . This true God is called Jesus Christ, true Man and true God, Giver of being and life, Redeemer and Savior of the world. As He is God, He had no beginning. He is eternal. He made heaven, earth, and hell. He made us—that is, all the men of the world. He also made the demons. He sees and knows all. He is completely perfect. Inasmuch as He is also Man, He has his royal home both in heaven and here on earth below. He has his kingdom here which commenced when the world was made; and He wishes that you enter it now, that is, those among you who want to consider yourselves as indeed happy.

The catechisms which were used ideally included the following subjects: preliminary discourses about God, Jesus Christ, immortality of the soul, freewill; the seven articles of the faith which define the divinity of Christ; the seven articles which define his humanity; the love of God and the three commandments which are related to it; the love of neighbor and the seven commandments which define it; the works of compassion; the joys of heaven; baptism; the Mass and the Eucharist; the sign of the Cross; the Lord's Prayer, and the Creed.

Catechisms also ideally included the sermon to be given to those catechumens about to be baptized, the marriage ceremony, communion, penance, the capital sins, confirmation, and the enemies of the soul.[73]

It should be clarified that it is unlikely that the catechumens actually learned more than the barest essentials about the Christian God before baptism. The catechism in reality served as a text or guidebook for those who were able or cared to learn more about Christianity.[74]

These *Platicas* or Sermons to which we have referred, took the place of the *Hueyhueytlatolli* or moral speeches of the elders, which were so important before the conquest. The people met daily at the sound of the church bell. They gathered in the church atrium, and for one hour were taught the catechism. Then the adults and children separated, and the latter were taught prayers and poems in the relevant Indian languages. Ideally, there were two daily catechism sessions, one in the morning and the other in the afternoon. In the villages where the priests were visitors and not residents, the *fiscales,* who were appointed and trained by the clergy, directed the activities of the church in the priest's absence.[75]

The manner in which the missionary dramas were presented will be clarified in the description of certain individual productions which follow. In brief, the priests were known to have written plays and/or adapted existing religious dramas from Spain with which they were already familiar. In adapting liturgical dramas, they simplified the theological subtleties and symbolism depicted, focused upon biblical narratives, and very often transformed the latter into social situations and terms more readily comprehensible to the indigenous audience.

Sometimes the missionaries composed entirely new dramas utilizing ideas and problems which they recognized as present in the remaining substratum of indigenous culture, and perhaps linked these to biblical themes or typical Christian virtues. The Indians themselves enacted the various roles, and contrived the scenery and settings as well. When it was necessary to enact a female role, the young male students accomplished this, as the assistance of females was not yet permitted.[76]

Two other genres of theater developed contemporaneously with the missionary drama: the humanistic theater and the comedy. Although these will be mentioned later, they will not be dealt with to any extent; instead, emphasis will be placed upon the didactic homiletic theater fostered by the missionaries primarily for an indigenous audience.[77]

The original manuscript sources from which information concerning the missionary theater of the sixteenth century can be obtained are three in number: the journals of the missionary-historians who themselves saw and described these dramas and/or their presentation; the laws enacted by the sixteenth century Spanish *cabildos;* and the few extant manuscripts of plays, the content of which dates back to the sixteenth century. Various secondary sources have been used such as the few available articles and studies which refer to the subject in question.

Apart from descriptions of particular celebrations which included dramatic presentations, there are a few references by the chroniclers to the general utility and value of the theater as a didactic device. For example, the following is an account from *The Naturall and Moral Historie of the East and West Indies,* by José de Acosta, a Spanish Jesuit missionary who passed through Mexico on his return from Peru in the sixteenth century:

> For this reason the prelates have labored to take from them these dances all that they could; but yet they suffer them, for that part of them are but sportes of recreation, for alwaies

they dance after their maner. In these dances, they use sundry sortes of instruments, whereof some are like flutes or little lutes, others like drummes, and others like shells, but commonly they sing all with one voyce, and first one or two sing the song, then all the rest answer them . . . . Our men that have conversed among them have laboured to reduce matters of our holy faith to their tunes, the which hath profited well; for that they imploy whole daies to rehearse and sing them. . . . We must therefore conclude, following the counsel of Pope Gregory, that it was very convenient to leave unto the Indians that which they had usually of custom, so that they be not mingled nor corrupt with their ancient errors, and that their feasts and pastimes may be to the honor of God and of the Saints whose feasts they celebrate.[78]

Further, there is a brief but relevant statement from Fray Juan Bautista, one of the early missionaries; this is included in his *Confessionatio en Lengua mexicana y castellana,* published in 1599:

It is my wide experience that with the dramas which these and other examples Our Lord has made (them) represent the events of Lent, he has brought forth through his mercy great results; has cleansed and renovated consciences for many years habitually in his offense. . . .[79]

Prehispanic Mexican culture was one in which men sang and danced their religious and esthetic devotion. As we have seen, the missionaries had the choice of completely outlawing this manner of expression, or of using the Precolombian forms of religious celebration by superimposing the elements of Christian content upon them. By and large the latter alternative was chosen, and only when the form and content became dangerously confused with the pagan or too blatantly reminiscent of Prehispanic roots did the priest or church officials object to or limit its expression.

The First Church Council which terminated in November of 1555 defined the official position at the onset:

The indigenous peoples of these parts are greatly given to ritual dancing and to other rejoicings which they have held as their custom since their gentility. They now wish to mix with these dances elements which are reminiscent of their Pre-Christian history. With the permission of the Holy Council, let us instate and order that when the Indians dance they shall wear no ancient masks, nor use any insignia which might arouse suspicion. Nor shall they sing hymns pertaining to their ancient rituals or history, without their first having been examined by either priests or persons who well understand their language; and such songs which do not directly treat of the Gospel or the Mysteries of our Faith they shall not be premitted to dance before dawn, *nor after the High Mass*, but *only after these hours* and until Vespers.[80]

We know that the priests and their most advanced students struggled to compose poems, sermons, catechisms, and plays in the indigenous languages to furnish the Indians with an adequate corpus of ritual compositions. Poetry was an important part of the Prehispanic tradition, and had to have a counterpart in the early colonial period. There was, according to Garibay, a substantial body of newly "baptized" Christian poetry which in general preserved the form and rhythm of Prehispanic poetry, but which included praises and supplications to God, Jesus Christ, the Virgin Mary, and the saints. The same joy, the same inspired sensitivity to compose lyric analogies in terms of the natural world was still apparent. The christianized Indians had maintained their own poetic tradition with limitations, and the priests were clever enough to ape this commendable manner of expression.

It becomes increasingly clear that although the Spaniards had few qualms about destroying the material culture of the Indians whom they conquered, they sought rather to substitute than to eliminate certain elements of the non-material culture. The social organization of Prehispanic Mexico was almost completely destroyed: the family structure, the social and religious hierarchy, the system of government, the concept and waging of ritual warfare, all were demolished. In one area the priests sought to parallel, substitute, and subtly to satisfy the void left by the colorful and absorbing ritual pattern of a destroyed cult. Their goal demanded that they not destroy religiosity *per se*, but that they take it and change its content and orientation. The Prehispanic Indian had seen his relationship to the divine as one of dependence but as collaborative; according to the Christians, they now had to see it as one of utter dependence upon a gracious two-edged Will of Love and Justice.

While the awful burden of ritual warfare and human sacrifice was alleviated, the necessity of heavy tribute and the burdens of assuming a new religious and social system remained.

In place of the Prehispanic didactic and epic traditions was substituted a new didactic literature including catechisms, new histories, homilies, a wealth of sermons, and a smattering of the ideas and cultural traditions of Western Europe. For the ritual and lyrical poems and paeans directed to the pantheon of Precolombian deities, as well as those describing their cosmological and metaphysical ideologies, the Spanish fathers substituted a *new poetic tradition* in old vestments. Gods became saints, calendrical celebrations were converted to saints' days and to Christian holidays. Dancing and music were permitted and were, in fact, encouraged within confined and controlled patterns. Processions continued, and dramatic enactments were used to great advantage to convey Christian ideas.

A few manuscripts exemplary of what must have been a rich literature representing the early colonial period remain in various archives. Some of these are anonymous, others are both dated and signed.[18]

Farces and burlesques with much joking continued as general secular entertainment. The poems dealing with colonial history and figures tried to emulate the style of literary adornments and epic grandeur notable in the Prehispanic oral tradition.

Of greatest interest here are the religious poems, many of which have a vivid freshness of attitude and description. A few examples of these will be included here, the originals of which are in Nahuatl and found in manuscripts of the National Library of Mexico. The following examples had their provenance in Azcapotzalco, which was dominated more by the Dominican tenor of thought than by the Franciscan; that is, they believed thought was a more powerful basis in the formation of imagery than pure emotion.[82] One poem describing the creation of the world, obviously according to Christian ideology, was composed by one Francisco Plácido:

> Come and hear this, oh you of Nonoalco and Tepaneco!
> Hear of the new budding-plant (idea) which my heart values.
> I shall sing of how the heavens began,
> And of how the earth was created. . . .
> God first created the light.
> On the second day He created the heaven.
> The third day He created the earth and the sea.
> And on the fourth day He brought into being the sun, the moon, and all the many stars.
> The fifth day He created the dwellers of the waters, and the myriad kinds of birds which go about flying.
> On the sixth day He created the many beasts which walk the earth.
> And it was then that He created the first man!
> 'He shall truly be our substitute, truly our image.
> This shall be his perfect work, entirely his possession.
> Here is our creation, that which dwells upon the earth.'[83]

So it was that the new Christians learned of their religious concepts through songs, much as their grandfathers had been taught theirs through generations of songs and singers.

The following is a paean dedicated to the celebration of Christmas in 1553. Here the poet speaks wih God and says:

> Your many birds—the beautiful golden finches—trill in your honor, oh God!
> The angels are those who sing, *'Gloria in excelsis Deo!'*
> Rejoice! Take pleasure!
> Thus it was when the light of heaven fell upon the earth;
> A host of flowers burst forth.

> The angles sing, *'Gloria in excelsis Deo!'*
> The Kings heard this there in the east.
> From the heavens it was shouted: 'God has appeared upon earth!'
> They took gold, incense, myrrh, and went to Bethlehem.
> With their own eyes thay saw the true God, the true Man.
> They knew you first, oh God!
> They saw you as a jewel;
> They saw you as a quetzal.
> The Kings made supplications to the Holy Virgin Mary, who affirmed the glory of the true God and true Man.
> Oh, brothers, let us all give praise!
> But in Bethlehem, the plumage of the quetzal was laid waste.
> As a necklace of fine jade were the children destroyed.[84]
> Oh, what precious bracelets are resting there in heaven!
> The mourning song is spun.
> They are remembering those beloved of God with flowers of bitterness.
> Oh, what precious bracelets are resting there in heaven![85]

We have an example from 1550 of a song performed on the Day of the Holy Spirit or the feast of the Annunication. At this time the announcement of the future birth of Jesus Christ to Mary was celebrated. The pronouncement or annunciation was sung in this manner:

> A red and blush-warm mist stretches over your house, oh Holy Mary!
> Blue birds, many forms of birds trill;
> You are invoked by them, oh Holy Mary!
> Now Saint Gabriel is coming! He comes in search!
> You are invoked by him, oh Holy Mary!
> 'Hail Mary!'
> Truly even we from here (heaven) praise you with love.
> Oh Queen, oh Sovereign Lady!
> "Hail Mary!". . . .
> The many-colored Bird, He of many jewels—
>   the Holy Spirit soars!

And now He comes upon the apostles;
Only with divine aid could the apostles—beloved
  of God—die for the faith here on earth.
Only with divine aid!
As a red flower the dawn burgeons forth;
You are there! Deep in heaven, oh God!
Like bits of shining emeralds the seedlings burst
  into shoots.
Many and festive are your creatures!
You fill them to overflowing.
They shall never cease to flower.
The angels intone beautiful flowery songs.
All men prostrate themselves before you,
  oh only God!
Like bits of shining emeralds the seedlings burst
  into shoots.
Many and festive are your creatures!
You fill them to overflowing.
They shall never cease to flower.[86]

Garibay makes the point that the same images utilized before the conquest were used in the religious-lyric poetry afterwards. The same metrical pattern and versification were also frequently employed.

There is extant an early colonial poem which was perhaps composed by Pedro de Gante. This poem was probably written before 1550, and was to have been sung by the children who were students at the San Francisco Convent, and on the patronal feast of St. Francis. This poem clearly uses the classical Nahuatl image of Tlalocan, the watery "paradise" inhabited by certain individuals after their death.

We shall give pleasure to the only God,
Here upon the budding green meadow.
Most joyful is that which is murmured about.
Oh, perfumed and delicious flowers,
We are to gather them there, are we the children.
The red blossoms of God spring forth there.

> The red-branched weeping willow which bends
>   is suspended between the green fronds.
> We must gather it, must we the children!
> On the flowery strand waits St. Christopher;
> He helps one pass over the ford to the beloved Jesus Christ.[87]
> The colorful butterflies fluttering weave a web.
> On the flowery strand I humbly speak to you, oh God;
> Oh, St. Christopher!
> Enough! You have helped pass the ford to the
>   Lord of the universe!
> The colorful butterflies fluttering weave a web.[88]

These two fragmentary examples are illustrative of how the imagery and manner of expression are reminiscent of classical Nahuatl poetry with a baptized content of Christian ideas.

It is apparent that the Indians, both children and adults, had deep emotional ties to some of the priests who were educating them and extending to them the succor which was so important in the difficult days of forced acculturation to an alien social and religious system. The following fragment is a point in issue:

> Your heart is a many-colored book,
> Oh, brother Pedro!
> So many are the hymns you offer to Jesus Christ;
> You have them sung in San Francisco.
> You give us great pleasure there!
> With your timbrel you are gracious to the children;
> And we feel ourselves delighted . . . .

> Ho there, children of Huexotzinco,
> Let us give a little pleasure.
> Let us hunt butterflies with nets.
> We shall await our brother Pedro, our beloved father.
> This will appease the majesty of God!
> Come, little children; let us gather flowers.
> Then let us dance with them;
> As will brother Pedro, who is our father.[89]

Garibay judges that, although these various fragments were composed in the third person, they were very likely written by Pedro de Gante. That the Indians particularly loved and respected this priest is attested to by other sources.

Finally, a lovely fragment again to be sung by the children follows:

Like the plumage of the quetzal we bend earthward,
Do we the children!
We humble ourselves.
We pray to the Eternal Virgin, Holy Mary.
With the beauty as of iridescent plumage does
  our understanding gird us.
Like a necklace of pearls do we entwine ourselves.
Do we the children!
We pray to the Eternal Virgin, Holy Mary.[90]

As early as 1526, the Spanish were celebrating the *fiesta* of *Corpus Christi* in Mexico. The first mention of such a celebration is included in the records of the *Cabildo* dated February 9, 1526. This statement refers to a request for financial aid to build a hermitage and a hospital, and mentions *Corpus* in its context. If, as is fairly certain, this custom was carried over from Spain and immediately established in the new world, it follows that it is also likely that such commemorations involved the enactment of both processions and plays as did their paradigms.

We know from a subsequent act of the *Cabildo* in 1529, referring to the order in which the *Corpus Christi* procession ought to be organized, that in fact these processions were being celebrated.[91]

In the year 1530, *an auto* entitled the *"Conversion de San Pablo"* (*"The Conversion of St. Paul"*) was presented in the atrium of the largest cathedral in Mexico City, the *San José de los Naturales*.

Although it is a subject of conjecture whether this play was written or adapted by a Franciscan or an Indian, it is certain that it was written in Nahuatl and presented by the Indians themselves. In this play, for which we have extant a probably derived version, Paul is represented as a great nobleman and warrior who deserted his previous idolatrous beliefs in order to become a good Christian. The implications of this dramatic object lesson were clearly that the Indians, and especially the Indian nobles and leaders, should emulate this decision.[92]

John Hubert Cornyn, in a published reference to this play, includes the following initial paragraph in his translation of the text from the manuscript in the archives of the National Institute of Anthropology and History of Mexico:

> Paul mounts his horse, stumbles and falls. Paul's body is thrown to the ground and smashed to bits. The devils (Aztec Priests) come and gather these up and place them on a blanket and Paul goes straight to heaven. When the Lord God sees him he says to him: "Paul, why did you kill St. Sebastian? He builds my houses for me and he sweeps the road to heaven so that my people may come straight to my home here."[93]

It might help to understand this rather obscure excerpt to know that shrines to St. Sebastian were often built over places where previously Quetzalcóatl had been worshipped. Quetzalcóatl had been the one who swept clean the road to the gates of Dawn, over which the dead warriors travelled on their way to the Sun.

Such a representation of St. Paul as a noble warrior epitomizes the method of didactic Christian history dramatized, with the accent on emotional empathy and understanding by using Prehispanic cultural patterns to inculcate Christian ideas.

There is another *Cabildo* record on June 10, 1533, mentioning in greater detail the order in which the *Corpus* procession was to be assembled:

> . . . the officials and judges of the Indians (come), then come the gardeners, and behind them the giants, and behind the giants the shoemakers, and behind the shoemakers the smiths and metalworkers, and behind these the carpenters . . .[94]

The care in organization as well as the impressive size of this procession and celebration can be deduced from this brief quotation.

We know of another early drama variously entitled *"El Juicio Final"* (*"The Final Judgment"*); *"El Juicio Universal"* (*"The Universal Judgment"*); and *"Representación del fin del mundo"* (*"Representation of the End of the World"*). Since varying dates are also given for the presentations of this play or plays, it is most likely that we have references to different versions, perhaps adapted by more than one priest.

Fray Bernardino de Sahagún in his *Historia general de las cosas,* while enumerating the chiefs of Tlaltelolco, states that in the time of Juan Quauiconco there was a presentation "of the Judgment in the mentioned city of Tlaltelolco, and that it was something [worthy] to see."[95]

A manuscript in the Academy of History in Madrid (Folio 15R) contains the following quotation which Garibay has translated from the Nahuatl:

> When Don Pablo Xochiquen ruled in Tenochtitlan, there was presented in Tlaltelolco something very beautiful; that is, the great and instructive *auto* of the *"Fall of the World."*

We can ascertain the date of this presentation in the following manner. Xochiquen ruled in Tenochtitlan or Mexico City from 1528 to 1531. Cuaúhiconoc was in Tlaltelolco from 1530 to 1537; therefore, the presentation very likely took place in 1531.[96]

In the *Septima Relación Histórica de Chimalpáin,* translated from the Nahuatl by Rémi Siméon, there appears the following statement about the year 1533:

> . . . There was given in Santiago Tlaltelolco, Mexico, a representation of the end of the world; the Mexicans were left greatly wondering and admiring. . . .[97]

Garibay gives the year 1535 for the presentation of *"El Juicio Final"* in the chapel of San José de los Naturales in Mexico City. This play was presented in Nahuatl and is believed to have been the work of Fray Andrés de Olmos. Olmos, who had arrived in Mexico in 1528, was reknowned for his rapid and thorough learning of the Indian languages. Indeed, according to the chronicler Mendieta, Olmos knew Nahuatl, Totonac, Tepehua, and Huastec.[98]

It is further possible that this version of *"El Juicio Final"* might be the same as that found in copy form in a manuscript of the Library of Congress which bears the same title of *Nexcuitilmachiotl Motenhua Juicio Final,* as mentioned by Sahagún. The closest translation of the Nahuatl part of the title is: "Exemplary scene or doctrinal model presented before the eyes."[99]

There is a reference to this or a similar play, as having been produced in Mexico City in the year 1546, in the *Bibliografía mexicana del siglo XVI* by Joaquín Garcia Icazbalceta. In this work, Icazbalceta states that he took his information from a photographic copy of a catalogue owned by Francisco González de Vera, a Spanish bibliophile, containing the words:

. . . with a farce entitled *"El Juicio Final,"* composed by the Reverend Father las Cassas *(indigno)* religious priest of this New Spain, and dedicated to the illustrious and Most Reverend Lord Fray Iuan de Cumárraga (Zumárraga), the first and most meritorious Archbishop of this great city of Tenochtitlan of New Spain, in the year of 1546.[100] . . .

If this play was presented, as is suggested, to a large audience as a welcome and entertainment for the installation of the new Archbishop and the first Viceroy of Mexico, Don Antonio de Mendoza, the date could not have been 1546, as stated by the quotation, unless it is, as Icazbalceta says, "an anachronism or a prophecy"; the Bull instating Zumárraga as Archbishop was not given until 1547, and did not arrive in Mexico until May of 1548. Since Mendoza came to Mexico in 1535, and Zumárraga died in 1548, one can only say that the presentation took place sometime during this interim. Garibay and others choose the date 1535 as the most correct.

Both Mendieta and Torquemada mention the production of this play to which we refer; Mendieta in particular describes the huge crowd which attended the drama and observes that it had undoubtedly converted many to Christianity.[101]

Education and Culture Change

From the foregoing analysis, it would seem likely that the theme of the final judgment was perhaps well-known and popular in the corpus of missionary drama of the sixteenth century and that we have only one version extant of what were probably several. Other similar versions of dramas with this theme are known to date back to medieval times. Since *"El Juicio Final"* is included in translation in this study, further discussion of the plot and ideas of the play will be included within the introduction to the drama itself.

In the years 1538 and 1539 several plays were presented in the city of Tlaxcala. Fray Toribio Motolinía has left us the most detailed accounts of these which we possess to date on this subject. Because of the earliness of the plays, as well as the extensiveness of the data which we have about them, they will be described at some length. They are generally typical of the missionary theater of the early sixteenth century.

Motolinía describes the festivals of *Corpus Christi* and St. John as they were celebrated in Tlaxcala in the year 1538. He describes the *Corpus* procession in detail, saying that "had the Pope and the Emperor been there with their courts they would have been delighted with the sight."[102]

Both Torquemada and Las Casas give the date of this celebration as 1536. Since Torquemada received his information from Motolinía, as did Las Casas very likely, Motolinía's dates will be accepted as the more correct.[103] Of the procession Motolinía continues:

> In the procession were the Blessed Sacrament and many crosses and images of the saints on their platforms. The veils of the crosses and the ornaments of the platforms were all of gold and feather work. . . . All the road was strewn with reeds and rushes and flowers. . . . There were many varieties of dances which enlivened the procession. . . . Along the road were chapels with their altars and altarpieces well adorned . . . and there many additional singers appeared and sang and danced before the Blessed Sacrament. There were ten big triumphal arches very neatly made, and . . . they had the whole length of the road divided into three

lanes, like the naves of the church. The central lane was three feet wide; along it went the Blessed Sacrament and the clergy and crosses and all the pageantry of the procession, and along the two side lanes, which were each fifteen feet wide, went all the people. . . . The division was marked by medium-sized arches of about nine feet, and there were by actual count 1,068 of these arches . . . all covered with roses and flowers of various kinds and colors.

At each of the four corners or turns that the road made, there was constructed a mountain and from each mountain there rose a high cliff. The lower part was made like a meadow, with clumps of herbs and flowers. . . . It was a marvelous thing to see, for there were many trees. . . . On the trees were many birds, both big and small . . . and in the wood much game. . . . In order that nothing might be lacking to make the scene appear completely natural, there were hunters with their bows and arrows well concealed on the mountain.

In the procession was a part-song choir of many voices with its accompanying music of flutes which harmonized with the singers, and horns, and drums, and bells, little and big.[104]

Motolinía goes on to describe how the Indians then presented four one-act plays the following Monday, which was the day of St. John the Baptist. On Friday these plays were written, and the Indians memorized them all on Saturday and Sunday.[105]

. . . [They] represented very devoutly the *Annunciation of the Birth of St. John the Baptist* made to his father, Zacharias. The play took about an hour and ended with a pretty motet sung in parts. Then on another stage they represented the *Annunciation of Our Lady,* which was very well worth seeing and took as long as the first play. Later, in the churchyard of the church of San Juan, where the procession went, they represented upon another stage the scene of the *Visitation of Our Lady to St. Elizabeth* . . . it was quite a sight to see how beautiful the stages were adorned and covered with roses. After Mass, they represented the *Nativity of St.*

John, and instead of the circumcision they baptized a week-old boy named John. Before they gave the dumb Zacharias the writing materials that he asked for by signs, it was very amusing to see the things that they brought him, pretending that they did not understand him.[106] This scene ended with the singing of the *Benedictus Dominus Deus Israel,* and the neighbors and relatives of Zacharias, who rejoiced at the birth of the son, brought presents and many kinds of food, and set the table and sat down to eat, for by then it was dinner time.

The next record we have of a play presented in 1538 is also from Motolinía. It concerns the presentation of a play by the Confraternity of Our Lady of the Incarnation. Since the Indians could not celebrate this during Lent, they kept the celebration for the Wednesday of the Easter octave in 1538. There was first a general distribution of alms in the form of clothing and food. Then, near the door of the almshouse, they presented a drama in Nahuatl:

[The play] represented the fall of our first parents . . . The dwelling of Adam and Eve was so adorned that it really seemed an earthly paradise, with different kinds of trees full of fruits and flowers, some of them natural and some of them counterfeited in gold and feathers. In the trees were many different birds, from owls and other birds of prey to little ones. . . . There were two ocelots tethered there. . . . Once Eve carelessly collided with one of them and the well-bred beast moved aside. This was before she had sinned, for if it had been afterward, she would not have been so lucky [sic].

There were four streams or springs which flowed out of Paradise, each with its sign saying: Pison, Gihon, Tigris, and Euphrates. In the middle of Paradise stood the tree of the knowledge of good and evil, with many and very beautiful fruits made of gold and featherwork.

Round about Paradise there were three big cliffs and a great mountain all full of every thing that one can find on great and verdant hills. . . .

It [the play] took a long time, because before Eve ate the fruit or Adam consented to do so, Eve went back and forth three or four times between her husband and the serpent. . . . Adam always resisting . . . she throwing herself into his arms, importuning him, so that finally he went with her to the forbidden tree, and she ate some and gave him some also. . . . As soon as they had eaten they realized the evil that they had done . . . they could not prevent God from seeing them, and He came, accompanied by many angels . . . and God cursed them and gave to each his penance.

At this point players and audience alike were apparently weeping as Adam and Eve exited from Paradise, each accompanied by three angels, and all singing the psalm *Circumdederunt* in parts. To the left of the stage they had represented another world, the world of toil and labor; and as the play ended they all went off singing in parts a *villancico*, the text of which Motolinía fully reports, and it is therefore all we have remaining of the actual text of this play:

> Oh, why did she eat
> —that first married woman—
> Oh, why did she eat
> The forbidden fruit?
> That first married woman
> —she and her husband—
> Have brought Our Lord down
> To a humble abode
> Because they both ate
> The forbidden fruit.[107]

The next play which Motolinía reports from Tlaxcala was meant to celebrate the Treaty of Aigues Mortes of July 14, 1538 through which the Pope helped to negotiate a successful European alliance against the encroaching Turks. Since the news of this treaty reached Mexico only a few days before Lent in 1539, the Tlaxcaltecans waited to see what the Spanish in Mexico City would do to celebrate this event, and then emulated them. In Mexico City they presented *"La Conquista de*

Education and Culture Change

Rodas" (*"The Conquest of Rhodes"*). So the Tlaxcaltecans decided to stage *"La Conquista de Jerusalén"* (*"The Conquest of Jerusalem"*), another conquest drama. We do not possess a detailed description of the Spanish presentation of *"La Conquista de Rodas"* in 1539; that the effect was elaborate, however, can be judged by a quotation from the *Actas* of the *Cabildo* dated March 27, and referring to the money appropriated for the production of this play:

> For this the city gave the sum of four hundred *pesos* and *"medio de oro commún"* which was spent on materials and adornments, and other things needed for the play.[108]

The people of Tlaxcala waited to present their play until *Corpus Christi* of 1539 in order to increase the solemnity of the occasion. So there follows in Motolinía a detailed description of what must have been an extremely elaborate staging of the siege of Jerusalem. This included great numbers of costumed people enacting the various groups involved in the fanciful Tlaxcaltecan conception of such a battle. They constructed a "Jerusalem" for the occasion, replete with five towers. Not only was the scenario for *"The Conquest of Jerusalem"* complex, but the entire huge cast was completely outfitted with elaborate costumes including properly simulated weapons.

Many scholars feel that Motolinía is the probable author not only of this play but perhaps of all those which he describes. Their assumptions are based on his prolific references to and evident interest in these presentations; his ability to write in Náhuatl, the fact that he was in charge of the monastery in Tlaxcala during the period to which we have reference; and lastly, the fact that the Count of Benavente, who was the titled leader of the village in Spain in which Motolinía was born, and to whom he dedicated his *Historia,* was made Captain General of the Spanish forces in *"The Conquest of Jerusalem."*[109]

The procession preceding the *Corpus Christi* celebration of 1539 was elaborate to the point of incredibility; the Host was carried along a roadway divided by fourteen thousand arches, and marked by six chapels with altars. Three mountains were constructed at appropriate junctures, realistically styled, and on these three additional plays were performed.[110]

On the first, they represented *"The Temptation of Our Lord."* In this, the devils held counsel, decided that Lucifer should be the tempter, and he went forth cleverly disguised as a hermit except for his horns and claws which stuck out quite noticeably. After depicting the various temptations which Christ resisted, the devil fled.

Although he (the devil) remained concealed in the cliff which was hollow, the other devils made such noises that it seemed as if the whole mountain were falling down, with Lucifer, into hell. Then the angels came with food for the Lord, apparently from heaven, and after doing reverence to Him, they set the table and began to sing.

On the next mountain, they presented *"St. Francis Preaching to the Birds."* The dialogue of this play included homilies on the reasons for thankfulness to God, and included one interlude in which St. Francis tamed a wild beast and extracted from it a promise never to be destructive again. Dramatic and didactic relief was afforded by an interlude in which an actor pretending drunkenness interrupted St. Francis by singing and acting as the Indians did when intoxicated. This ended with his being cast into hell by fearful devils. Several witches, and other evil characters, such as those who dispense drugs for abortions, also interrupted St. Francis and fared likewise.

The dénouement of this drama was:
Hell had a secret door by which those inside exited, and when they got out, the place was set on fire and burned so terribly that it seemed as if no one had escaped. . . . The devils and the souls of the damned cried out and shrieked, which produced a feeling of horror and fear even in those who knew that no one was being burned.[111]

The third and final play presented was listed as the *"Sacrifice of Abraham,"* which is described only as having been well acted.

Among references to early indigenous missionary drama

ought to be mentioned the *"Diálogos en lengua mexicana entre la Virgen Maria y el Arcángel San Gabriel,"* *("Dialogues in the Nahuatl Language between the Virgin Mary and Saint Gabriel")*, composed by the Franciscan Luis de Fuensalida who was one of the first twelve missionaries to arrive in Mexico. It is known that Fuensalida died in Puerto Rico in the year 1545, that he knew Nahuatl well, and that he wrote in this language.[112]

Beristáin y Souza stated that he had seen the manuscript of this play and described it, saying, "The angels presented to the most Holy Virgin various messages from the Fathers *(Padres)* of Limbo in which they request in prayer permission to admit the Archangel Gabriel into her presence, and to secure her consent for the Incarnation."[113]

It is said that the manuscript is curious and unusual and that it is perhaps the one which entered into the second place of presentation in the Tlaxcala *Corpus* celebration of which Motolinía speaks. The play was said to have been brief, and Motolinía mentions that its presentation took only one hour. The location of this manuscript is no longer known.

Soon after the year 1555 a drama entitled *"Tlacahuapahualiztli"* in Nahuatl was produced. Since a manuscript of this play is extant, it has been examined by several scholars, including Garibay, and an English translation of it was published by John H. Cornyn and Byron McAfee.[114]

Two manuscripts of this play are in the Library of Congress: one, thirty-six pages in length, includes a prologue; the other, thirty-one pages long, commences where the prologue terminates. The style of both the prologue and the "stage" directions differs from that of the play itself, and were therefore probably introduced at a later period. Both manuscripts lack titles; however, since it is known that a previously lost play of the sixteenth century was entitled *"Bringing up Children,"* the same title was chosen for this particular drama because of its themes and concluding statement of purpose. This statement is translated by Garibay as: "You who educate men, you who indoctrinate men, be not foolish." Cornyn and McAfee add: "Unintelligent! Open your ears; listen to the sermon and the good example and you will not fall into the pit of fires as I am about to do."[115]

For several reasons, this play probably belongs to the period closely following the Conquest. All of the early dramas had specific and definite teaching purposes in mind, and very clearly illustrated the values of the social system with which the missionary-teachers wished to inculcate their indigenous converts. The purpose of the *"Tlacahuapahualiztli"* is to illustrate how one ought properly to educate youth. The education proposed as the most valuable is clearly a religious one, which recognizes individual and cultural needs, but at the basis of which are undeniable supernatural principles reminiscent of the Roman Catholic doctrine of natural law.

The machinery of the play depicts a sixteenth-century mission under the pressures of the early post-Conquest days. The language used is refined and educated in tone and exhibits the old esthetic pride of the Aztecs in the beauty of the Nahuatl language. The play includes statements reminiscent of the Aztec *Hueyhueytlatolli,* of which the priests were most certainly cognizant. The *Hueyhueytlatolli* as it survives today is a collection of maxims and proscriptions which regulated the interpersonal behavior and social relationships of the Aztec youth in Prehispanic times.[116]

The *"Tlacahuapahualiztli"* is superbly representative of the manner in which the missionaries utilized Prehispanic ideas and values, refurbishing them with Christian values and thus baptizing them into the curriculum of the incipient Catholic Church in Mexico. The Aztecs has been a superstitious people, dominated by a priesthood much given to seers, and using the visionary and the miraculous. The early priests recognized the deepseatedness of this cultural trait, and often sought to present to the Indians a similar and therefore understandable concept of the saints and their miraculous powers. Among other things, they added to this belief system a great reverence for the power of the Mother of God, Mary, and the postulation of a place of eternal castigation for the unworthy.

Thus, the *"Tlacahuapahualiztli,"* as most of the early plays, contains many supernatural beings in its cast of characters. The machinery of the play is simple and consists primarily of a series of scenarios. A definite insistence upon obedience and respect to the dead, whether directed to their remains or their souls is shown. For the abovementioned reasons, Garibay concludes that the play was presented perhaps not long after the First Ecclesiastical Council of 1555. This council insisted strongly upon fulfillment of the wills and the necessary prayer-saying and masses for the memories and souls of the deceased. This drama, as well as others to which we shall refer, seems to have been influenced by this emphasis.[117]

Since the *"Tlacahuapahualiztli"* is one of the very few missionizing dramas available to the English reading public, we shall not dwell long on its plot or content: It consists of a series of scenarios enacted either on earth or in heaven. Devils and angels contend for the souls of disobedient and sacrilegious youth who scorn both the sacraments and parental authority. Jesus and Mary, in heaven, discourse with sober dignity and theological rectitude upon the values of proper reverence to the sacraments, especially with respect to the burial litany and to the rosary, and to respect in general toward persons and ideas of authority. An old and moribund couple prepare themselves for death with homilies and careful attention to ecclesiastical detail.

In one interesting monologue, a picture of the dead and their past deeds is exclaimed by the figure Death, much in the same manner as the old-speakers-of-wisdom or *ancianos* of Preconquest times. Death speaks:

> Be happy, you who have been saddened for the bones scattered about here and there, and perhaps left in mounds!
> Now they speak not; neither do they move, nor smile, nor run.
> Nor do they go to the four directions seeking to conquer.
> They have lost their strength; they hold in their hands neither sword nor *macana*.[118]

Their dress is no longer beautiful as it was.
Now they lie in the dust, broken as small particles upon the earth.
While those who live upon the earth pass, tread, and rest upon them.
But they are neither angered nor do they cry out; nor do they move.
But when they lived upon the earth, no one dared to pass over them, and no one surpassed them in eloquence.
They held themselves to be as gods, but now come and see!
I come to all. I take away your strength and quit your life.
But weep not now, nor feel saddened.
I shall return shortly, perhaps tomorrow or soon thereafter;
Swiftly shall I come...[119]

This eulogy of life compared to death could very well be a description of the Aztec lord or honored warrior formulated according to their own value system. At any rate, the message is purposeful and clear: that no one, not even those magnificent embodiments of the highest Aztec values, the noble warriors, can escape death. Once dead, all men are as dust under the feet of the living, and there is no special heaven for the valiant as had been previously conceived.

The following is a sample of the measured dialogue between Jesus and Mary as they discuss the values appertaining to human souls, and they intercede for them:

MARY: Beloved Son, my flesh and my blood,
　　　The sins of the world weigh heavily upon you!
　　　Oh, that your justice might reach even to them who are in purgatory, the place in which they are purified with fire.
　　　I place before your eyes my tears, my pain.
　　　Let them, your beloved creatures, be close to you and happy at your side in heaven.

JESUS: Beloved and glorious mother,
　　　I shall do as you wish!

> I hold in my memory the affliction which I gave
> you when you bore me in your arms;
> And how you suffered and were pained when my
> enemies gave me torment.
> Men do not appreciate what you did for them.
> Let them—my beloved ones—go free, those
> who gave me happiness through your
> beloved and precious Rosary! [120]

As yet, there is no way of knowing either the exact dates, occasions, or places of the presentations of these two dramas. This is true of the majority of extant Nahuatl plays. We shall again refer to the problem of dating in the particular introductions to the plays included in this study.

Another extant manuscript of a Nahuatl play probably from this same period, also deals with the honoring and respecting of the dead through masses. Its title is *"In Animatzin Ihuan Alvaceasme,"* which is translated as *"Souls and Testamentary Executors."* This drama is included in this study and will not be discussed further here.

Although the Jesuits were not especially famous for their work in small rural villages or directly with indigenous peoples, they did in some instances present theatrical performances in indigenous languages. For example, in about 1573, shortly after their arrival in Mexico, the Jesuits in the College of Pátzcuaro were directing the initiation of an image of the Virgin sent to them by the head of their order. They had decided to use Epiphany as the occasion for this installation and had planned a program which included dances by the Indians of the region, and, in the afternoon, a play of unknown authorship in dialogue form, written partly in Tarascan and partly in Spanish.[121]

Under the date of December 8, 1574, there is a record of a play produced upon the occasion of the presentation of the Archbishop's pallium[122] to Pedro Moya de Contreras. This play represents a kind of missionary theater not principally aimed at the indigenous population, but which does not yet qualify as purely humanistic religious drama. This Spanish play, entitled *"Desposorio espiritual entre el Pastor pedro y la Iglesia mexicana"* (*"Spiritual Contract between the Shepherd Peter and the Mexican Church"*), was composed for this occasion by Juan Perez Ramirez. It is known that Ramirez was a Mestizo priest whose mother was Indian and whose father was a Spanish soldier. He knew the Nahuatl language well and was also able to write in Spanish and Latin. Ramirez was perhaps the first author of a drama of this genre whose heritage included both indigenous and Spanish genetic and cultural elements.

The *"Desposorio"* is interesting as an example of semi-humanistic drama in which the cast of characters includes such classical abstractions as the Mexican Church, Faith, Hope, Grace, and Charity. These roles were portrayed by shepherdesses; and the shepherds included such notables as Peter, Prudence, Justice, Modesty, and the like. The cast is completed with Divine Love, a chorus of singers, and thankfully, a buffoon.[123]

As to the last third of the sixteenth century, there are several references to theatrical productions contained in the records of the *Cabildo* proceedings of the most important towns in Mexico. Many of these refer to *Corpus* or Epiphany celebrations, or to the ceremonies performed to welcome viceroys, archbishops, or other visiting dignitaries. In these records, the names of specific actors are sometimes mentioned, as are the authors of the plays. The tone of the theater was changing from that associated with a narrow didactic conception to one calculated merely to entertain. Since this study is devoted primarily to the missionary theater, there will be few references to those other humanistic dramas, and to very few of the genre known as *"comedias."* [124]

It is interesting to note that in July of the year 1575, the municipal government of Mexico City offered a certain Diego Juarez a prize for his play and its presentation, including certain interludes and farces, during the *Corpus* celebration of that year. This play, *"La Cayda del Hombre"* (*"The Fall of Man*), was presented on a *carro*. The prize awarded for it consisted of fifty gold *pesos* (*cincuenta pesos de oro común*).[125]

Other prizes of this nature and their approximate values are mentioned, especially with respect to *Corpus* commenorations. Records of 1586, mention that 450 *pesos* were provided by the government of Mexico City toward the preparations for the *Corpus* celebration of that year. For the year 1593, the records show as large a sum as 1,300 gold pesos allotted for the preparation and presentation of the *autos* for the *Corpus* of that year. The extent of the patronage mentioned supports the idea that on all social levels present in sixteenth century colonial society, theatrical presentations were an important part of all principal *fiestas,* and that both for the Indian and the Spaniard they commanded great interest, as well as a substantial outlay of material wealth.

To return briefly to the year 1575, the *Corpus Christi* celebration in Etla, Oaxaca, was described in various records because of a tragic event that occurred at the time.

At that time Fray Alonso de la Anunciación was vicar of this territory. He was well-known for his extensive knowledge of the Zapotec language and was the author of the play to be presented on that occasion. His play was an *auto* including figures relevant to the Holy Eucharist, as found in the Old Testament. On that occasion, Fray Alonso had requested that a gallery be constructed near the convent in Etla, from which the many guests, himself included, could view the *auto* which followed a procession. The gallery was evidently poorly constructed and collapsed under the weight of the great crowd. One hundred and twenty died, and many were wounded in this accident. The dead included Fray Alonso himself, who had managed to escape from the collapse of the gallery, but who was then killed by two falling columns which had supported the roof.[126] The history written by Dávila Padilla mentions some of the *fiestas* celebrated by the Dominicans in Mexico, and particularly this one which he describes as being presented "outside, in the east part of the church patio."[127]

In November of 1578 a drama was presented by the Jesuits, which, while it belongs more to the category of humanistic rather than missionary theater, is mentioned because unusually complete data about it are available. These data include a translated text, substantiated by a carefully documented introduction and a set of notes.[128]

This play, entitled *"El Triunfo do los Santos"* (*"The Triumph of the Saints"*), was presented as a demonstration celebrating the receipt of the relics which Pope Gregory XIII had sent to the Jesuits of Mexico. This drama, actually a tragedy in five acts, represented the religious persecutions in the time of Diocletian as compared to the greater prosperity of the reign of the judicious Constantine. The *"Triunfo,"* which is composed in Spanish, is eclectic in flavor, has humanistic overtones, and commences with a prologue in octaves. It was not presented so much for popular missionary consumption as for a demonstration of the virtuosity of both the students and their Jesuit instructors in the *colegio* sponsoring the drama.

Father Juan Sanchez de Baquero, who was an eyewitness of the celebration, writes of it in his *Fundación de la Compañia de Jesús en Nueva España;* a text of the play is included in the extremely rare sixteenth century work of Father Pedro Morales entitled *Carta del Padre Pedro Morales de la Compañia de Jesús.* There are articles and detailed studies on, and even translations available of, the *"Triunfo,"* which was apparently one of the great successes of its day.[129]

A Dominican chronicler of the sixteenth century, Augustín Dávila Padilla, describes a *Passion* play in his *Historia* which he witnessed on Good Friday, April 13, 1582. This drama was presented by the Confraternity at the Church of Saint Dominic in Mexico City. Dávila Padilla pictures the scene of the church along side which were the three crosses bearing Christ and the three robbers. Nearby, there stood an articulated image of *La Soledad,* the Sorrowing Mother, which moved its hands as if to dry its tears. The midday sermon described the Passion; and at the mention of the burial, priests came out of the sacristy, kneeled down upon each step, and slowly took down the implements of the Passion story. Then they made a procession with the Christ figure through the streets to the Church of the Conception, where the image was interred until the following Sunday. At that time it was returned to Saint Dominic's.[130]

In the year 1587 Fray Alonso Ponce, who was commissary of the Franciscan missions in New Spain and visitor of the province of his order, describes a theatrical presentation which he witnessed in Tlaxamulco, while on a trip through Mexico. From his account we can clearly recognize both *"Los Pastores"* (*"The Shepherds"*) and the *"Adoración de los Reyes"* (*"Adoration of the Kings"*). We have historical references that during Epiphany it was and still is customary to present one version or another of these Christmas dramas. The celebration of 1578 will not be described here but will be dealt with in a detailed manner subsequently. Probably, the production referred to by Alonso Ponce is precisely the same *"Adoración de los Reyes"* the translation of which is included in this study.

It is known that the Christmas story was of especial interest to the Indians, and that they greatly enjoyed the *fiestas* connected with this holiday. Mendieta, in his *História eclesiastica indiana,* makes the following allusions:

> During the night of the Nativity of Our Lord, they [the Indians] are accustomed to place many torches in the patios of the churches, and some also in the terraces of their homes; so that, since their houses are numerous and extend for more than a league, it appears as if it were a starry sky. . . . In the church, they constructed for that night and for the successive nights until *Los Reyes,* a portal with a manger representing that in Bethlehem, and with the baby Jesus, his Mother, Joseph, and the Shepherds. . . . They also celebrate greatly the festival of *Los Reyes,* as if it were truly their own. For this, they present the *auto* of the Offering, in which there are [portrayed] the first offerings of the people and the foreigners [*gentiles*] who came to seek out and to adore the Lord and the Savior of the world.[131]

Among the contemporary dramatic repertories then, the

themes of the Nativity, including the aforementioned *Adoración* and *Pastores,* ranked high as favorite yearly rituals.

From as far away a mission as that in Sinaloa comes a report, in the year 1596, that the Christmas holidays were celebrated there with dances (*mitotes*), the singing of carols, and, moreover, with the presentation of a *coloquio* in the indigenous language of the area.[132] This *coloquio* must have been composed by one of the Jesuits teaching in the area. Although the data which are available pertain primarily to the valley of Mexico, references to the Mixtec area and to Sinaloa attest to the geographical spread of the use of didactic liturgical drama.

We have records from the period during and after the last decade of the sixteenth century which were kept both by the government of Mexico City and by the Church; these records contain references to various dramatic presentations enacted for special *fiestas.* For example, there is a record of two religious *"comédias"* produced in 1588 in the College of San Juan de Letrán; the 1594 records of Mexico City mention a contract with one Luis Lagarto for the *coloquios* for the *Corpus Christi* of 1596; and in 1600, the records acknowledge a drama about the *"divino"* which was to be presented again on *Corpus.*[133]

We have no detailed records of presentations of what can most accurately be designated as missionary theater in indigenous languages during the last part of the sixteenth century; however, through secondary references we can be certain that these productions were continued.

Mendieta, writing in 1585, mentioned that a *Padre* Juan de Ribas had been presenting a series of *autos* or mysteries and lives of the saints to further his teaching. No actual titles were listed.[134]

Torquemada also referred to Juan de Ribas and his work in the Convent of Tlaxcala; he stated that he was known by many to have possessed a good command of Nahuatl, and to have preached and produced representations of "mysteries of Our Holy Faith, and the lives of some Saints on their proper *fiestas,* that they, as exemplary things, might be better received and remembered as more vivid for the memory than mere words."[135]

Toward the end of the sixteenth century, Juan de Torquemada initiated a kind of theatrical production designated as *neixcuitilli* or "examples." These "examples" were mute dramas presented every Sunday afternoon, probably to accompany and illustrate the moral or religious themes of the sermon of the day. The presentation of these *neixcuitilli* in San José de los Naturales lasted at least for a century after their initiation.

Perhaps at the same time and in the same chapel in Mexico City, the Franciscan Francisco de Gamboa initiated the practice of presenting certain *pasos* every Friday night in memory of the Passion of Jesus Christ. For the purpose of supporting and preparing for these *pasos,* Gamboa founded a *Cofradía* or Brotherhood of *Nuestra Señora de Soledad* (Our Lady of Sorrows), which remained associated with San José. This practice too endured for many years.[136]

Many additional specific historical records of the sixteenth-century didactic religious theater are undoubtedly buried in various church or civic archives of smaller cities and *pueblos*; but these are most difficult to locate and consult. The references quoted are sufficient to assure us of the continuing and lively usage of this dramatic technique. The organized incorporation of plays into the weekly ritual cycle of the Church is a witness to the success of drama as a satisfactory teaching technique.

Although we do not know any of the titles of Torquemada's "examples," we do know that his teacher, the Franciscan Juan Bautista, in the year 1599 had printed three books of religious *"comedias"* which he had composed, as he stated, with the assistance of Agustín de la Fuente. Some of these themes might also have been used by Torquemada. The titles of the three volumes are *De la penitencia y sus partes* (Concerning Repentance and Its Meanings); *De los principales artículos de nuestra santa fé y parábolas del evangelio* (Concerning the Principal Articles of Our Holy Faith and Parables of the Gospel); and *Vidas de santos* (Lives of the Saints).[137]

We know further that Fray Juan Bautista was a lecturer in

theology in the College of Tlaltelolco and that Agustín de la Fuente was his educated Indian secretary and aide.

Through the writings of Francisco de Burgoa, we learn of the work of the Dominican Martín Jimenez. Jimenez worked for many years among the indigenous peoples referred to as the *Chochos*. He learned their language (Chocho Popoloca), and used drama as a technique to teach them. Martín Jimenez then travelled to the area of the Mixteca in Southwestern Mexico. He stayed there long enough to learn the Mixtec language.[138] His teaching method continued to include the use of drama with songs and music, as well as the presentation of *autos* about the Eucharist and the mysteries of the Gospel.

Many other Dominicans went to see and learn his methods of teaching. It was widely known that his plays were ingenious and that his method of instructing the Indians in proper intonations and delivery was unique. Other Indians flocked to see the strange phenomenon of their costumed peers enacting Gospel stories in their own language as well as to enjoy the content of these productions. Unfortunately, none of these plays is known to be extant today. This particular work was accomplished sometime near the end of the sixteenth century, or perhaps at the beginning of the seventeenth because Fray Martín Jimenez died in 1624.[139]

Copies of very few dramas in Nahuatl are extant the contents of which, if not the manuscripts themselves, can be dated from the sixteenth century. Some of these are religious and missionizing in their themes; others have fragmented off from the mainstream of liturgical subjects and deal with historical events, especially with battles. The various versions of the *"Danzas de moros y cristianos"* (*"Dances of the Moors and the Christians"*, as well as the *"Batalla contra Tepozteco"* (*"The Battle against the Tepozteco"*), which are still presented in Mexico undoubtedly date back to the sixteenth century. The same is true for the play *"Invención de la Cruz por Santa Elena"* (*"How the Blessed Saint Helen Found the Holy Cross"*). To this list can be added the *"Cuaderno de marqueses"* (*"Notations of the Marqueses)"*, which is still known in both the Spanish and the Nahuatl versions. The theme of this dramatic dance concerns the entrance into Mexico of the conquistadores.[140]

There are extant several versions of dramas dealing with the Passion of Christ, which was as popular a theme for didactic presentation in the sixteenth century as it is today. Two manuscripts treating this subject are of particular interest. One of these, 115 pages in length, is now in the library of Tulane University. This drama was celebrated at Tepalcingo and appears to be a very old version of a text not known to be extant now. The second manuscript bearing the date 1732, has content which is certainly much older.[141] The themes of both these manuscripts include many legendary elements, the intervention of angels, unknown personages, and other interesting features which denote changes at the hands of the *pueblo*.

Dramas which portray the miraculous revelation of the Virgin of Guadalupe are still popular. Examples of these are: *"Coloquio de la aparición de la Virgen Santa María de Guadalupe"* ("Coloquio of the Apparition of the Holy Virgin Mary of Guadalupe"), and the *"El portento mexicano"* ("The Mexican Miracle").[142]

Fragmentary references to other plays possibly of sixteenth-century origin are found in the unpublished notes and manuscripts of Francisco Paso y Troncoso in the Archives of the National Museum of Anthropology and History in Mexico City.[143] The most complete and up-to-date bibliography of plays written in Nahuatl is Pimentel's the *Piezas teatrales en lengua nahuatl: Bibliografía descriptiva.*[144]

During the last quarter of the sixteenth century, the Jesuit theater, which grew and flourished, seemed to have shared in all the elements of the various types of drama celebrated during this era. The Society of Jesus began work in Mexico only as late as 1572, but the extent of their work in education, especially in the founding of colleges, was prodigious. From the beginning, they taught their students the classical and humanistic subjects and traditions. Although they used dialogues, *coloquios,* tragedies, and comedies as didactic vehicles, their purpose was never simply that of converting uneducated peoples, but rather of teaching and giving intellectual exercises to students interested in learning the Western Christian historical tradition.

Toward this end, the earliest Jesuit-sponsored plays were usually composed in Spanish, and, in a remarkably short time, in Latin as well. The Jesuits were sometimes called upon to present a play to commemorate a civic occasion such as welcoming visiting ecclesiastical or political dignitaries. Within the colleges themselves the usual occasions for the presentations of dramas were the opening and closing of each semester on October 18 (St. Luke's Day) and on July 25 (St. James' Day) respectively; and on Assumption Day, Christmas, Epiphany, Easter, and *Corpus Christi*. The patron saint of each college and town in which the college was situated were commemorated in this fashion.[145]

The aforementioned *"Triumph of the Saints"* is an excellent example of such plays, being clearly eclectic and studiedly classical in style. The Jesuit dramas were usually of a moral or religious tone, the mutability of man being an especially favored subject. The Church and the Bible furnished further themes for theological or humanistic interpretation.[146]

Early in the sixteenth century it was not difficult to distinguish the religious from the profane theater. The earliest plays were patently religious in nature and their purpose didactic. But the period of transition came early too; the Spanish-dominated persentations of *Corpus Christi,* and the later public theatrical productions for clearly profane celebrations also oftentimes involved religious figures and symbols.

When professional actors began to play roles and the interpretation of characters began to change, then the introduction of elements of buffoonery and broad humor placed much of the drama outside the category of religious theater. Some of theplays or dramatic themes began as genuine *"comedias"* of evangelization but lost their original meanings and evolved into dramatic entertainments featuring fireworks and colorful costumes amid great pageantry. The various *"Dances of the Moors and Christians"* exemplify this category.

The works of Hernán González de Esclava, who was born in Spain in 1534 and arrived in Mexico during the 1560's, bridge the gap between the religious and profane theater although they do not qualify as missionary or evangelizing drama. Of Esclava's works, sixteen *coloquios* and one *entremés* have been published. García Icazbalceta did the definitive work of collecting, editing, and republishing these plays. Although Esclava's dramas are entitled *Autos Sacramentales* and *Coloquios Espirituales,* it is clear that they do not all properly fall within this classification. Many were composed solely for such political occasions as viceregal birthdays.[147] That they are of a superior literary quality in comparison with the homely and oftentimes crude missionary dramas is also undeniable.

By the end of the sixteenth century some works of the classical non-religious dramatists of Spain had been translated into the indigenous languages. It is doubtful that this practice was widespread. There is a Nahuatl manuscript containing two comedies of Lope de Vega in the Bancroft Library at the University of California at Berkeley. In the same manuscript is also contained a Nahuatl version of *"El Gran Teatro del Mundo"* by Calderón de la Barca, as well as a play of non-Spanish origin called the *"In ilamatzin ihuan Piltontli"* (*"The Old Woman and the Child"*). The translations of these plays as well as the *entremés* we owe to Bartolomé de Alva Ixtlilxochitl, born about 1600 in San Juan Teotihuacan.[148]

A manuscript of another interesting drama, the age and provenience about which diverse opinions exist, is included in the García collection of the Latin American Library at the University of Texas. This manuscript consists of twenty-three folios in handwritten Spanish and is included with other writings attributed to Gutiérrez de Luna, a "creole." The paper of the manuscript of the drama is distinct from that of the other writings with which it is included, and Carlos Castañeda judges it to be the first part of the sixteenth century, and to have been wholly incorporated into the writings by Luna and not copied by him. Castañeda feels that the Spanish of the play is more polished and literary than Luna's, and that the historical details of the plot are too complex for Luna to have known. This *coloquio* is entitled *"De la nueva conbercion y bautismo de los quatro ultimos reyes de Tlaxcala en la Nueva España"* (*"The New Conversion and Baptism of the Four Last Kings of Tlaxcala"*). All action is accomplished in one scene and no stage direction are included. Castañeda who has published an English translation of the play [149] concludes that there is good reason for attributing this *coloquio* to Motolinía, who was so active in Tlaxcala in the sixteenth century.

The play concerns the conversion and baptism of the four last and very famous Aztec kings of Tlaxcala. The cast of characters includes kings Xicotencatl, Maxiscatzin, Zitlalpopocatzin, and Tehuexolotzin and the demon idol Hongol; two angels who sing; an ambassador; the Marques del Valle (Cortés); Juan Diaz, a cleric; Marina (Malinche, the Indian interpreter and mistress of Cortés); and another ambassador.

Garibay does not feel that the *coloquio* is a sixteenth century play, or that it can be attributed to Motolinía. He judges that the style and versification are reminiscent of a period closer to the middle of the seventeenth century. The *"Bautismo"* could be an adaptation of an earlier play in Nahuatl. Garibay adds that "Hongol" was not a known god in Tlaxcala.[150]

It is true that the historical records concerning the actual baptism of these four Tlaxcaltecan kings are contradictory. It is highly unlikely that, as legend has it, they were converted and baptized within twenty days of Cortés' arrival in Tlaxcala. No surviving document for a generation subsequent to this time mentions the event; and, although the four names do appear in literature, no record agrees on the Christian names of these four rulers.[151]

It is plausible that the play and the ideas which it contains date back to the sixteenth century, but that the manuscript is of much later origin. The last four kings were used as symbols of great power and prestige brought to the fold and glory of

Christianity. Their names and fame as great leaders and warriors have not been forgotten, for contemporary Nahuatl speakers in the area of Tlaxcala are aware of the historical importance of these names.[152]

Albeit "Hongol" was not a known god in Tlaxcala, there is, the author believes, a simple and sound explanation for the use of this character in the drama. *"Hongo"* is the Spanish word for "mushroom"; the "l" was probably added to make a proper name out of this term. This new term ("Hongol") was very likely formed by the process of linguistic analogy to Nahuatl morphology, which includes "l" as a final phoneme of proper names and nominals. It is known that at the time of the conquest, as well as today, there existed a widespread ritual usage of an hallucenogenic mushroom for divining or curing purposes in certain areas of the Valley of Mexico.[153]

The Nahuatl name of the hallucenogenic variety of mushroom is *"teonanacatl,"* the most widely accepted translation of which is "divine flesh" or "flesh of the god." These *teonanacatl* were taken orally (eaten or drunk), and greatly venerated as obvious repositories of divine power and revelation. The general portent of the play is to eulogize the Christian Eucharist and rituals, and to calumniate those of the indigenous pagan heritage. The final *villancico*, sung by two angels accompanied by guitars, sums up this idea nicely:

> Ask, oh soul, and you shall receive
> Far more than you ask.
> If you ask for bread in God's name,
> God's own substance shall be given you as bread.

> New life is this day given
> To man in a single morsel,
> Though the guest is mere man
> He feeds on God Himself.

> Come one, come all,
> You are all invited to the feast.
> If you ask for bread in God's name,
> God's own substance shall be given you as bread.

> Behold the feast is free,
> If he who wishes to partake
> Is unable to attend
> It shall be given at his home.
>
> The poor are rich in this,
> Come, partake of the feast,
> If you ask for bread in God's name,
> God's own substance shall be given you as bread.[154]

It is probable that the writer of this *coloquio* was a priest accustomed to thinking of religion in terms of the sacraments, and who knew something of the history and the customs of the area of Tlaxcala. He substantivized and personalized the ritual sacrament of the taking-of-the-flesh-of-god in mushroom form into "Hongol." He opposed this demon-Eucharist to Christianity, epitomized and symbolized through its sacraments of Baptism and the Holy Eucharist. This is mentioned in some detail as an excellent example of the use of existing indigenous ideas and symbols for the purpose of teaching and evangelizing for Christianity.

In spite of the intense religiosity of both the missionary fathers and the evangelizing dramas which they planned and presented to the indigenous public, there was a constant temptation to interject a light or comical motif. These farcical interludes sometimes included a rather broad genre of humor, and this travesty, real or imaginary, came to be regarded as dangerous by the Church. In this manner, religious drama in Mexico came to be legally censured just as it had been in Europe for similar offenses.

In 1544 or 1545 Zumárraga, the first bishop of Mexico, added the following statement to an appendix of a treatise he sent to Dionysius Cartujano:

> There exists a thing of great profanity and shame; for it appears that in front of the most Holy Sacrament (apparently the Host as carried in processions) go men with masks, dressed as women, and dancing and leaping about shamefully and lasciviously, making a confusion and disturbing the

hymns of the church. They represent profane triumphs, such as of the god of love, with great immodesty; and to immodest people belongs the shame for seeing them. What could be worse in the presence of our God? Further, these things they do with no little cost both to the Indians, and to the city officials, and to the poor people; for they are compelled to pay for the *fiesta*.[155]

Zumárraga continued his censorship of farcical elements in the missionary theater. He was fearful that, precisely because the Indians were accustomed to celebrating their Prehispanic festivals with songs, dances, and farces, they might therefore misunderstand the basic ideas of Christianity and judge that in such *"burlerias"* consists the sanctification of the *fiesta*.[156]

He was the only one among the chroniclers to speak so harshly of the Church-sponsored drama. The rest of the Church fathers spoke most highly of the theater as a powerful weapon of edification. Zumárraga, always a zealous man and protective of his ideas, continued to censure the theater until his death on June 3, 1548.

During the period in which the episcopal see was empty, dances and representations, especially for *Corpus Christi*, were permitted. But in 1555, Alonso de Montúfar, the Dominican who suceeded Zumárraga, renewed the legislation prohibiting dramatic performances. He stated that because he had heard of "certain excesses" portrayed in the theater, no representation would be permitted without punishment for all concerned, unless special permission was first given by the Church. The categories of persons who were liable for punishment if they were found guilty of disobeying Montúfar's edict included the authors; the actors involved; the clergy directing; and even the *mayordomos* responsible for the sponsorship of the representations. He added that any presentation permitted could be enacted only during the daylight or at dawn.[157]

That this conflict concerning acceptable teaching methods and entertainment had even reached the ears of the King of Spain is evident from the following fragment:

To the President and Judges of the Royal Court of New
Spain: It has been told to us that there are a great many
(and the expense is great) instruments of music and singers
in the monasteries not only of the big but also of the little
towns. This is too expensive, leads to the wasting of time and
to loose morals in general. Very lazy are those who grow up
from childhood in the monasteries with nothing to do but
this. Such men do not pay tribute, therefore leaving it for the
poor to pay. Therefore, call everyone together and change all
this to quiet and rectitude for the Indians.

Toledo, the 19th of February, 1561,

I, the King (rubric)[158]

In spite of such legislative discouragements and censure, the liturgical and didactic drama continued. It is uncertain exactly when full privileges for dramatic presentations returned, but by the year 1565 the *Cabildo* was far from opposing the production of *autos*. They voted to give every year "a prize of gold or silver, of value up to thirty crowns for the best representation or work which someone had composed to present on the day of *Corpus*."[159]

In 1574 the Court of Mexico proposed and approved a law which stated that:

. . .There be presented in the cathedral neither *autos,* nor *comedias,* nor other dramatic pieces without their first having passed the censorship of a hearer.[160]

Again, in 1575, a letter of chastisement was sent from the King of Spain—this time to the Archbishop of Mexico:

To the Archbishop of Mexico, with respect to a certain comedy presented on the occasion of the presentation of the Pontifical Cloak to the Archbishop, about an interlude concerning Tax Collectors: We are informed of a farce which was presented, and also of an interlude about a Tax Collector, which has caused ill-feeling and murmuring among those to whom it was presented. If the Archbishop had not first seen it to check it, then the fault in duty lies there. There must be a good example for the Indians who imitate what they see in the religious leaders.

Written in Villaseca, the 26th of April, 1575,
I, the King (rubric).[161]

From the quotations which we have, it would seem that the censure of the king was impelled as much by economic interest as by religious piety.

Finally, the legal curtailment initiated by Zumárraga was reduced to its proper limitations by the Third Church Council of 1585. This council followed the precedents established by other councils and prohibited such presentations *in* the churches; that is: "of dances, ballets, representations, and profane songs, either on the day of the birth of Our Lord, or on the *fiesta* of *Corpus Christi*, or on other similar occasions."[162]

This censure actually affected only presentations which could be considered "profane," and specified that they should not be presented *in* the churches, thus leaving an opening for presentations outside the church proper.

To this they added the following clarification:
. . .However, if there would be a presentation of some sacred story, or other things holy and useful to the soul, or the singing of certain devoted hymns, then these should be presented one month ahead of time to the Bishop, that they might be examined and approved by him.

It is uncertain how widely these censures were either known or enforced, for in spite of the legal probitions first initiated by Zumárraga there are records of *autos* and even farces being presented *in* the churches and in their portals after this was expressly forbidden. The following is an example of such exceptions from the legal records of Puebla de los Angeles, a city too near Mexico City not be *au courant* with its legislation:

This day it is decided by common consent to celebrate the *fiesta* of the Most Holy Sacrament, the day of *Corpus Christi* of this year of 1588, and to do a comedy *(comedia) in* the cathedral.[163]

For the succeeding year a similar statement appears concerning the same *fiesta,* and about a *"comedia"* presented *in* the cathedral. By the year 1600, it was true that the majority of presentations were done in the doorways and courtyards of the churches. The reasons for this are various, however, and concern elements other than legal prohibitions.

At this point we notice a difference between the usual places for presentations of dramatic representations. In both Spain and Mexico, liturgical dramas were enacted within the cathedrals. The masses themselves sometimes comprised interludes within the action of the plays; heaven and hell could be the altar and the place beneath it. In Spain it then became customary to present plays on *carros* or wagons which could be drawn about the city, placed in squares or other open places, and used as stages for the dramas. This method, although there are records of its use was never as popular in Mexico as it was in Spain.

The *tablado,* actually an elevated stage constructed for dramatic presentations, was earlier used in Spain, but more widely accepted in Mexico. *Tablados* were often built in areas where a procession was to move, and the drama would be presented as interludes in the procession itself. More than one *tablado* could therefore create a kind of multiple staging method. As previously defined, platform stages and dramatic processions were in keeping with the Prehispanic indigenous heritage of religious presentation, and for this reason were understood and appreciated by the Indian audience.[164]

The net result of all the legislation and ecclesiastical censure of dramatic presentation was to scotch but never destroy the procedure. The hillsides and church courtyards of the *pueblos* of contemporary Mexico still become stages for dramatic rituals during the most important *fiestas;* and processions, dances, music, mock battles, and the whole theatrical *entourage* are supported by patronage and the cooperation of *cofradías* and *mayordomías* just as they were in the sixteenth century.

The early chroniclers describe the great crowds of Indians who gathered at the churches in their intense eagerness to share in the ritual life of the Christian sacraments, to hear the messages of the fathers, and to view the representations illustrating their ideas. Probably the immensity of the crowds concerned more than the element of legal censure soon dictated that most religious representations be held outside the churches in the courtyards. Indeed, this situation was so prevalent that it influenced the architecture of many churches in Mexico and expedited the invention of the "open chapel" (*capilla abierta*). This is an architectural phenomenon which does not exist outside Mexico.

In some areas it was necessary that the church buildings remain more secure because of the ever-fresh memories of marauders and hostilities. Nevertheless, the open chapel flourished in most parts of Mexico. A few examples of this kind of architecture still exist in Mexico, notably Acolman near Teotihuacan, which still has a terraced amphitheatre-like area for the seating of the audience.

These *capillas abiertas* usually had a small central nave, with broad lateral arches which gave them the atmosphere of an open air theater. In this way there was a greater capacity to accommodate the multitudes who gathered for *fiesta* occasions.

The scenario of the missionary theater in Mexico exuded its own unique flavor. The Indians, not particularly capable of or interested in theological subtleties and abstract symbols, imbued the scenarios of their dramatic representations with a realistic extravagance which dazzled the spectator. It is clear from the reports of missionaries that the Indians themselves not only played the roles but also created and constructed the scenarios. They turned their imaginations not to investing simple settings with imagined furnishings, but rather to the ingenious construction of realistic staging, utilizing as many natural elements as possible. Here we can recall the descriptions of the complex and detailed scenario and staging of the *Corpus* representations of 1538 and 1539, which Motolinía includes. The Indians often used what can technically be termed "multiple staging."[165] For example, they used different but clearly visible settings to designate "earth-level": one for Paradise before the

Fall; another for earth, but subsequent to the Fall. The use of real animals tethered to real rocks and trees and actual fire to portray the tortures of hell, and the construction of "mountains" for stages, and actual towers for the settings of cities, all must have enhanced the effects of the stories and actions so ardently apostrophized by the missionary teachers. The contrivance of a series of ropes and towers by which the star was suspended above the heads of the Magi and finally over the manger of the Christ child in the Nativity dramas is exemplary of the elaborate lengths to which stage props were detailed. This will be referred to later in this study.

The consistent and lively inclusion of much music, dancing, firework displays, instrumentation imitating celestial sounds, vivid portrayal of hellfire itself, off-stage voices, mysterious appearances and disappearances of supernatural characters, all contrived to insure an interested audience of a memorable experience, not only homiletic but entertaining.

The virtuosity of the Indians as musicians, singers, and dancers was noted by the chroniclers. Descriptions of the curricula of schools and colleges conspicuously include classes in music and chorus. We know from extant manuscripts that the representations were frequently interrupted by musical interludes, and occasionally by lengthy dances. This practice, more alien to the esthetic canons of Europe, is again closely in accord with the Prehispanic indigenous practice of including music and dance as important and valued elements both in the educational curriculum and in the ritual celebrations.

The characterizations in liturgical drama as it had been presented in Europe were standardized to a great degree during the medieval and renaissance periods. Biblical figures were clear-cut representations, and their manner of conducting themselves was predictable. Since much of this symbolism and gesturing was extraneous to the indigenous culture, adaptations in characterization had to be made. Most of the missionaries were wise enough to see that whatever was alien to the social organization of the Indians would fabricate a weak symbol, difficult to understand and lacking in dramatic empathy.

The rigidity of the Prehispanic social organization with its prevailing religiosity is reflected in the *language* used in the missionary theater. This will be further clarified in the final section of this study by the translated texts of some of the plays. The seemingly tireless necessity for repetition, the great formality in the patterned salutations and blessings are all reminiscent of general elements in Nahuatl literature, as well as of the one play which we possess in Maya, the *"Rabinal Achi"*. Adjustments in narrative content to the pattern of Indian literary devices will become evident as we turn to the last section of this study, that is, to the plays themselves.

Each of the seven plays contained in this study was translated from the Nahuatl. None of them has ever been published in English before, and four of them have remained completely unpublished until now. The remaining three plays were published in Spanish, but in such limited editions that they are not now readily obtainable.

Although it is fairly certain that each of them is essentially a sixteenth-century play, in no case is the manuscript from which the translations were made from that same century. They are later copies or versions of which perhaps several variations were extant during the first century after the conquest.

Each of the dramas is preceded by a brief introduction including whatever data are available with reference to either dating or stylistic elements. Notes have been added to the translations to help clarify some of the more obscure allusions to Prehispanic or sixteenth-century indigenous culture.

As is inevitable in translation, a considerable amount of the flavor of the original Nahuatl texts is regrettably lost. The translations are literally faithful, however, and many awkward phrases and circumlocutions have been deliberately included, as they are characteristic of the original Nahuatl.

In no case is any of these plays a rare gem of great literary beauty; so violence to the esthetic value of the original text is minimal. In each case, the *content* of the play is the thing to be noted and appreciated. The value of these dramas lies in the information which they communicate to us about the method and the content of the acculturation process of the sixteenth century as studied from the standpoint of the religious-didactic nexus.

As has been mentioned, many of the dramatic and ritual celebrations of contemporary Mexico have their direct antecedents in the homely but entertaining missionary plays of the sixteenth century. These *fiesta* commemorations further epitomize the remarkable amalgam which has persisted for over four hundred years between Prehispanic indigenous ideas and the version of Roman Catholicism practiced in Mexico today. And so to the plays themselves.

III

"THE SACRIFICE OF ISAAC"

introduction

The *"Sacrificio de Isaac"* was copied from a manuscrpit belonging to the library of Alfredo Chavero, which is an orthographic copy of the middle of the eighteenth century. The manuscript states that the play had been presented in 1678, but that the original copy was no longer in existence. Thus, the manuscript which served for the translation from Nahuatl to Spanish was copied on February 1st, 1760, by one Bernabe Vasquez.

In the microfilm division of the library of history at Chapultepec in Mexico City are the following copies of this play: one copy in Nahuatl (Roll V) of the original which is said to be in the Archives of the National Museum of Anthropology and History (the author has been unable to locate the original of this manuscript); secondly, a paleographic copy of the Nahuatl, including an introduction by J. H. Cornyn, dated 1932 (Roll XIV); thirdly, a copied version of the play including both the Nahuatl and a translation into Spanish by Chimalpopoca (Roll III).

The internal evidence of the play indicates that it dates back to the sixteenth century. For this reason, the date 1678 on the manuscript does not indicate the date of the first presentation in Mexico, but probably that of a local attempt to renovate the memory of its previous presentations. There are other reasons for dating *"The Sacrifice of Isaac"* back to the sixteenth century. The first is that it is immediately preceded in the manuscript by a drama whose theme concerns the celebration of Epiphany. This play very closely fits the circumstances and description of the Epiphany drama presented by the Indians in Tlaxomulco on February 6th, 1587. Further, the Nahuatl words chosen to refer to Ishmael, son of Hagar, are carefully couched so

83

that the fact that he is also the son of Abraham is concealed. Ishmael addresses Isaac as *"no' kniuhtcinen,"* which is derived from *"ikniuhtli";* the latter is used in the sense of friend rather than brother. Ishmael also uses the same term to designate other children and to refer to their status as friends and nothing more.

This kind of verbal ambiguity and deliberate suppression of historical tradition is understandable in a period of history when the missionaries were most energetic in their attempts to combat the Prehispanic custom of concubinage.

Certain phrases used in *"The Sacrifice of Isaac"* are particularly reminiscent of the *Hueyhueytlatolli,* which is of Prehispanic origin. This *Hueyhueytlatolli* consists of the advice of the elders to the youth with respect to their deportment in important social relationships and situations. It is clearly didactic in purpose, and the language used was typical and therefore easily understood by a people accustomed to this traditional phraseology.

Again we note that, whenever possible, the action is played in settings calculated to be familiar and therefore comprehensible to an indigenous audience; e.g., the banquet scene of a noble (Abraham) entertaining other nobles; the use of flowers for important decorative purposes, as well as the presence of music accompanying various units of action and dialogue; the formality of salutation and conversation used by the characters of the play; and specific reference to the worship of the sun.

The title of the drama placed on it by the author or copyist is *"Del Nasimiento de Isaác del Sacrificio que Habrahan su Padre quiso por mandado de Dios hazer."* In the title page of the work only *"Sacrificio de Isaac"* is used, and the drama does not in fact include the birth of Isaac. Indeed, as the play opens, Isaac is not only already born but nearly grown to manhood.

Francisco Paso y Troncoso presented the Spanish translation of this play for the Twelfth International Congress of Orientalists, which was held in October of 1899 in Rome, Italy. It was then published in a very limited edition under the title of the play *"Sacrificio de Isaac,"* by Salvandor Landi of Florence, Italy, in 1899. The translation published here was made from this Paso y Troncoso publication.

Paso y Troncoso states that his translation of the play from the Nahuatl into Spanish is extremely literal. This manner of translation was chosen in order to conserve some of the original Nahuatl flavor of imagery and phraseology. For this same reason, certain phrases and repetitious expressions which seem circumloquacious have been preserved in English as well. As usual, many expressions and ideas which are typical of Nahuatl literature and culture in general are designated in the footnotes. The presence of many of these Nahuatlisms is also evidence that the age of this play is close to the time of the conquest when these phrases were current and still richly connotative.

The Sacrifice of Isaac

CAST OF CHARACTERS:

God the Father
An angel
Abraham
Sarah
Isaac
Two nobles
Hagar the slave
Ishmael
Two servants
A demon

(Enter ABRAHAM *And His Wife,* SARAH.*)*

ABRAHAM: Oh God, Almighty Father, who exists for all time! You who deigned to create the heaven, the earth, the sun, the moon, and the stars, and all things on earth visible and invisible! Let all the inhabitants of heaven ever praise You in Your royal home deep in Paradise—for it is thus that You created them, that they might ever rejoice in Your abode. And likewise we, Your creatures, whom You formed and created in Your power, we poor ones here upon earth praise You. And you, my beloved wife, from whom was born my first son—of my blood and complexion—take care not to offend in some way your Creator, almightly God the Father.

SARAH: Oh my beloved lord, you have already lived a long time here on earth where the almighty God created you; and for this reason I am now greatly grieved!

(*She Weeps And Dries Her Eyes On A Handkerchief.*)

ABRAHAM: Do not weep so! What pains you? Tell me!

SARAH: In truth, I weep because of my precious son, Isaac, the splendor and light of my soul—he who is truly my firstborn and of my own blood and complexion. What if I gave him my milk, what if I nurtured him with my own milk? Now we see by his countenance that he is already grown. Who will be able to say to us that perhaps we have merit because of our son if perhaps he will be of some service to Him. (that is) God, to the end that he prospers upon the earth? Perhaps he will not follow His law, as He has ordained us His creatures to do! If you should die tomorrow or soon afterwards, who will there be to teach him? Who will make him see the honorable life which has carried others to heaven?[1]

(*Here She Weeps.*)

SARAH: My soul weeps because my milk, my own milk, will be lost in vain. Truly it would have been better had I never conceived, never given birth!

(*Here An* ANGEL *Appears.*)

ANGEL: Your reasoning was clearly heard in heaven before the almighty and most Holy Trinity. Hear this, you people of the world! Something shall come to pass because of this child, Isaac. In order that the whole world be saved, from his lineage shall be formed the precious Son of God. He with his precious blood and death shall truly open Heaven where his portentous and holy Father is. And even if the precious and holy Son of God should not be formed from Him directly, first this one—the blessed and beloved child Isaac—must be shaped and developed. For this reason be consoled, oh mother and father.

(*The* ANGEL *Disappears*).

ABRAHAM: Do not vex yourself so much, for truly the almighty Himself must nurture and strengthen my jewel, my golden son![2] And now before anything else, let us go in and rest ourselves a little.

SARAH: So will it be. Please enter.

(*They Enter. There Is The Music Of Flutes.* ISHMAEL *Enters Alone.*)[3]

ISHMAEL: My heart is greatly pained. My face is inflamed because of the boy Isaac, a person of very good behavior, but one who never cares to become my friend. Nor has he ever sought to play with me as the other children do when we frolic together. It is true that if his father or his mother ask him anything he carefully fulfills their commands; nor does he disobey in the least thing. Then what can I do to be able to talk often with him?

(*A* DEMON *Enters, Dressed Either As An Angel Or As An Old Man.*)[4]

DEMON: What are you doing, young man? For I see your affliction is very great.

ISHMAEL: Most certainly my affliction is great! But how is it that you know if I have pain? Who told you this?

DEMON: Do you not see that I am a messenger from heaven? I was sent here from there in order to tell you what you are to do here on earth.

ISHMAEL: Then I wait to hear your command.

DEMON: Here then why it is that you are troubled. Do I astound you? Truly it is because of the beloved child, Isaac! Because he is a person of a good life, and because he always has confidence in the commands of his father. So you contrive and wish with all your energy that he not be obedient to his father and mother. Most assuredly I can tell you what you must do [to accomplish this.]

ISHMAEL: Oh how you comfort me when I hear your advice. Nor do I merit your aid. You are most truly a dweller in heaven and my protector!

DEMON: Open your heart wide to my command! Look now—his father and his mother have invited many others [to a banquet]; they are relaxing and greatly enjoying themselves. Now is the time to give Isaac bad advice so that he might forget his father and his mother and go with you to amuse himself in some other place. And if he should obey you, they will certainly punish their son for this, however well they love him.

ISHMAEL: I shall do just as you command.

DEMON: Then, indeed, I am going to return to heaven. For I came only to console you and tell you what you must do.

(They Leave. Thunder Is Heard In Various Areas. ABRAHAM *And His Son,* ISAAC, *Enter. They Are Well-Costumed.*

ABRAHAM: You, oh my necklace of gold! You, my bracelet of precious stones! Oh you, my girdle of silver, my beloved son, come here! I offer you my counsel, embracing you at the same time. You must believe that the following is the truth: that God the almighty Father created you and all the creatures of the earth, both visible and invisible. Hear then, oh my beloved and esteemed son! Watch with this purpose in mind, that you do not stain your soul, your spirit, in some way and in some time. Would that you always feel as a precious stone, and think as a pearl. For a child of God ought to be thus. And do not break the beloved, marvelous, and royal precepts of our Lord God. Engrave this well on your heart! Remember this for all times: that truly your Maker and Your Creator exists. He who made you is worthy to be eternally praised in heaven and on earth. And further, my beloved son, know that now persons of your kin are coming here to see you. So now they will come to know how much I love you, my cherished son![5]

ISAAC: Oh my beloved father! My begetter upon this earth! Truly now your substance and your possessions (land and earth) are made old! I have given you great pain and labor here on earth. Granted that you have nurtured me, and that you have given me my daily maintenance (lunch and dinner), as well as that with which I cover my body, which is as earth and dust. You fulfill your labor of mercy, and yet I give you suffering and pain. Oh my cherished father! Truly I have gained much from the beloved and cherished advice with which you counsel me. Yet, I bow your head, and stir up your breast! I shall certainly do whatever you command me, oh my beloved and honored father.

ABRAHAM: Look then, order my servants together so that they may prepare my dining room. Let us comfort ourselves a little there.

ISAAC: I go at once to fulfill your respected command, my cherished father.

(ISAAC *And* ABRAHAM *Enter (Exit)*. HAGAR *The Slave and Her Son,* ISHMAEL, *Enter.*)

HAGAR: Now while the great lord Abraham once again entertains many for the sake of his son whom he so greatly loves, we are only servants. He values us but little. And you, my son, merit nothing, are worthy of nothing. Oh that I might placate myself through you, and that you might calm all my torment upon earth! But so it is; your birth and its reward are eternal tears.

(*Here They Both Weep—Also The Son.*)

ISHMAEL: Oh you sun! You who are so high! Warm us even here with your great splendor as well as in every part of the world, and—in the way which you are able—prosper all the peoples of the earth! And to us, yes, even to us two poor ones—who merit nothing and who are worthy of nothing![6] Know now, oh my mother, what I shall do:

later, when they are all feasting, perhaps I shall be able to lead Isaac away with some deceit, so that we might go to divert ourselves in some other quarter. With this action he will violate the precept of his father, who will not then love him with all of his heart.[7]

HAGAR: What you are thinking is very good. Do it in that way.

(Here ISAAC *Enters.)*

ISAAC: What are you doing here? Is everything which is necessary already prepared? [Otherwise] prepare the table.

ISHMAEL: All is well. We are discussing this matter now so that nothing in the feast will be incorrect, and that all the players and musicians are notified so that they will all be here.

ISAAC: Do it accordingly then. Put everything in order quickly.

(They Arrange Everything. They Place A Table And Chairs Where They Are All To Eat. They Arrange Many Flowers There Also. Music Is Played. ABRAHAM, SARAH, *And* TWO NOBLES *Enter. They Embrace* ISAAC.*)*

ISAAC: You are most welcome here, my beloved and honored father; and you, oh cherished mother; and you also, oh beloved and esteemed nobles. Rest yourselves! We are awaiting you here.

FIRST
NOBLE: Oh how I enjoy his practical wisdom,—this young man! May He who exists forever, the Eternal One, the Lord God of all the world, grant him valor!

SECOND
NOBLE: Much good is manifest in him. His progress is truly great. Assuredly this precious blood came from honorable men!

ABRAHAM: Rest yourselves, esteemed gentlemen!

(Here They Are Seated. There Are The Sounds Of Music.

The Sacrifice of Isaac 91

HAGAR *Is At Hand, As Well As* ISHMAEL *Who Stretches Out His Hand To Isaac.*)

ISHMAEL: Come, oh my friend! While everyone is enjoying himself here, let us also go to some place and divert ourselves. Perhaps you must attend to something here? Or perhaps you must constantly venerate your father and your mother? Let us go. Let us enjoy ourselves as our friends the other children do.

ISAAC: I must not forget the precepts of my beloved father and mother! Leave me! Enjoy yourself alone!

(*The Music Sounds Another Time.* ISAAC *Withdraws A Little From The Table. He is Deeply Humiliated.*)

SARAH: You, oh lord! You, the greatly esteemed, oh you my cherished husband! I beseech you and those who are present here—so worthy of honor—that you would hear my humble homily about my precious son. Indeed, while we were eating here, the son of the slave seized your beloved son by the hand to take him from the house that together they might divert themselves. Truly I often weep because of such tomfoolery and hoaxes, for the reason that I fear your beloved son be lost.

ABRAHAM: Come here, slave, and with you your son. (Bow down) together here.

(HAGAR *And* ISHMAEL *Come Forward Together.*)

ABRAHAM: Now here this, you, oh mother! Your son, whom you view with joy, disports himself incessantly. If you do not strike him (in punishment) the guilt will be yours, and you will pay for it in Hell tomorrow or soon afterwards.

FIRST

NOBLE: You speak justly. The petty act, the low trick are the beginnings of evil. For truly, if we don't take our sons in hand the blame will be ours very soon.

SARAH: If you don't send them away, they will make your

cherished and valued son negligent. They will truly teach him a life of corruption and contumely.

ABRAHAM: I shall do as you wish.

SECOND
NOBLE: Dismiss them then. Or is it possible that those of the evil life, both the mother and son, might come to be loved? Perhaps, as they say, you will do them some good. Perhaps he (Isaac) will amount to something, and a good life will demonstrate to them the infamy which was done to God and to you by him.

ABRAHAM: Go! Leave me! And may I see you here no longer. Quit our village so that you do not teach your evil life to our true sons, you ignorant ones!

(HAGAR *Weeps Here.*)

HAGAR: Oh! I am completely disgraced! Because of the bad way in which I reared you, oh my wicked son, now I atone along with you for the knavery which has come about. Oh, woe is me!

(*Here Both* HAGAR *and Her Son* ISHMAEL *Weep.*

FIRST
NOBLE: Go! Leave us! Don't stay around here weeping.

ISHMAEL: It is done! Oh, I am miserable! Would that nothing had come of my impudence.

SECOND
NOBLE: Enter, oh gentlemen and nobles!

ABRAHAM: So be it, honored nobles. Let us go (in).

(*They All Enter. Music is Played. The Heavens Open And* GOD THE FATHER *Comes Out And Speaks.*)

GOD THE
FATHER: Truly, I order everything in heaven and on earth, so that nothing is ever lost from it. And all of the dwellers of heaven make me successful in this. They never disobey my precept of love. So it is that I command so that all the peoples of the earth might do, might accomplish, and might enact my law as my Supreme Will desires it.

(*Here* ABRAHAM *Comes Out.*)

ABRAHAM: You exist forever, high in heavenly Paradise. And You see all of Your children everywhere. I shall disclose for You an affair touching upon Your creatures, that one whom You gave to me upon earth, my beloved son Isaac. As he lives here upon earth, it is in my visage and my heart (person) that I believe he might give You sadness.[8] Perhaps sometime he will not fulfill your loving and divine law as You command it.

GOD THE
FATHER: Abraham! Abraham! Abraham! I speak. I am calling you!

ABRAHAM: Who are you who calls me?

GOD THE
FATHER: If it is true that you fulfill my divine precept perfectly, take your son who is named Isaac, and whom you love so deeply; take him to the top of the mountain which is called Miriah. There you shall kill him. With this deed my heart shall be satisfied; it will know if it is true that you obey my divine will.

ABRAHAM: I shall do Your bidding because it is my faith and understanding that You are forever worthy to be believed, and because of Your great power when I hear Your word.

(*The Heaven Closes. Music Again Sounds.* ABRAHAM *Goes In (Off-Stage). Here The "Te Deum Laudamus" Is Played And Sung.* ABRAHAM *and* ISAAC *Come Out Accompanied By Two Servants Ready For A Journey.*)

ABRAHAM: Now you know that I am taking you to the peak of the great mountain which is over there. We shall go there to pray.

ISAAC: Your will be done, oh my beloved and honored father!

ABRAHAM: And you (the servants) bring some firewood here, also some ropes, and a strong knife.

FIRST
SERVANT: Very well, oh lord.

(*They Go To Collect A Bundle Of Wood And Some Ropes. Music Sounds Briefly Here.*)

SECOND
SERVANT: Here is what you asked for.
ABRAHAM: Good. Let us go! Come and follow me now. Where I shall go, you will also go. Be not weary.
ISAAC: Your wish will be carried out as you command me, oh my beloved and cherished father.
(*Music Sounds As They Walk Toward The Mountain.*) [9]
ABRAHAM: Now we have come to the foot of the mountain. We shall pray (up) there. You (servants) wait here, for you are not to accompany us. Bring me my weapon of iron, the fire, and the firewood. Place them upon the shoulders of my son, and thus he will make himself useful.
(*Music Sounds Briefly.* ISAAC, *With His Shoulders Burdened, Proceeds To Walk Up The Mountain.* ISAAC *Then Stops And Speaks.*)
ISAAC: Oh my cherished and honored father! Truly I am already fatigued because of all this firewood which I am carrying. What are you going to do with it?
ABRAHAM: It will, indeed, be of use to you in order that your body be turned into ashes; in order that I may offer you up.
(*Here* ISAAC *Seems Not To Understand, Or The Speech Made By* ABRAHAM *Is An Aside.*)
ISAAC: But what then, oh my beloved father? Will you perhaps offer only the fire and the wood?
ABRAHAM: Oh my beloved son! How greatly you grieve my heart! In truth, that which is the will of God must be perfectly followed; and thus it is that he commands me. Let us go.
(*Music Sounds Again. They Proceed On Their Way. Then* ISAAC *Places The Wood On The Ground. Then* ABRAHAM *Speaks.*)
ABRAHAM: Bring the firewood and throw it here.
(ABRAHAM *Breaks The Wood Into Pieces.*)
ABRAHAM: Come and kneel down here. Thus has God commanded me. And with this I shall fulfill His will!

Isaac: May the sovereign will of God be done as He and you desire it!

Abraham: Now here me, my beloved son! Truly this is what the almighty God has commanded me in order that His loving and divine precept might be fulfilled; and so that He might see whether we—the inhabitants of the earth—love Him and execute His Divine Will. For He is the Lord of the living and of the dead. Now with great humility, accept death! For assuredly He says this: "Truly I shall be able to raise the dead back to life, I who am the Life Eternal." Then let His will be done in every part of the earth.

(Here Abraham *Weeps. The Music Of The "Misericordia" Is Heard.*)

Isaac: Do not weep, my beloved and honored father! For truly I accept death with great happiness. May the precious will of God be done as He has commanded you.

Abraham: Come here! I shall bind your hands so that you won't move.

(Abraham *Binds* Isaac's *Hands.*)

Isaac: Oh my adored and reverend father! It would be good if you could blindfold my eyes so that I shall not be afraid. When you lift your sword with your hands—cover my eyes!

Abraham: So shall it be done, oh my cherished son!

(Here Abraham *Blindfolds His Son. Then* Abraham *Raises His Weapon.*)

Abraham: You will now die according to the word of God, oh beloved son.

Angel: Abraham! Abraham!

(Here An Angel *Appears And Seizes* Abraham's *Hand So That He Is Unable To Kill His Son.*)

Abraham: Who are you, you who speak to me?

Angel: Now know the following by the authority and word of God. For He has seen how much you love Him; that you fulfill His divine precept; that you do not infringe it; that you brought your cherished son—he whom you love so much—here to the peak of the mountain; and that you have come to offer him here as a burnt sacrifice to God the almighty Father. Now truly for all this, by His loving Will, I have come to tell you to desist, for your cherished son Isaac does not have to die.

ABRAHAM: May His adored will be done as He wishes it. Come here, oh my beloved son! Truly you have now been saved from death by His hand.

(*Here He* [(ABRAHAM *Or* ISAAC)] *Unties The Cloth With Which He Was Blindfolded, And Loosens The Ropes With Which His Hands Were Bound.*)

ANGEL: Then understand this: as a substitute for your beloved son, you shall prepare a lamb as God wishes it. Go, for I shall accompany you and leave you at your house.

ABRAHAM: So be it. Let us go.

(*Music Sounds As They Are Descending From The Peak Of The Mountain.*)

ABRAHAM: Now may the glorious name of God the Father almighty be forever praised in every part of the world! His mercy is most great! If all we—dwellers upon the earth—could fulfill His divine and beloved law, then truly how we might rejoice! And you, my beloved son, you have seen how I saved you from death through this same means (obedience). Now then, in all of your future life, may you ever love God with all your heart; and may you never take his name in vain; and may you love your neighbor as He commands.

ISAAC: Truly I shall fulfill all of the commandments of God as well as yours. Enter now, for we have come to our house. Rest a little.

(*They Go In, And The* ANGEL *Speaks.*)

ANGEL: All you who are here, see this portent clearly! It is this: Live your lives according to His divine commandments, and violate not a single one of them. Take care of your children that they live not sensually, but rather that they live moderately so that they might serve God our Lord, and thus merit the Kingdom of Heaven. So be it.

The end. Praise be to God. In the year 1678 this *auto* was composed. It is now translated on Friday, February the first, in 1760; and faithfully have I translated it, this *auto*.

Bernabé Vásquez

Commentary

The reasons for the presentation of *"The Sacrifice of Isaac"* to the Indians are several. This play emphasizes unquestioning obedience both to the mandates of God as well as to those of one's elders, or other persons in positions of authority. Note the complete obedience of Isaac to Sarah and Abraham and how he clearly epitomizes the ideal youth. Ishmael is the disobedient and disgraced figure, and Hagar is also chastised for being permissive with her son. Abraham is a noble figure, a great warrior-type, but wise and subservient to the commands of God in his daily life.

Obedience to authority and respect for age and tradition were perhaps the two most important values for the Mexican Indian. The purpose of most indigenous education was precisely the instilling into youth of the necessary rights and obligations contingent upon his or her social role and status. Each individual was taught not to disturb the social fabric by non-compliance with these important values.

"The Sacrifice of Isaac" is notable also in that it emphasizes particularly the grace of God rather than his punishment or retribution. God is loving to those who obey him; he blesses their seed and makes them happy and honored in their old age. That God does not desire human sacrifice is also patent from this play. This fact was clearly a point in issue for an audience recently given to ritual human sacrifice on a stupendous scale, for the Aztec gods in the days immediately preceding the conquest had seemed ever to demand the precious blood offerings of the believers.

The measured cadence of the formalized greetings, the literary quality of the homily of father to son, and the typical form of the banquet scene, the characterizations of the lord Abraham and his noble young son Isaac, are all reminiscent of the Prehispanic Aztec culture. Some of the many nahuatlisms the text contains have been explained in the footnotes.

IV

"THE MERCHANT"

INTRODUCTION

The Nahuatl manuscript from which this translation was made bears the title *"In Pochtecatl,"* and is in the manuscript collection of the Library of Congress in Washington, D. C. The following is included in the manuscript:

"The Merchant." A moral play about a merchant. I write it now. It is my property. My name is Don José Gaspar. My home is here in Tulancingo (Hidalgo). Here I record the day and the year: today, Saturday the 15th of November, 1687.

Again we have the similar situation of a copyist dating his copy of a manuscript, but the content and actual body of the play date back to the sixteenth centrury. The text of the play contains the following line: "Put it in the deed that I purchased them three years ago, in 1627." This statement places the presentation of our version of the play as early as 1630; and internal evidence of the language and style and content attest to its even greater antiquity.

There is a microfilm copy of the manuscript made by Byron McAfee in the collection of the Historical Library at Chapultepec Park in Mexico City. This English translation from the Nahuatl was made by Byron McAfee. The author secured the translation and the rights of editing and publication from Mr. McAfee. No other publication of the play is known.

"The Merchant" is a drama obviously sponsored by the Church but contains no clue as to whether or not it was celebrated on a particular holiday. It might also have been a "moral example" presented not so much as a part of a *fiesta* but as a sermon or an answer to social problems which were troublesome during the first centrury following the conquest.

"The Merchant" is essentially non-liturgical and non-devotional; nor does it teach historical elements of Christianity

from texts of the Old or New Testaments. It is rather a presentation of human interrelationships, with a clear-cut homiletic theme.

The plot concerns an avaricious merchant who gains his riches but loses his soul by cheating and overcharging his clients. It is interesting to note that he is condemned to eternal punishment in spite of the fact that he had confessed and received extreme unction, because he did not make restitution for his many thefts. The lesson is clearly that one must conduct oneself honestly and without taking advantage of one's fellow beings. The priest plays the role of the gentle helper who does all he can to save the merchant, but who fails only because the power of evil deeds is too great at the last moment.

The idea of sin in *"The Merchant"* seems to have overtones of that which can affect and defile the body. The physical state of illness seems causally contingent upon previous evil deeds. Even when the merchant is moribund, he cannot understand his sudden illness except on these grounds.[1]

The guardian angel of the merchant's soul and the devils which struggle for possession of it are interesting examples of how the early priests probably taught the Indians about the struggle of the conscience against sin. It is evident from this and other plays that the belief in the existence of a guardian angel for each person was prevalent; and that wrongdoing was due to the presence of the devil in various guises and manifestations. Similar ideas were present in Prehispanic indigenous Mexico, where individuals often had associated spirit forms, animal or plant, with which their personal destinies were linked. These often had calendrical relevance, for example, to the day of birth of an individual, much as a saint's day has today.

This is the only play which hints that the Church is the necessary but *not* sufficient condition for salvation. (The priest is powerless if the devil succeeds in tempting the dying man.) Perhaps there were too many deathbed confessions being heard, so that it was judged expedient to present the moral lesson about conducting one's daily affairs with prudence and charity. Both this play and the *"Final Judgment"* emphasize the imminence of doom and possible damnation, both on a personal basis and on a cosmological scale. *"Wills and Testamentary Executors"* even affords us a peek into the machinations of Hell itself.

This play consists of a series of scenarios or tableaux, and was probably presented outside of the church (see the notes to the stage directions). Characters enter and exit without careful directions, and time lapses are poorly marked. We can assume, on the basis of what we know about contemporary theatrical production, that the characters were carefully costumed; this device would help to clarify their roles.

The simultaneous appearance of beings from both the natural and the supernatural realms is fanciful; and the use of fireworks to symbolize the departure of the soul of the wicked merchant at his death must have been effective.

The linguistic characteristics of the Nahuatl in which *"Wills and Testamentary Executors"* is composed suggest that the play is of an early date. Pat repetitions as well as elaborate phraseology and salutations support this evidence.

THE MERCHANT

CAST OF CHARACTERS:
The Merchant
The Merchant's Wife
The Merchant's Sons
The Priest
An Old Man and Old Woman
A Young Girl
Two Sick Men
A Weakminded Man
Mayor
A Mother (Widow)
Servants
A Notary
A Constable
A Doctor
A Nobleman
First, Second and Third Devils
Guardian Angel of the Merchant

PROLOGUE:

May God the Holy Spirit show you His way of leading a proper life. You are gathered together here; you have come to receive and to hear the will and the words of the Lord God. Here before you we will present and enact a moral play of fearful import, showing how the Lord our God punished a rich and prosperous usurer who robbed others of their property and wealth. Although he had confessed and partaken of communion through the blessed body and blood of our Saviour Jesus Christ, yet he did not receive pity. In spite of all he was condemned because he had not given back the wealth and property of others. Terrible, dreadful was the punishment reflected on his body and soul.

Take warning from it, all you who are here, lest the punishment of the Lord our God herein depicted be visited on you, oh unbelievers. Through it (the play) may you be filled with fear which will prevent you from falling into the great sin of usury, of overcharging. And now, with the help of God, may we open our hearts to the lesson presented in this play.

(Enter the MERCHANT.*)*

MERCHANT: In the greatness of my power no one can come close to me. There is no one like me in great wealth and property, gold and silver, emeralds, turquoise and precious stones, and all the many and varied things which are my joy. No one can equal me in fine blankets and fashionable clothing. Who is the first one who is thought or spoken of when there are invitations to a banquet, if not I? And when there is a wedding or when there is singing, who is the first invited,—who is the first sought after, if not I? I merit, I deserve great things. I am everywhere and at all times celebrated throughout the land. People of small importance give me great pleasure. They look to me to make loans to them. When they do not pay promptly, I increase the debt so that they must pay and I can maintain my wealth and property. They would not come to me if I waited for them!

The Merchant

(*Enter An* Old Man *And An* Old Woman.)

Old Man: My lord and my master, I bow low in your presence. I beseech you earnestly, for the love of our Lord God, lend me ten *pesos* so that I can get my son out of jail, so that they may not keep him shut up, so that they may let him out. I shall return it to you in fifteen days.

Merchant: I hear what you say. But am I going to go about hunting up money to make a loan to you? I can't give you anything! Get out! If your son is in jail, is that any of my business? Let them sell him! Let them keep him shut up or let him out! Do I know you? Are you any relative of mine? Get out! I will not give you any money!

Old Woman: Master! For the love of God lend us the money! We shall pay whatever interest you ask!

Merchant: Very well. What you say is all right, old woman. I shall give you the money; but you must pay fifty centavos interest on each *peso*. All right. I shall let you have it, but only for fifteen days. Then you must return it; and if you go beyond that time—although it be only for a few days—you will give me twenty *pesos*. If you agree to this, then I shall give you the money.

Old Man: That's all right, sir. Let it be done just as you wish. Here we are—my wife and I—and we promise to return it on time. The fifteen days will not have passed before we return the fifteen *pesos* to you. If we keep the money longer, we shall add five more *pesos* for the overtime.

Old Woman: Many thanks for your help. You have been kind to us. You have done us a favor. Now we must be going.

Old Man: May the Lord God give you strength! We must leave you now.

Merchant: May you continue in good health! May God be with you!

(*There Is The Sound Of Trumpets. Enter A* Young Girl.)

Young Girl: May God the beloved Father give you strength, my lord and master! I bow low in your presence. I am your humble servant. For the love of our Lord Jesus Christ help me! My mother and father are very poor, and our Lord God has sent a great sickness upon them. I have come to ask you to lend me twenty *pesos* which I shall return promptly in twenty days. Here, I give you my underclothes as surety, as well as my shawl and my blouse. I beg you to do this for the love of the Blessed Virgin.

(*The* YOUNG GIRL *Begins To Cry.*)

MERCHANT: What do you want, girl, that you come here crying to me? Although God has given you a handsome face, I am not looking for that! What I greatly desire is that my money might greatly increase and become much more. If you want me to lend you money you will have to do two things. The first is that you are to return thirty *pesos* to me for the twenty I lend you. If you want to do the second thing, I shall make a considerable deduction from this sum. If you will come and sleep with me, then you won't have to pay me so much. If you do not want to do this, then get out! I'll not give you any money!

YOUNG GIRL: What you ask me to do is impossible! I am not an immoral woman, and I am not selling my body! If you will not lend me the money, then don't! I shall bid you good-bye.

(*Exit the* YOUNG GIRL. *Enter Two* SICK MEN *Who are Begging.*)

FIRST
SICK MAN: For the sake of God the Father have pity on us!

SECOND
SICK MAN: For the sake of Saint Mary, the Virgin Queen of Heaven,—for love of her—look with pity on us so that God the Father may have like compassion on you!

MERCHANT: Servants! Don't you hear them shouting there at the door like coyotes? Run them off! Make them get out! Those harebrained people,—that scabby lot! Am I to give my wealth and property to them? Chase them

The Merchant

away! See that they get out—that they leave here! Give them such a scare that they will not come back!

(The SERVANTS *Drive Them Away*.)

SERVANT: Go away from here! Get out! Don't hang around here shouting! You are giving the master a headache. If you come here again, we'll break your heads for you!

FIRST
SICK MAN: Woe is me! God! Oh our Lord! You who judge rightly, look with searching eyes upon this foolishness—this madness of Your creature. Let him understand! Do not curse him!

(*Exit* SICK MEN. *Enter The* WEAKMINDED MAN.)

WEAKMINDED
MAN: My lord and master, God be with you! I bow low in your presence. Here is some money of mine. Please be so kind as to keep it for me. I am not going to take it with me, for I am going to Guatemala to get my wife. This is why I have come to see you. You are an honorable man and a very good Christian. Here are one thousand *pesos*.

MERCHANT: Well, if that's the way you want it, all right. Give me your money. I'll keep it for you; and when you come back and ask for it, I'll give it to you at once. I have just received one thousand *pesos* in keeping for you.

(*Enter The* OLD MAN *and The* OLD WOMAN.
Exit The WEAKMINDED MAN.)

OLD WOMAN: Dear husband! My dear man! The fifteen days in which we are to return the money to the merchant are already up. Yesterday I heard it reported in the market place that not long ago they sent a man and a woman to prison and then they sold them, all because they couldn't pay the money owed. Don't let this happen to us! It is time to go and look for the rest of the money, for I have only seven *pesos*. Go and hunt for the other eight *pesos* at once, so that we can get together the fifteen we owe. Let's not give him any occasion to be angry with us for he's not human! He's terribly bad!

OLD MAN: All right, wife, I'll go and get the money at once for the fifteen days are up.

MERCHANT: Come here, servant! You know that the fifteen days fixed for the payment of my money are past. Go at once and ask them for it. If they don't give it to you immediately, put them in jail. Don't let them work the pity racket on you. Although they may cry to you and put on a sad face, see to it that you don't get softhearted. If you have pity on them, I'll make *you* cry! I'll make you sorry for it!

SERVANT: All right, master. I'll go right now and see them.

(*The* SERVANT *Goes To The* OLD MAN *To Ask Him For The Money.*)

SERVANT: (At the home of the old man.) I have come to ask you for the fifteen *pesos* which you owe. If you do not give them to me at once I'll put you in jail, or I'll seize your money and property.

OLD MAN: My dear sir, here is the money for our lord and master; don't get worried about it.

(*Enter The* MAYOR.)

MAYOR: Dear sir, may life be pleasant to you! I have come to kiss your hands and your feet. You will help me! I am in need of four thousand *pesos*. I want you to lend them to me for one month. I shall pay you back promptly. Kindly do me the favor of signing your name here.

MERCHANT: You have told me what you want, Sir. I have heard what you have to say. You want me to lend you money. All right. But you must know that through this practice I make my money. If I lend you four thousand *pesos* for one month, there will be added to it a charge of four hundred *pesos* for the month.

MAYOR: All right, let it be as you wish.

(*He Receives The Money And Goes Away. Enter The* WEAK-MINDED MAN.)

WEAKMINDED
MAN: Respectable sir and master! How are you? Has God the Father given you strength? I beg you to give me the money which I left in your care, for I have brought my wife and now I want to buy some things.
MERCHANT: I am well. God give you strength. Have you had a good trip? What is this money you are asking me for? I don't even know what you're talking about!
WEAKMINDED
MAN: Sir, master, perhaps you have forgotten? Remember that—just four months ago today—I gave you a thousand *pesos* to keep for me. For God's sake give them back to me!
MERCHANT: I have already told you that I know nothing about it! Perhaps you were drunk,—or maybe you are crazy! Leave me! Go away!
WEAKMINDED
MAN: I am certainly not drunk; nor am I crazy. I gave you the money all right! You are just pretending! Swear on the cross that you did not receive it!
MERCHANT: I am telling you the truth and nothing else. I swear it! Here, I make the sign of the cross and kiss it. I swear by God that I know nothing about this money of yours. You certainly never gave it to me! I have none that I am keeping for you!
WEAKMINDED
MAN: All right then! I am satisfied that you are stealing my money. But there is a God. I leave the matter with Him! May He see your robbery! I am not going to make a scene here.
MERCHANT: Get out! Go away! If you do not leave at once I have servants who will pound you to pieces immediately. Here servants! Throw this fool out,—this drunkard!
(*They Run Him Out, Striking Him. Enter A* MOTHER *And* SONS.)
MOTHER: My lord, my master! May the grace of God the Holy Spirit be with you. We have come to salute you,

we poor people—my children and I. May your heart have compassion for us, for we are very poor. Give me what was left for me in the will of my husband, his wealth and his property, his lands and cultivated fields, his money and his precious jewels. For you know very well that he did not die in my presence. I had gone away into town to work for my children. For the love of the Lord God have pity on us, your poor servants!

MERCHANT: What is this you are saying, woman? Probably you do not remember too well! Most likely you have made a mistake, for I have no will. The lands and planted fields of which you speak are my property through a purchase which I made from your husband a long time ago. And as for the money and precious stones,—well, I know nothing about them. Perhaps you lost them! Or perhaps no will was ever made. Or perhaps you and your lover together squandered the money. Run along now! I know nothing at all of what you are talking about. Perhaps you are drunk. Go away and sleep it off! Don't trouble me about it.

MOTHER: All that I have told you is true. I am certainly not drunk! You certainly do have the will. For God's sake have pity on my children!

MERCHANT: I have already told you, woman, that I do not understand what you are talking about. Go away! Don't bother me! You give me a headache. Get out! Go out and hunt what you need for your bastardly children! It's none of my business. Go away! I don't want to see you here any more. Servant, come here! Call my dear friend, the notary.

SERVANT: All right, master, I shall call him.

(Enter The NOTARY.)

NOTARY: God keep you, sir! What are your orders? Here I am come to hear them.

MERCHANT: Friend, I want you to make a will. In it you are to state that I bought the house, the land which overlooks the garden, and the big field which faces the nose of the mountain. You are to say that I paid the sum of one thousand *pesos* for all these aforesaid properties. Put in the deed that I purchased them three years ago, in 1627. See to it that you do this correctly. Don't make any mistake! For you know that you are my dear friend whom I love very much, and that I shall pay you.

NOTARY: My dear sir! Don't worry about it, for I shall do as you say. You know that I am your humble servant. But I beg you to have some consideration for me, your humble slave, so that I shall be able to buy something for my children.

MERCHANT: Don't let that worry you, for I shall certainly give you something. So draw up the deed right away.

(*Enter The* ALCADE, *Or* MAYOR.)

MOTHER: My lord, I have come here to tell you that six months ago my husband died. He had left money in the care of the merchant for the help of his soul, as well as the other wealth and property which he willed to me and my children. Now he does not admit having my house and my cultivated fields. He has taken possession of them and is keeping them for himself. For this reason I humbly bow before you; I beg you to order him to present himself before you to give an accounting of his trust. I have nothing with which to bring up my children,—these poor servants of yours present here. For the sake of our Savior and his beloved Mother, I earnestly beseech you to do this for me!

MAYOR: Very well, my poor woman. I shall certainly help you. Don't you worry about it. Constable, go and call the merchant whose house is by the market place.

CONSTABLE: (*At the house of the merchant.*) The mayor wants to see you, sir. You must go there. I can't leave you here!

(*The* CONSTABLE *Takes Him Away.*)

MERCHANT: You have sent for me, sir? What is it that you want? If I can be of any service to you, I am at your command.

MAYOR: Now that you are here, you must know that this woman has filed a complaint against you that her husband, when he died, left his wealth and property in your charge, and that now you do not acknowledge the obligation. Make the sign of the cross before those who are present here. Place your hand on it and swear under oath what of his wealth and property, his houses and fields, were left in your charge.

MERCHANT: I kiss this holy cross. May the devil carry me off if what this woman says is true. Here is the notary before whom I bought her lands, her cultivated fields, and her house. I have nothing belonging to this woman.

MAYOR: Is what this gentleman says really true? Where is the will?

NOTARY: Here is the will. It is true that before me and in the presence of witnesses this woman's husband sold his house and his cultivated lands to this merchant for the sum of one thousand *pesos*. He received the money in my presence, and took it away with him. In his will, which was also executed before me, he didn't leave anything except money enough to pay for his burial expenses. I am telling you the truth. Is there any reason why I should lie for this merchant?

(He Presents The Copy Of The Will.)

MAYOR: You have seen the will. It has been read in your presence. Nothing for you has been left in the care of this merchant. You may go now.

(Enter The PRIEST.*)*

PRIEST: Sir, may God the Holy Spirit be with you! I do not want to trouble you or molest you, for you are an honorable man. You are a child of God, and our Lord has given you this wealth and property. You are the steward of our Lord God. Have pity, therefore, have mercy on this poor woman. You have taken from her the house and the lands of her husband. You know that the house is quite valuable. Help her and her children! All that you give her God will receive. For his sake do this, my dear son.

MERCHANT: Reverend father! I have heard what you said. I know what you wish. But I tell you truly that I am very poor just now. My money is lent out to many people and they have not paid me yet. But even if I had collected it, I wouldn't give any of my money to her. Let her go and spin! Let her go and weave! Perhaps some time I'll remember her,—but leave me now for I have much work to do.

PRIEST: Know, sir, that when you die you will take with you none of your wealth and property. All you will take with you is a winding sheet in which to wrap up your body. Just as water extinguishes fire, so the grave extinguishes pity. Therefore, help her, so that God in some measure help your spirit, your soul. Help yourself! No one else will help you! I must leave you now.

(*Exit The* PRIEST.)

MERCHANT: Oh my servants, I feel very sick. I did not sleep all night. All night my head ached as if it would split into pieces. Call a doctor for me!

(*The* SERVANT *Goes and Knocks On The* DOCTOR's *Door.*)

DOCTOR: You have made trouble enough, young man; what do you want?

SERVANT: The merchant has sent me to ask you to come to him for he is sick.

(*The* DOCTOR *Accompanies The* SERVANT *And A* NOBLE.)

DOCTOR: My dear sir, may God the Father give you strength! How do you feel? What is the matter with you?

SICK MAN: You have done me a favor. You have been very kind. I am very sick, sir. My whole body is in pain!

DOCTOR: Brace up, sir! May our dear Lord God help you. Go to the house of God and confess. Prepare yourself and partake of the blessed body of our dear Savior Jesus Christ. For thus we are commanded, so that the sick will first confess so that afterwards their bodies may be helped.

SICK MAN: Let what you suggest be done afterwards. Help me here immediately, for I am on the point of death!

DOCTOR: What are you saying, sir? What are you thinking? It is not right! Let them take you to the house of God at once, for sickness comes out of the soul.

NOBLE: My dear sir and master, what the doctor tells you is quite true. For it certainly seems to me as if the justice of God were following you. So let us take you there at once. For we must first of all confess. You must prepare yourself so that afterwards your body may be helped. This is god's will. So now let us take you there at once.

SICK MAN: You give me a headache! You are both headache-makers! Well, I'll go! What I wanted was to be cured right away. But I'll go now.

(*They Take Him To The Church And Carry Him Inside. As They Go In, Three* DEVILS *Also Enter.*)

FIRST DEVIL: Oh, it's all over with us! Unfortunate that we are! Our servant, the usurer, has made up his mind to confess! If he should confess all of his sins, our power and influence over him would come to an end. All the time that he served us well would be lost.

SECOND DEVIL: It is certainly not possible that all of our work should turn out so badly and be lost! What does he think of us? Are we not strong and mighty? We certainly can't let him go now! As for me, I'll give him a fright and make him so ashamed of himself that he won't confess that he cheated and robbed people. And would he dare to confess later in a court of justice that he hadn't told or acknowledged that he made a false oath to justify his robbing the wealth and property of others.

THIRD DEVIL: Let us go at once! We are wasting our time! Let us go straight to where they have taken him and see to it that he makes a false confession. Keep our aim before you! Be courageous, brothers!

(They All Exit. The DEVILS *Go Ahead And The* ANGELS *Follow Some Distance Behind. They Lay The* MERCHANT *On His Bed.)*

SICK MAN: Oh, it's all over! Unfortunate that I am! What have I done? What have I been doing? My heart pains me deeply. My soul is suffering intensely. It doesn't let up for a moment. Why have they taken me away? What have I gained out of the things of this world? What have I found in them? Alas! Oh unfortunate that I am!

WIFE: Dear husband! Why are you so troubled? Why are you so worried? Is there anything you want? Are you thinking of something which brings painful memories? What is it? This is the way that things are in this world of God! Is this not so?

SICK MAN: You have pity on me. You are kind to me. What you say is true.

(Enter The PRIEST.*)*

PRIEST: Praised above all be the name our Lord Jesus Christ. How are you, my dear son?

SICK MAN: Loved and respected father! You are very kind to me! I thank you. I have become very rich and prosperous through the favor of God; yet my soul is about to be lost. My body has fallen into the mire.

PRIEST: My beloved son, brace up! Put your strength in the Lord God. Learn to have pity so that He may have pity on you. So that He may let you remain on earth a little while longer, and that He won't curse you. He wants you to be saved so that you can make yourself worthy and deserving of His royal palace. If perchance you shall die suddenly, He gives you time to save yourself, that is, to confess. So tell all your sins. Although you may already have confessed, is there anything which you have withheld because of shame? If so, confess it now, for you are about to die!

FIRST DEVIL: Don't let him worry you. Don't be upset, for you're not very sick. Have you not been unwell many times before? But you became better right away! For God gives you strength. The same thing will happen to you now. You will surely get better right away!

GUARDIAN
ANGEL: Believer in God, don't trust your enemy the devil, for he is only trying to deceive you. He wants to destroy you morally so that you will die in your sins; then he will carry you off to Hell! Do you not see that he is the deceiver, the destroyer, the tempter? Numberless are those he has sent to perdition where he mocks them in the nethermost Hell while they suffer everlasting torment. Confess at once, for you will not live another day! May Jesus help you!

SECOND
DEVIL: He is a liar! You are not going to die now. You are out of danger! Are you an old man? No, you are still young. Your are going to live longer. You are not going to die yet!

PRIEST: Just take a good look at him. He is the devil who is doing everything to send you to perdition. He wants to confuse and deceive you so that you won't make a true confession. Do not believe him! Tell all. Confess everything now if there is anything which you have withheld because of shame. Now is the proper time for salvation. If you are withholding something because of fear, if you are keeping back your sins because of shame, you may be sure that when you die you will go straight to Hell. There you will suffer forever and be in torment among the devils. I have done my duty by you before God.

SICK MAN: I thank you, father. You have been kind. Let me say that I remember only that I have spoken ill of people. That I mocked them and looked with anger at them. This is all, dear father.

PRIEST: My dear son, let not the spirit of evil, the devil, lead you astray and deceive you.

GUARDIAN
ANGEL: Have pity on yourself! Look with compassion on

yourself! You are dying, your life is coming to an end. Remember that once you are dead you will certainly not be able to confess your sins. Then there will be no crying for you, no pity for you. You will be lost forever! May God make you see! May He give you light!

Sick Man: I have not left out anything at all, dear father. I have confessed all my sins.

Priest: All right. You know. I have done my duty before God. May He, in His love, keep you. I am leaving you now.

Sick Man: Very well, then, go! Oh! I am dying of thirst. Give me a little water. My lips are very dry. My thirst is dreadful!

Guardian
Angel: If with only a little sickness you are so very dry and thirsty, how are you going to stand the fire and the dry lips of Hell? Nothing will cure you except boiling molten lava which gives constant and unlimited torture to people, until it bursts their hearts. This is what they will give you to drink.

Sick Man: Is it possible that God might still have pity on me?

Guardian
Angel: Certainly! Cry out to Him and He will help you!

(*Exit The* Guardian Angel.)

Third
Devil: Don't believe it. The angel is lying to you! You are already ours. God has cursed you because you have not done penance.

Sick Man: It is true! I belong to Hell! For my sins are so many that they are countless. Oh! Call my sons, the young gentlemen. I leave all my wealth and property to them.

(*Enter The Two* Sons.)

First Son: What is the matter with you, sir? Why have you sent for us? Here we are. Be of good cheer! May the Lord preserve you! Cry out to Him so that you may not lose your salvation. Place yourself altogether in His hands. He is kind and compassionate. He will have pity, He will have mercy on you. And may our sovereign Lady, Saint Mary, intercede for you with her beloved Son so that He may have pity on you. What is it that you want? Here we are.

SICK MAN: My dear sons, I do not feel well in my body. I am extremely weak. I am on the point of death. All my wealth and property I leave to you. You will draw up a will for me stating that you will share and share equally in all my possessions which I leave to you.

(*Exit The* SONS *And Immediately The* DEVIL *Chokes The Sick Man.*)

SECOND DEVIL: Put your hands about his neck and choke him! Let us carry off the soul of this great sinner, the most evil man.

(*They Take Out His Soul. When He is Dead, Many Sky-Rockets Burst Black Symbolizing This.*)

WIFE: Oh a thousand times unfortunate that I am! My beloved husband is dead! I do not know what happened that the Lord should have sent such a sudden death upon him. Go at once and summon all of our relatives to come and bury his body. Have the death bell rung. Call the singers and the wise men—the priests—at once!

(*Enter The* GRAVEDIGGERS. *They Repeat The Prayers For The Dead As They Bury Him. Enter The* ANGEL.)

GUARDIAN ANGEL: Alas! It is finished with me! Oh unfortunate that I am! I deserve nothing! I, your servant. Blessed are the others, my brother angels here. They are guardians of the good who live on earth. Now that the end has come, oh, unfortunate am I! I am useless, deserving of nothing. Do we not cry out to them daily? Do we not warn them? Do we not encourage them and make them conscious of all that is good and proper? But they do not care to listen! They would rather obey the devil who makes them deaf and blind! Oh! Alas! There in Hell he opens their eyes. Is there any chance of salvation for them? Certainly not any longer! While on earth, they lost through neglect the most precious gift which might have been theirs!

So the play *"The Merchant"* ends on the desolate note of a defeated guardian angel. The last sacraments of the Church were nullified by the untruthfulness of the last confession.

It is uncertain why the figure of the merchant was chosen as the villain for this play. Clearly there could not have been so many professional usurers in the sixteenth century as to make them villainous *per se*. Yet the more generalized picture of the rich taking advantage of the poor was undoubtedly typical and widespread. This drama must also have been meant as a warning to the poor to attempt to conduct their affairs with prudence and no little naïveté.

It is true that the merchants in Prehispanic Mexico held a peculiar position in the social organization. Sahagún and others attest to this fact. They not only bought, sold, and traded, but they acted as military spies for the Aztecs during their business trips. For this, they were offered special privileges such as deferment from military duty, as a result of their economic and political importance. They reported their findings directly to the Emperor. The merchants lived in their own *barrios* or areas as the rule, and were perhaps held in some suspicion by the majority of the people because of their activities.

Some Spaniards complained that both Indian and Spanish traders took advantage of the general ignorance of legal rights and privileges as well as the naiveté of the indigenes toward the new money economy which was replacing the Prehispanic system of exchange of native currency. Barter, the use of cacao bean currency and metallic coins existed side by side in markets during the colonial period. The ratio of cacao beans to coins fluctuated and generally declined through the sixteenth century; and, although the Indians tried to maintain their vigesimal numeration in exchange rates, this must have been confusing to the lower-class indigenes.

The ownership of land was always a crucial problem. Little by little, the Indians who had owned land through inheritance lost it through defaults of various kinds. The socially subordinate position of the vast majority of Indians made them frequent objects of fraud and trickery.[2] Reasons such as these made such a character as our unprincipled *Merchant* a genuine threat.

V
"ADORATION OF THE KINGS"

INTRODUCTION

The manuscript of the *"Adoración de los Reyes"* was included in the same folio as that of the *"Sacrificio de Isaác."* Therefore, the manuscript used for the translation is not the original, but rather probably belongs to the second half of the eighteenth century according to its form of the handwriting. It is written in the same script as the *"Sacrificio"* and must have been done by the same copyist, Bernabé Vásquez, whose hand and rubric are found at the end of the other *auto*.

The translation from the Nahuatl into Spanish was made by Francisco Paso y Troncoso and presented to the Twelfth International Congress of Americanists in Paris, in 1900. It was then published in a limited edition by Salvador Landi (Florence, 1900). It is from this publication that the present English translation was made. The author knows of no other publication of this play.

The theme of the drama is Biblical, taken especially from the second chapter of the Gospel according to St. Matthew, where the story of the Magi is related. These verses tell of Herod and of the flight into Egypt by the Holy Family. With this impending event our play ends.

That the drama dates back to the sixteenth century is ascertained both on the grounds of internal evidence of language and content, and on the fact that we have a description of a play produced in the sixteenth century which is so similar to the *"Adoración"* as to be another version of the same play.

Fray Alonso Ponce, who was a *comisario,* referred to this or a similar play in his *Relación breve de algunas cosas de las muchas que sucedieron al Padre Fray Alonso Ponce en las Provincias de la Nueva España, siendo Comisario General de aquellas partes.* (Brief account of some of the many things which happened to Fray Alonso Ponce when he was Commissary General in New Spain).

The *fiesta* he describes took place in Tlaxomulco (Jalisco) on January 6, 1587. Because of its great interest for sixteenth-century missionary theater in general, and because of its similarity with the drama with which we are here concerned, relevant translated passages from Ponce's account will be included here.[1]

> The Indians of Tlaxomulco have had the custom *for a long time* of presenting yearly in their village the story of what happened on the day of Epiphany, as it is taught by our Mother the Holy Church. That (drama) which they produced for this occasion while I was commissary there happened in this manner. They placed the portals of Bethlehem in the patio of the gateway of the church, almost at the foot of the bell tower. In this setting they placed the Child, the Mother, and Saint Joseph. This setting was constructed of poles covered with other smaller poles; these were all covered with (what is called in Nahuatl) *paxtli,* which grows both in other lands and in Mexico on oak or other trees, like little rootlets or a beard of fine thin wisps. This *paxtli* is used for many things.[2] Somewhat separated from the ramparts of Bethlehem and off to one side of the patio, they built an archway wherein Herod was seated on a chair and surrounded by a large retinue representing pomp and majesty. From the peak of a mountain which was near the village, the Kings came slowly wending their way down on horseback. Because of the slowness of their descent and of the height of the mountain, it took them almost two hours to come down and arrive at the [patio of the church.] The three Kings had an Indian on foot in front of them as their guide; and behind them was an old man of eighty years bearing a basket in which were the offerings they were to give to the Child.
>
> During the interim in which they [the Kings] were approaching, there was presented a ballet of angels, who danced about singing verses in Nahuatl in front of the ramparts, while making many obeisances and genuflections to the

Child. Then they presented another dance of shepherds, who were dressed in shepherd's costumes with their crooks, and who were carrying leather pouches with squash and other things. When they were altogether in the middle of the courtyard, there appeared an angel in a little tower made of wood, singing the *Gloria in excelsis Deo.* At the sound of the voice, the shepherds fell as if senseless to the ground. The angel exhorted them, telling them the news about the birth of the Child. They came to themselves again, rose up, went together to the ramparts, and with great happiness and rejoicing offered what they were bearing to the Child: one giving a little lamb, another a kid, some bread, another a cap, and other things, but all with such reverence that it provoked devotion in the onlooker. Then again they commenced dancing about and singing in the same Nahuatl in praise of the Child, some asking questions of others and recounting what they had seen and heard. They reacted with great happiness, repeating what the angel had said and chanting, '*goria, goria, goria.*' They gave great leaps and bounds using their shepherd's crooks, as of the greatest joy and pleasure. . . . They wove intricate patterns with steps and with acrobatic antics, some leaping over the shepherd's crooks of the others, and all together forming circles and squares in a most commendable fashion. . . .

The head-shepherd gave orders to each one as he came out leaping and jumping, calling each by name—to one *Dominguillo,* to another *Gonzalillo*—and to others with names which were very pleasing. They all obeyed him. And finally, when they saw that the Kings were approaching, they made a circle or corral by joining their hands as in a wheel, leaving two of their number inside with their crooks; these ran after those of the circle as if they were bulls. Either of them brought to the ground with their crooks anyone whom he could catch. Thus they went about circling around from one place to another terminating their celebration which was certainly something to see.

The Kings, having been guided by a star which the Indians

had made of shiny tinsel (or brass), arrived at the gate of the patio. They moved the star along by two cords which reached from the mountain to the tower of the church. They had placed little wooden towers at intervals, and made the star move along on its cord from these. As the Kings arrived at the gate of the patio, they hid the star by putting it in one of these little towers; they then sent their messengers in to see Herod. After some speeches and questions, they too entered into the patio, appeared before Herod, and asked their questions (about the Child).

Herod summoned his wise men, who in turn came in each bearing a big book. One of them, at the behest of Herod, searched out, found, and related the prophecy to him. Herod was so angry with him that he would have liked to have laid hands upon him. He threw the book upon the floor, and commanded the priest to read the prophecy again, which he did while kneeling on the floor. The black priest was trembling, shivering, and turning the pages of the book. Finally he found the prophecy and showed it to Herod. Herod, furious with him, took the book from his hands and gave it to another priest, who, kneeling with the same trembling and perturbation searched and found the same prophecy. So also did two or three others to whom Herod had given the book. Sometimes he threw the book upon the table or upon the floor, always exhibiting such rage and anger, pride and presumption both in the aspect of his deeds as well as his words that it was as if he were actually enraged and actually Herod. When the Kings left the presence of Herod, the star appeared from the little tower, and continued on its journey until it came to rest over the bell-tower of the church, at the foot of which was—as I have said—the ramparts of Bethlehem. The Kings prostrated themselves before the Child, and presented him with their gifts which were jars of silver. Each King, while kneeling, made a brief prayer in Nahuatl. The old man who bore the carrier for the gifts had done the same thing (had played the same role) on this day every year for the past thirty years. He bore the *chicuitle* a short way from the ramparts, then turned about in front of the Child, and at his feet spoke in Nahuatl, saying that he had no other thing to offer him than the carrier itself; and thus he offered it to him, his work having finished with it.[3] Later, an angel appeared in the aforementioned tower, and said that they (the Kings) should return to their country by another road than that by which they had come. Thus they left the patio, and the celebration was finished. There were ten or twelve *frailes* present as well as many Spaniards, and more than five thousand Indians from that place and others; for in that area they all supported this *fiesta*.

The reader can compare this description with the body of the play as it is read. The translation from the Nahuatl is literal according to Paso y Troncoso, and, as usual, the circumlocutions and patterned greetings have been maintained in English in order to preserve some feeling of the original dialogue.

Adoration of The Kings

CHARACTERS WHO DO NOT SPEAK:
The Child God (Jesus)
The Virgin Mary
Saint Joseph

CHARACTERS WHO SPEAK:
The Three Kings:
  Gaspar
  Melchior
  Balthazar
The Messenger (of the Kings)
An Angel
King Herod
Herod's Steward
Three Priests of the Jews

This is the beginning. Here commences the story of the three Kings and of how they came to hail the precious and glorious Divine Child, the Son of God our Lord Jesus Christ. From there, from the birthplace of the sun, they left to come here. At this point their story begins—that is, of how it came about that the three Kings came here from the East. Their messenger, their guide, came leading them; but the star guided them better. And when the three Kings had come here to the valley, which is close to the city of Herod, the star hid itself. Here he (Gaspar) speaks.

GASPAR: For some time I've continued on aware that I no longer see the precious Star, our miraculous guide which until now has led us forward. For this reason, I think that we have arrived at the birthplace of the marvelous Child whom we seek. It is certain at least that this is the city of Jerusalem, and I surely doubt that we shall immediately find what we are searching for. You, our servant, come here! Go into the city of Jerusalem and tell this to Herod. Explain to him that we have come here from the East, and that we kiss (salute) both his hands and his feet many times.[4] Ask that he give us his royal permission to go and search for that which is our desire, and (tell him) that here in the valley of the city of Jerusalem we await his royal summons in order that we might proceed to make our search plans clear to him.

MESSENGER: Your royal command shall be fulfilled. I shall do whatever you order me, for truly I am your slave.

(*The* MESSENGER *Goes To The Entrance of* HEROD's *Residence. He Salutes The* STEWARD *And Says To Him:*

MESSENGER: Oh sir, may the gods strengthen you, for you have searched out a life of labor. Know that I am a servant of the three Kings.

STEWARD: Come here, oh my friend! Your anguish must be very great for truly it can be seen in your face.

MESSENGER: Oh sir, oh great sir, may the gods strengthen you, for you have passed your life with work! I have come from the East, for my home, the name of which is Persia, is there. I have led three noble lords here to your territory. Now lead me, therefore, into the presence of your great monarch Herod, because I have come to salute him by command of the noble lords.

The Adoration of the Kings

STEWARD: Good, my friend! Wait for me here a little while until I see if the great king Herod is able to talk to you.

(*At This Point, The* STEWARD *goes* (*Up*) *To The Presence Of* HEROD. *He Doffs His Hat, Makes Reverence Three Times, And After This Says:*)

STEWARD: Oh lord, oh great lord, oh King! Truly your fame, your glory, and your omnipotence are found, are manifest, and resound loudly everywhere. All the peoples of the world—gentlemen, nobles, and princes—all respect and honor you. Know therefore that our God, our Lord, has deigned to perform a great miracle for us. A messenger from the three Kings has come here to your palatial residence, to your royal home. They journeyed from very far and have come here. Truly no one ever before has come to your city in this fashion (as a messenger). He is certainly the first of his language, form, and visage who has come thus. And in truth I doubt if he is an idolator. Further, he desires to speak in your presence. He awaits your royal command there in the doorway. Shall I perhaps summon him? May he perhaps enter and come into your presence?

HEROD: This is a great portent, a great marvel, which you have announced to me. Let him enter. Let him come into my presence in order that I might know where he comes from, and what he (now) wishes.

(*The* STEWARD *Goes Down And Speaks With The* MESSENGER.) [5]

STEWARD: Have the goodness to enter, oh my friend, for Herod the King summons you.

MESSENGER: This is good, oh my friend.

(*The* MESSENGER *Goes Into The Presence Of* HEROD *And Kneels Down.*)

MESSENGER: Oh lord, oh great lord, give me—your servant—your hands and your feet to embrace.

(HEROD *Arises And Again Seats Himself.*)

MESSENGER: You pass your life in labor, oh lord, oh great lord! Oh prince, oh Herod, may the gods strengthen you! You ought to know why the three lords and nobles, who have come here to the valley near your city and who await you there, have thought to send me here. They have come from very far away—from there, from the East. They repeatedly embrace your hands and your feet, and with much humility request that you give your royal permission for them to come and appear before you, and to give you notice of their purpose.

HEROD: Oh my friend who has come here, may our Lord God strengthen you! You shall say to your superiors—to your lords, to your kings—that I acknowledge greatly the royal and distinguished manner in which they have come to honor my city, my residence, and the interior of my dwelling place. Would that they come here so that I might merit seeing their royal visages and know what their desire is. Truly I await them.

MESSENGER: This is good, oh lord, oh my master!

(*Here* HEROD *Calls To His Nobles.*)

HEROD: You now, oh lords, nobles, and princes! Come! Come to meet and salute the Kings. Play (make music) and dance! Entwine them with flowers, and show them honor! For truly I await them.[6]

(*Here The* MESSENGER *Goes To Call The Lord Kings In The Valley Near The City.*)

MESSENGER: I went there where you commanded me. I appeared in the presence of Herod, the great prince, the great lord, and he was greatly pleased with your courtesy. Further, it pleased him to say, "Let them enter. Let them approach that they might come and rest in my home. And whatever is of my property and my holdings, all this is at their disposal. Say all this to them."

(*The* KINGS *Journey Onward Briefly Here. Then They Dismount From Their Horses. Here They (Herod's Nobles) Play Music (flutes and drums). They Entwine Them With Garlands Of Flowers.* HEROD *Comes Down To Salute Them. He Makes Reverence, Salutes Them, And Says:*)

The Adoration of the Kings

HEROD: You have finished your labors when you came here, oh you honored ones, you princes, you kings! Oh that God might strengthen you, that great ruler our Lord God! Perhaps He will give you power—He who is near at hand, He who is nigh to all things![7]

MELCHIOR: Take heart, oh lord, oh great prince, oh Herod! Truly we receive great honor through the feeling which your heart emanates. We are truly your servants, your vassals. We definitely needed your good will; and we indeed kiss your noble hands and feet many times.

HEROD: May it please you to come to our residence, to our city! Deign to enter and be served a banquet. For truly, this is as your home to which you have come.

(*The* THREE KINGS *Enter. They Rest, And The Others Perform Them Many Honors.*)

HEROD: Now speak, oh princes, oh lords, oh honored ones, oh nobles! Why have you come here from so very far away? I receive great honor from your courtesy.

MELCHIOR: We are certainly greatly indebted (to you). You have done so much for us, oh lord, oh great lord, oh Herod. It is true that you are noble, that you are king, that you have seen fit to honor your elders. Know this, then, that for a long time our grandfathers, the ancients, have preserved (something) in their hands, and for ages too the great wise men have left a prophecy as a heritage. The name of our prophet was "Balam." He spoke thus: "From the patriarch Jacob shall be born a marvelous Star. From Israel shall he descend and come forth; and he shall mature as a noble, a great lord, who shall castigate and destroy the governors of Moab; he shall completely ruin the sons of Seth." In reality and truth, the old ones, our grandfathers, have taught this prophecy with the idea that they were to await the great and noble Lord and his Star. In order that they might know and be honored whenever this presage—the sign or star in the sky—might appear, they placed twelve learned ancients on the peak of a mountain in order constantly to inspect the East, and be waiting whenever the wonderful Star appeared to be admired. Furthermore, sixteen hundred years have passed since they awaited it. It (the sky) is unceasingly watched from the peak of this mountain. And now for several days, that One by whom we all live has permitted it to come about—has He who is most near and who is most nigh to all beings, our Lord. In the middle of the night when all were sleeping in the city, the twelve ancients saw a star very worthy of admiration. The Star shone so brightly that it completely outdid the sun! It sent a light which radiated to all places. They saw that there was the greatest portent in the interior of the Star: a marvel, a most beautiful and desirable Child was within it![8]

Immediately they (the sages) left for my house. They ran! They awakened me and the others who were there —that is, the lords and nobles who were near me, and who had come to salute me. I called them at once and awakened them. We saw the Star and most portentous Child God who more or less inspired us with love. We met together immediately and discussed this with one another. We dressed ourselves. We gathered provisions and left on the journey to search for the Child.

The prodigious Star has truly guided us to this place. We have been watching from afar, and we have come here. Upon nearing your city of Jerusalem, we lost our marvelous guide; for we saw it no longer. For this reason, we think that here in your city we shall discover what we search for. Oh prince, oh lord, oh Herod, repeatedly we beg you to tell us where He has chosen to be born; where the King of the Jews deigns to be!

For truly then it is as we have said. We saw this Star afar off in the East, and we have come (here). We have come to adore him. We have come to humble ourselves before him. We have come to worship him.

HEROD: Oh great lord! Perhaps you are out of your mind. What are you saying? Who is the ruler, the King of the Jews if not I? By virtue of the mercy of his lordship the Emperor of Rome, Caesar Augustus, I was made (king). Perchance this is not my dominion or property? Perhaps I am not the great lord nor do I reign? Perhaps I have already perished or am dead, or already finished? Perhaps I am no longer sensible (sane), nor am I Herod, nor king? Who rules over me? Let the principals of my Jews, my priests and wise men, come and explain to me without delay. Let those who have the divine books—the noble and spiritual ones—the prelates, come and declare to me what star, what child, what great noble is he whom the Kings designate! Immediately! Wretched me! Ay, ay, ay, ay. . . . For already I wish to die. I am already dismayed!

STEWARD: It is well, oh great lord, that they should be summoned. Do not despair!

(*Then The* STEWARD *Leaves To Go And Call The* PRIESTS.)

STEWARD: Indeed, they are already coming, oh great lord! Do not forsake all of us, your servants, your vassals, your Jerusalemites!

FIRST
PRIEST: May the only true God, the God who rules, strengthen you! Oh lord, oh great lord, oh Herod! Truly you see before you us—your servants. Be glad! Rejoice and console yourself! For truly it is evident that our Lord God protects you! Give us your hands and feet that we might embrace them. What do you desire? We hear in order to obey it!

HEROD: Oh you—Jews, princes of the priests, wise men, diviners! You are made many times foolish! And moreover you ought to jeer at yourselves! You go about deluding others excessively. You no longer know the word of truth, nor are you worthy of respect. Am I not always perhaps telling you that I am your prince? You love me well! How well you lie! It is true that three kings have come. They left the East which is their land. In the middle of the night they saw a Star there. The Star says that the King of the Jews is now born! Who is this Child? Who is the Lord who rules over me? Tell me this at once! Perhaps you have not seen the new Star? Perhaps you sleep night in and night out! Sluggards! Lazy ones! Pigs! Perhaps then you don't pray your matins during the night? Jews! Sons of the devil! Ask at once and satisfy my (curiosity). Let it not come about that you'll be completely destroyed, oh rogues!

SECOND
PRIEST: Do not be angry, oh our lord! What is there to be gained from that? Whatever comes about is not in our power, nor is it our fault. You must know that our Lord God has promised us that here upon earth He will sometime give us the Son of God. That He will deign to send him here so that for our sake He will come and be Incarnate. And if He has deigned to come now, shall *we* wrest away his Divine Will? It was indeed a prophecy and must be made manifest when our Lord God is pleased to bring it about.

HEROD: Search, oh rogues, in all of your holy books (and find out) where our Lord will be born!

FIRST
PRIEST: Go and take the Divine Book and let us search. May God illumine us and whoever interprets the information about the Child. With this we shall calm our great King Herod.

THIRD PRIEST: It must be here! Let us search. May God enlighten us!

(The Jewish PRIESTS *Search In The Divine Books.)*

FIRST
PRIEST: Oh lord, oh Herod! It says this in the book of the prophet Isaiah: 'Of his root shall be clearly formed, shall be born and brought forth a man, a noble man; and

there shall be born, shall bud a marvelous flower. For this reason He shall be truly manifest as a noble and a lord. He shall be born from the lineage of David and shall belong to it.'

HEROD: I know this, you knave, you little man of no account, that He has to belong to the lineage of David! Where is He to be born? In what city? Search at once and tell [the answer] to me or you shall be seared, flayed, and turned into pork-cracklings, oh great Jews![9]

THIRD
PRIEST: May our Lord God favor us for fear that Herod will mistreat us! He is most angry. He will surely scorch us and make us into cracklings!

SECOND
PRIEST: Oh esteemed lord, oh Herod! I have here what our Lord commanded, and that about which you inquired. Know then what the prophet—the sublime prophet Michael—says in one chapter: "And you Bethlehem, you over all the land of Judah, you are most certainly not small in the excellent things of the lords of Judah. For truly from you shall come forth the Ruler, the Chief, the Lord—He who will govern the Israelites spiritually." On these grounds it is clear that the royal person [is] born there in Bethlehem in the land of Judah. Who will go to seek him if you should desire it?

HEROD: In Bethlehem? Search, knaves—now I shall have you seared! Why have you said nothing to me before? Pigs! Sons of the devil!

(Again And Again They Pursue The Holy Book. Then HEROD *Again Affronts The Priestly Jews.)*

HEROD: Leave me at once! Go! I shall speak with the kings!

(The PRIESTS *Go Out And* HEROD *Turns And Speaks To The Kings. He Will Act Much Humbled.)*

HEROD: Please be honored by me, you princes, you lords! Forgive me if I became a little angered with my nobles before you because they had not informed me of the prodigiousness of that which has come about. And now truly I greatly entreat you to tell me when the Star which was seen in your land appeared? When did you see it? I implore you sincerely to tell me the truth!

GASPAR: Oh prince and my lord, oh my esteemed Herod! Please know that we shall not displease you. Be not angered on our account! Most assuredly we appreciate your courtesy and we do not speak falsely to you. Oh lord, please be honored by us! May it serve you to know that thirteen days have passed since we saw the marvelous Star there in the East. Because of this, little time (has passed) since we arrived here still seeing it. Now at dawn just when we came to the entrance of the city of Jerusalem we lost our precious guide, oh Herod many-times prince!

HEROD: Oh lords and princes, you have favored me! Now let it please you to go there to the city of Bethlehem which alone is close to the city of Jerusalem. Would that it go well with the Child. And when you see him tell me of it at once so that I too may go and salute and adore God, the Prince. I shall go and take him as my Lord. Please if you will, go there now!

BALTHAZAR: May a peaceful life accompany your beloved person, and may He who is near to all things—that One by whom one lives—our Lord God, strengthen you! Oh my lord, oh prince, oh king, oh great lord! Most assuredly we kiss your feet and hands. Now we shall leave, oh king, oh my prince.

(*Here* HEROD *Leaves The Kings At The Walk* (?) *Of His House. Then They Turn And Enter The Church. The Star Appears To Them In The Arch Of The Portico. At This Point* BALTHAZAR *Speaks. He Holds The Star As A Good Omen And Says:*[10]

BALTHAZAR: Oh! Please my beloved friends, look and see what has led us here, our marvelous guide the wonderful Star! In truth now it goes guiding us again. Oh may it please you to see it, oh my beloved and esteemed friends!

MELCHIOR: Now we greatly rejoice, for truly we see it anew. He who is nigh and near to all beings—that One by whom we live—made it appear to us! Our wonderful guide, how straight it came in its path! Now it moves, now it rests! It is raised over a poor shelter; it is lowered over it. What does this mean to say? Does it perhaps not want to descend over the great palace near the entrance to the city?

MELCHIOR: (again) Look, oh you my servant! Enter, look about, and see what miracle guards our Lord here, our great Lord!

MESSENGER: This is good. I shall go in and look about immediately.

(*Here The* MESSENGER *Will Enter The Church And Go And Look About. He will Come Out Again And Speak This Prayer.*)

MESSENGER: You, oh lords, oh Kings! Truly I did as you commanded me. I went and I saw. Most surely I shall never see anything like this again; nothing will ever be able to equal it! When I entered and looked about, there was truly a great light, exactly as when the light is shining out here. The splendor as of the rays of the sun were spread out everywhere. And I saw a most marvelous, beautiful, and Holy Virgin carrying a Holy, precious, and blessed Child! And next to her was an old man, and round about them were beautiful children with wings. Near them there were two four-footed beasts. The heavenly and beautiful Virgin completely surpassed every delightful flower—the dusky ones, the golden ones, the beautiful flowers of violet hues, and all those which are like bright red plumes spread out. The most beautiful, resplendent, kind, and most excellent face of the blessed and precious Child is most certainly completely graceful. And his beautiful and most perfect hair is like gold when it is shining, or like the snow when it is pure. Indeed, the place where He was born is most humble. The beautiful Child-God was born in a manger! Let us go then, oh Lords, let us go to salute and worship him; to humble ourselves and to bow down in his presence, oh lords!

MELCHIOR: Oh that our admirable God, our Lord God, be forever praised, and would that what we search for might be thus discovered. Let us enter, oh my lords and friends! Let us go and adore him, and to humble ourselves in his presence. Let us go and make him an offering of some kind!

(Here The Kings Dismount From Their Horses. They Enter Into The Church and Humble Themselves Greatly. They Then Proceed As Lords And Go To Place Themselves Upon Their Knees At The Foot Of The Altar. Then The Mass Is Pronounced. After This The Gospel Is Read, And All Concludes With The Creed. They All Reverently Salute The Beautiful Child God, And Each In Turn Speaks A Prayer. They Commence:)

GASPAR: Oh noble one, oh our Lord! Oh precious jewel, rich plume! Oh fine turquoise, oh bracelet![11] You have done well to come here! (And how good) that our beloved Father God—He who is near to all things and He by whom we exist—deigned to give you your place here! They have long since parted and gone to rest, have those who awaited you, your forefathers the prophets and the patriarchs. It has been ages since the noble lord David and the noble lord Abraham went to know the beyond. They prepared and left upright the load-bearer to handle the loads, the axe to cut with, and the apparatus to bear the weight (tumpline), (all) in order that there be no slackening, and that nothing would be liable to argument.[12] (Yet) is it still possible that some one comes, that he goes about following behind them at their shoulders (the prophets') or in their footsteps? Is it possible that he visits your houses and your fields when there is shade or in the dark places, even after You now exist? Is it still possible that he might enter some forest, walk about, and while he goes completely destroy the axe and the load-bearer?[13] Ah so it is. For the world has neither father nor mother, neither vassals nor servants. It has neither eyes nor ears. It is basically mute; it neither makes sounds nor does it speak. It is as something decapitated, like something which no longer has a head and goes about walking cautiously.[14] Oh my God, oh my Lord, oh beautiful Child God! In your hands shall be placed the tribute which is given to your beloved and worshipped Father God; and truly You yourself will present it. And indeed I declare in your presence that in all times past I have lived in a place of darkness, as in an obscure night. That is, I knew you not! And now, truly, you illumine my spirit, my soul, as also You have come to enlighten those within heaven and all your other creatures. Therefore, oh my God, truly I beseech you benevolently to accept my spirit, my soul, and my life, in order that it be proven that I make an offering to you of this *copal* called incense.[15] Deign to accept it with grace, oh my God, my Lord!

(*Here He Kneels. He Will Make An Offering To The Beautiful* CHILD GOD, *And Will Kiss Him. He Will Then Step Back And Say:*)

GASPAR: Oh my God, oh my Lord! I also declare before You that You are the true, the great minister of God. You are the true priest. Truly you will deign to care for the service made to your beloved Father God and my Lord. Of your own will you will be pleased to make the offering of the Cross in order to make your beloved Father God happy. Thus oh my King—He who is near unto all things, that One by whom we exist—receive with mercy my spirit, my soul, and my life.

MELCHIOR: Oh my beloved and most holy God! Oh You most truly Man and most truly God! I certainly believe in

You with all my heart, and that You acted in Grace to make heaven and earth, the visible and the invisible. Most assuredly You have within You the sovereignty to govern and maintain the world and all your creatures. Truly we awaited You a long time! A long time we walked about sighing for You! Now You have come! You have deigned to come! Your precious Father God did well to send You here. In truth the counsel and word of your Holy Father God has come upon You. Indeed, You will bear a great burden for all; moreover, You shall bear the load-bearer as well.[16] For it was to this that your ancestors, your elders, bound You. The patriarchs, the prophets, the princes, and the lords of Israel pledged You. You did your duty toward them—to those who since many years have known the thence (death). In truth, before all You must bear your cross, the instrument of salvation; upon your shoulders shall You place it. Your beloved Father places his sovereignty, his burden, his servants, and vassals, all in your lap to be saved. It is true that for a little while You will hold your city in your hands which is our Mother the Holy Church. And yet for a little while You will be able to hold it in your arms, separating the grain from the chaff. The Word, the breath of your beloved Father God—He who is nigh to all living things—has come upon You. Truly He has pointed You out with his finger and has sustained You. Perchance you are able to leave your undertaking? Certainly not! And now, oh my precious God, oh my Lord, truly much is attained with your wonderful love! And yet, what thing will be restored to You because of this! I humble myself before You. I adore You! I dedicate everything to You; and I give over my spirit, my soul, and my life completely! Receive this gold with kindness, oh God my Lord, and may it secure my forgiveness. Amen.

(*Here He Kisses The Child And Makes His Offering.* MELCHIOR *Will Say Nothing More. Then* BALTHAZAR *Speaks:*)

BALTHAZAR: Oh noble Lord, may You preserve heaven and earth, the greatness and the Sovereignty! You are most truly God, He who is near to all beings, and that One by whom we exist. I completely have faith in You with all my spirit, soul, and life. Indeed for our sakes You have deigned to leave your royal kingdom and marvelous home. And truly you agreed to remain here upon the earth to teach us. And for our sakes your enemies the Jews will bind your hands and feet, and will scourge You. For us too You will be hanged upon the Cross with your hands outstretched, and You must die. This (is) only for the sake of the inhabitants of the world. For so it is that You will save your creatures by your death. And now, what thing can I give You? Certainly nothing but that which is here! I offer you the much-prized bitter unguent which is called myrrh. When your precious body will be interred in the sepulchre, they will anoint You with this. Now, oh precious Lord, what thing have we really come to offer You? Only our spirit, our soul, and our life! Mercifully forgive us, oh my beloved and honored Father!

(Here He Kisses The Little Child as GASPAR *And* MELCHIOR *Have Done. He Steps Back And Again Says:)*

BALTHAZAR: You, oh precious and blessed Virgin, original sin never reached you! Oh that your precious grace might fill everything completely—both there in the interior of heaven and here in all parts of the world! Oh that it would never cease; that your glorious dignity as Queen shall never waver. What thing then shall I offer you? Truly it is as nothing! It is only our spirit, our soul, and our life. Would that you ever forgive me, oh my precious Mother! Truly we shall now leave. Thus it is done. Amen. Jesus, Mary, and Joseph.

(Here The ANGEL *Is Seen And Will Give Orders To The Three Kings Saying)*

ANGEL: Oh you lords, oh you Kings! What you did for the precious and blessed Virgin and for the most dazzling, precious, and unique Son since you arrived is most commendable. You came to salute him and to make offerings. So now I greatly beseech you not to return there where you came from, but rather that you return by another road in order not to fall into the hands of Herod —great ruffian—who deceived you when he said, 'I also shall certainly go to worship Him.' The truth is that he is enraged, and that he wishes to sentence him (Jesus) to death. Furthermore, the truth is that now, at this very hour, it is not time that He should die, for He must first save the inhabitants of the world.

(*Thus Ends The Mass. Here The* ANGEL *Calls Several Times to* JOSEPH, *And Will Give Him His Orders Saying*)

ANGEL: Oh Joseph! Oh Joseph! Oh Joseph! You must take flight with the precious Child God for the perverse Herod is coming! Indeed, he comes searching for him! Take him away to Egypt. Hide him there within a grove of palms, in order that they not sentence him to death. For now Herod is going to kill all the babies. Hurry Run! Oh lord Saint Joseph!

Commentary

Ponce's description included before the play is of interest to us as it defines some of the techniques by which the sixteenth-century indigenous Mexicans embellished the settings of their dramatic presentations. The device of the Star on a double cord extending from the mountain top to the church courtyard is remarkable. The devotional and entertaining songs and dances which were presented while the Kings wended their way down to the church *patio* were important as they amused, set the scene for the dramatic interlude to follow, and were readily comprehensible to an indigenous audience. It was undoubtedly prudent to ameliorate the Christian *fiestas* with music and color in order that the catachumens would not feel the lack of such spectacles to which they had been accustomed in Prehispanic times. It is possible that our copy of the *"Adoration of the Kings"* is precisely a skeleton script and that the interpolations of musical interludes, etc., and the embellishment of the Mass could be added by the group who were doing the presentation according to their own taste and customs.

Some differences are notable between our play and the one described by Ponce. The ramparts of Jerusalem, according to Ponce's description of the Tlaxomulco production were in the courtyard of the church; more action takes place within the church according to our manuscript. The Star is thus suspended over (*encima*) the arch or door of the entryway to the church. The messenger therefore enters the church on his errand, and then returns outside to relate to the Kings that which he has found. The Kings enter with the idea of adoring the Child, apparently disappearing from the sight of the audience remaining in the patio. It is likely, as mentioned, that the church was constructed more openly so that those in the patio could see what was going on inside the church. At this point, the entire audience could either follow and watch what the Kings did inside the church, or witness the mime of the Jerusalemites in their tableau outside the church. It is interesting that in contemporary Mexico it is the custom, during any presentation of the three Kings coming to adore the Child, that a good part of the audience follow the kings—perhaps in a turn or two around the square in front of the church—and then enter into the central nave as a company to bring offerings to the Holy Child. The Kings then usually ride away from the church and out of the village, still followed by the more interested members of the audience.[17]

In summary, then, our *"Adoration"* is essentially a mass, preceded and accompanied by scenes in the church courtyard and within the church. The scenes in the patio are of an entertaining and informative nature, while those which take place within the church are clearly devotional and inspirational.

In his *Historia de los indios* Motolinía in the fourth decade of the sixteenth century, mentions that the *auto* of the *"Ofrecimiento de los Reyes al Niño Jesús"* was almost never omitted by the Indians from their Epiphany celebrations.[18] We know therefore that the *content* of the text of our drama corresponds to that of the earliest epoch of the conquest period.

It is possible that our version of the play actually preceded the one described by Ponce as having taken place in Tlaxomulco in 1587 and that the subsequent placing of the ramparts of Jerusalem outside of the church was in answer to the sixteenth century prohibition against the presentation of the plays inside the churches.

VI

"THE FINAL JUDGMENT"

INTRODUCTION

The cast of characters in *"The Final Judgment"* is predominantly composed of supernatural personages. Only Lucia, who is the protagonist, and the priest are earthly inhabitants. The remainder of the cast consists of demons, saints, or abstract characterizations such as Time, Death, and Penitence.

The plot of the drama involves the downfall of Lucia, who has chosen the primrose path of the libertine instead of the moral life sanctioned by the Church. Unknown to Lucia, the time is drawing night for the Final Judgment of the world. As the hour for the actual judgment approaches, Lucia rushes off to find a confessor. She is unsuccessful in her last minute attempt to secure forgiveness and grace, and is subsequently carried off by devils, and a tremendous sentence is pronounced against her.

In this play, Lucia obviously epitomizes the practice of adulterous relationships so common both before and after the conquest in Mexico. The Prehispanic nobility had practiced concubinage, and the priests sought diligently to irradicate this custom. Although the nobility was severely truncated in size rapidly after the conquest, it still remained a powerful social force and symbol of indigenous cultural heritage. The use of drama helped to skirt the necessity of direct attacks on the undesirable customs of the nobility, and the use of a female as the direct object for the moral lesson was judicious. It could also be argued that the missionaries were making a special religious appeal to women so that, with the Christian view of womanhood epitomized by the Virgin Mary, a new concept of sexual purity could be forged.

The internal linguistic evidence of the drama strongly suggests that its origin was in the sixteenth century. The plot is simple and direct; the dénouement is developed through several scenarios, and not in a carefully integrated series of acts and scenes.

The number of references to other data on the *"The Final Judgment"* suggests that it was an important and popular theme among the missionary-teachers of the early colonial era.

The Nahuatl manuscript of *"The Final Judgment"* is located in the Manuscript Division of the Library of Congress (AC. 1139, III—48-C, 4). It is listed under the title *"Nexcuitilmachiotl Motenhua Juicio Final"* and has been attributed to Andrés de Olmos, who lived in the first half of the sixteenth century.[1] There is also a photostatic copy of the Nahuatl manuscript of the *"Juicio Final"* filed in the microfilm section of the Benjamin Franklin Collection now housed in the historical library of the Chapultepec Museum in Mexico City. There are no previous publications of this play.

The English translation published here was made from the Nahuatl by John J Cornyn and Byron McAfee in 1932. A copy of the translation was secured from the private collection of Byron McAfee, who resides in Mexico; he kindly extended both editing and publishing rights to the author.[2]

The translation has been left essentially as it was completed by Cornyn and McAfee. When minor changes in phraseology seemed advisable, care was taken not to alter the original meaning or the style. As usual in this study, notes have been appended where it seemed important to clarify for the reader some of the more obscure references.

While the action sequence of *"The Final Judgment"* lacks integration, some of the dialogue is lively and must have occasioned feelings of merriment among the members of the audience.

On the title page of the translation, there appears the notation "A moral play by Andrés de Olmos". Cornyn and McAfee apparently accept the attribution of this play to Olmos. It should be mentioned that, although there is no outside evidence attributing this play to Olmos, it is quite possible that he was in fact the author or adapter of the drama.

The Final Judgment

CHARACTERS:
St. Michael
Christ
Lucifer
Satan
Antichrist
Lucia
Three Devils
The Living
The Dead
First Angel
Second Angel
Priest
Holy Church
Penitence
Death
Time
Confession
Angels of the Court of Heaven
Devils of the Hosts of Lucifer

THE JUDGMENT DAY

(There Is A Sound Of Trumpets. The Heavens Open, And St. Michael *Descends.)*

St. Michael: Oh creatures of God, know—but then you already know—that, according to the sacred Commandments of the Lord Almighty, He our beloved God and Father will end, will destroy the world and all He has made.[3] Everything He has created will perish, will come to an end. All the birds and animals, and you too will be annihilated! Yet you may be sure that the dead will come to life; that God, the upright and just Judge, will take the righteous who served Him to His heavenly mansion the place of everlasting bliss, Paradise, abode of the blessed and of the saints. But the wicked who did not serve the Lord our God may be sure that they will receive the torments of hell! Weep because of this! Remember this: be in fear. Be in deadly fear! For the day of judgment will descend upon you, fearful, dreadful, frightful, paralyzing! Take warning and lead a proper life. The day of judgment is at hand. It is here now! It is upon you at this very moment!

(*There Is A Sound Of Trumpets*. ST. MICHAEL *Ascends. Enter* PENITENCE, TIME, HOLY CHURCH, CONFESSION, *And* DEATH.

PENITENCE: From now on it will not be possible to speak or to talk about all the follies of the people of the world. As for them, they are beaten down with many sins. What have they done? What are they doing? They can no longer quit their deadly sins, their hardness of heart, their blindness! Oh a thousand times unfortunate that they are![4] Ah! They will die in their sins! They are deaf; they are hard of hearing; they are blind; they are sightless! It may properly be said that through their sins their eyes have been destroyed. They have found sin pleasant to the taste and sweet-scented. They have received Sensuous Pleasure into their homes and clothed her. They looked upon her as their drink and food. They forgot their Lord God! Oh a thousand times unfortunate that they are! Their life on earth is now ended!

TIME: I am Time. I am he who continues ever-questioning the people. Our Lord God sent and established me to keep them, care for them, warn them, remind them day and night. Never do I stop speaking! I am continually shouting in their ears so that they may remember their Creator, their Maker, the Lord God. I take care that they cry out to Him; that they bless Him; that they serve Him; that they do as the Lord our God wishes. I urge them to go to His house and to praise Him; to ask for His Divine Grace. But as for them, they waste my life and my work. And so I say: "I leave them. I have done my duty to them. I am not to be blamed on their account. They must make their own defense in the presence of God as they are individually called and questioned. They know how they are going to purge their sins. As for me, I am going to render my account to God the Father. He has invested all His Power in me. The people will not be able to excuse themselves because of me. They are going to be called to be judged right away!"

HOLY CHURCH: I am the ever-merciful mother. My beloved Son Jesus Christ has established me here for the people of the earth. I am always weeping for them, especially when some of them die. For when I shed tears, I pray to my beloved Mother, the sacred fountain of joy, to have pity on her creatures and to give light to them. May the seventh Sacrament not be neglected! I am keeping it for them in case they may sometime wish it. The hungry I shall feed, and I shall give drink to the thirsty. Now I am waiting for them. Would that they might come and live proper lives! My heart is sad for them. Would that they might pray to be pardoned; that they might weep and repent of their shortcomings and sins!

PENITENCE: Oh mother of complete faith, all that you say is quite true! The people do not remember this. They do not want to. Their only desire is to sin. Do I not use all of my efforts? I am ever crying out to them! Daily I advise them to repent, to keep watch, to rise up early in the morning and do penance, to grow cool—that is, to spiritually purify their hearts and souls, to fast, to refrain from eating that they may be shown pity and pardoned. Otherwise they cannot enter the princely mansion of the Lord our God. They will certainly be lost if they do not first do penance. But if they are deserving, I shall take them to me; I shall bestow favors upon them, for to them belongs the celestial ladder which leads to heaven, the time is not far off when they will be called into the presence of the Lord our God that each may give an accounting to him of how they lived on earth.

May they not offer resistance to us in the presence of God.

DEATH: I am the officer of the law, the appointed one, the messenger empowered by heaven. Here on earth the power spreads forth to the uttermost limits as the rays of the sun shining forth in the heavens, and over the whole earth. Let the people of the earth remember that soon the beloved Son of God will come down to judge the quick and the dead. The good He will take to His celestial mansion in the heavens; and the wicked—those who did not serve Him here on earth—He will hurl into the nethermost hell. May the people of the earth remember that the day of judgment will descend upon them! This fearful thing must happen to them. Let them rectify their lives, for the time and hour of judgment is at hand when they shall answer as to how they served the Lord our God.

HOLY CHURCH: What you have just said, just expressed, is quite true. For you are the servants, the workers, of the only Son of my consolation, my beloved spiritual Spouse, Jesus Christ. He gave you your being in order that you might warn and call out to the sinners of the world whom He died to save. With great sin they have covered and besmirched their hearts and souls. Let us go now and cry out to them to come and prepare themselves spiritually with weeping and tears. I am waiting to purify them, to bathe them spiritually; to cleanse them through the seventh Sacrament, marriage, which I am reserving for them.

TIME: I am going right now to cry out to them; to remind them what they must do in order not to ill-use or waste the span of life which our Lord God has given me (for them).

(TIME *Alone Exits.*)

HOLY CHURCH: I am the divine light of the only faith. I enlighten and give spiritual vision to all Christians that they may come so that I may cleanse them; for they are dizzy and stupid with sin. If they weep and are sad, then my beloved Youth, Jesus Christ, will pardon them and give them the kingdom of heaven.

(HOLY CHURCH *Alone Exits.*)

DEATH: The people of the earth are deserving of great pity. They are blind. They do not remember that they will at some time be brought to justice. Sensuality soils their souls with sin. The people of the world are blind, sightless. They have blackened themselves with great sins, but their hearts and souls are not distressed because of this. Let them wash themselves. Let them bathe themselves in the divine light of goodness. Perhaps when the day of judgment dawns upon them they will remember, and they will weep. But then they may be sure that there will no longer be any pity for them. Oh, a thousand times unfortunate are the people of this world! Soon the day of judgment will visit them! Now the day is at hand! The time and place is now!

(*There Is A Sound Of Trumpets. Both Death And Penitence Exit. Enter* LUCIA, *Who Is Greatly Troubled.*)

LUCIA: Oh You, my God! Oh my Lord Jesus Christ! Oh, unfortunate that I am! What is happening to me now! My soul is terribly afflicted as if I were entering a cloud. What shall I do now? I shall go and confess! Perhaps that will ease my soul a little. I'll go now and look for my confessor for I am really suffering.

(LUCIA *Goes And Knocks On The Door. Enter The* PRIEST.)

LUCIA: May our Lord God be with you, dear father!

(*The* PRIEST *Comes Forward And Speaks.*)

PRIEST: May the Lord our God lead you here, my dear daughter! You are welcome here. What is it that you wish?

LUCIA: You must know why I have come, dear father. May I not make you angry, honored sir!

PRIEST: What do you want, dear daughter? Tell me! For the Lord our God has instituted us that we may receive the confessions of the people of the world.

LUCIA: Dear father! I want to confess before our Lord God and you, dear father.

PRIEST: My dear daughter, you make me very happy. I am listening to what is troubling you and afflicting you—that is, your sins. Let us go to the house of the Lord our God.

(LUCIA *Confesses And, While She Is Confessing, The* PRIEST *Suddenly Springs Up Very Frightened.*)

PRIEST: Lord! Lord! What is this you are saying? What have you done? Are you not a Christian? Do you not know that this thing which you have done is a cardinal sin? It is all over with you! Oh unfortunate that you are! Would that you had found salvation for your soul! Would that you had cleansed it! Why have you not received spiritual things? All you have done is to follow the devil! Why have you not accepted the seventh Sacrament, holy matrimony? It is all over! Oh a thousand times unfortunate you are! Up until now you have never wanted to be married here on earth. But you may be sure that you are going to be married down there in the nethermost hell. You deserve the torments of the infernal regions. And now what kind of account are you going to give to your Lord God? You cannot help yourself in any way; for the time is up, and God's judgment day has arrived! Now you will meet the blessed Son of our Lord God when He comes to judge the quick and the dead. Each must give an account to Him, his Maker. And you too must appear before the true Judge, Jesus Christ, the beloved Son of God![5]

(*Exit The* PRIEST, LUCIA *Remains.*)

LUCIA: Alas! Oh God! It is all over! Oh, I have been greatly unfortunate here upon earth! What have I heard? What has the beloved Son of God said to me? What fear it brings when God's Beloved speaks thus! Would that I had believed in God and listened to what my father, mother and relatives advised me to do. But all I did was

The Final Judgment

to become angry and curse the sacred Sacrament of Holy Matrimony. It is all over now! Oh, a thousand times unfortunate that I am! Accursed be my pride! What have a done? How has pride benefited me? Accursed be both earth and time! Now the world is coming to an end; it is about to terminate! All is finished! I am a thousand times unfortunate, great sinner that I am!

(*Sound Of Trumpets Is Heard. Enter The Living. They Sit Down On The Ground.* LUCIA *Is Also Seated. They Cover Their Faces. Enter The* ANTICHRIST. *He Wears The Cloak Of The Wicked And With It Only A Gown. He Lifts The Finger Of His Left Hand. There Are Fireworks As He Comes Out.*)

ANTICHRIST: My dear children, do you not recognize me? I am He who suffered for you on earth! For you I have gone through torment. And now you may be sure that I shall bring to an end and shall destroy the world. Have faith in me, my creatures, and I shall pardon your sins and your transgressions. Believe in me! Behold my dear blood, my dear flesh!

FIRST LIVE
PERSON: You are not the one we are waiting for! Our dear Lord God is coming. It is He who suffered for us, and who died on the cross. There they stretched out his arms because of our countless sins.

LUCIA: You are surely He for whom we are waiting! Our Lord and our God! Pardon our sins!

ANTICHRIST: Yes I am. I shall help you. Do you not know all my power that is in the world?

(*They All Begin To Sing* CHRISTUS FACTUSES. *The Heavens Open.* CHRIST *Appears.* ST. MICHAEL *Goes Ahead Carrying The Scales Of Justice While* CHRIST *Bears The Cross. He Stops At The Edge Of Heaven As The* ANTICHRIST *Goes Out Quickly. There Are Fireworks.*)

CHRIST: Come, my war leader, St. Michael, here into heaven. For now I am going to end and destroy time. This is called the day of judgment—the day of reckoning—as I have announced in my sacred law. I shall assuredly cleanse both heaven and earth. For the people of the earth, both the living and the dead, have defiled things through their evil lives.[6] Now wake up the living and the dead, the good and the bad. To the good I shall give heaven: the life of flowery bliss, the celestial jewel, Paradise, the heavenly palm![7] But the wicked may be sure that their reward will be the house of hell, the sufferings of hell! For they have not kept my sacred commandments.

(CHRIST *Descends.* ST. MICHAEL *Salutes Christ.*)

CHRIST: I have told you what you are to do, my war leader.

ST. MICHAEL: Yes, you certainly have, my dear Master. The dead are to be revived, and the living awakened. They are to gather together their bones and to assemble them in their places. They are to resume their dust and ashes (bodies) that You may give them their resurrection, as well as their holy spirit and their souls that they may answer to You; that they may declare what good they have done and what evil they have committed—that is, their deeds.[8]

CHRIST: It is true that through my power they shall arise from the dead, and that they will live again. Just as I myself rose on the third day, so also may my creatures rise!

(*There Is A Sound Of Trumpets. Exit* CHRIST *Through Another Door. He Does Not Rise Again To Heaven.*)

(ST. MICHAEL *Blows His Trumpet.*[9])

FIRST ANGEL: Wake up, you living, at the command of God! Take your bodies (your *flesh*) with you!

(ST. MICHAEL *Again Blows His Trumpet. He Calls Out To The Dead Where They Are.*)

SECOND ANGEL: *Surgite mortui! Venite a judicio!* Arise, oh dead! Come forth from the nether regions where you are.

Bring your bodies for it is the command of our Lord God.

(*The Dead Come Forth With Their Bodies.* ST. MICHAEL *Again Blows His Trumpet.*)

ST. MICHAEL: Now that you have arisen from the dead, come all of you together to give an account of what you have done to the upright Dispenser of Justice, the Judge! Don't any of you be excited now! Wait for your God and your Creator!

(*There Is A Sound Of Trumpets. Exit* ST. MICHAEL. *Enter The* ANTICHRIST *Who Comes To Deceive The Living And The Dead.* (*Enter* CHRIST *Somewhat Later.*)

ANTICHRIST: I have come in order to have you carry out my precious word.

(*They Chant The* TE DEUM LAUDAMUS. *The Antichrist Exits In Haste. There Are Fireworks. Enter The* CHRIST. *The First And Second Angels Come Forward.* ST. MICHAEL *Is Leading Them.*)

CHRIST: Come here, oh pearl of heaven, St. Michael the Archangel! Call the living and dead to assemble here before me that I may ask them to account for how they lived here on earth.

ST. MICHAEL: So be it, my dear master. I shall call them.

(ST. MICHAEL *Blows His Trumpet, And One By One They Go Before Christ And Sit Down. An Angel Weighs Their Sins On The Scales. The First Dead Kneels Down.*)

CHRIST: Come hither, you. Have you kept my commandments while you lived on earth and moved about? Speak! Answer me! Speak now just as you were in the habit of speaking on earth.

FIRST DEAD: My Lord! My God! I kept and observed, I fulfilled your divine commandments. I have done your will. Ask my guardian angel, my dear Master.

CHRIST: You have served me well. In heaven you will have eternal glory and bliss. Your happiness will never end!

(CHRIST *Blesses Him.* ST. MICHAEL *Puts Him On The Right Hand Of Christ.*)

CHRIST: Come hither, you living. Whom did you honor and whom did you love on earth?

FIRST LIVING: You, oh my God and Lord!

CHRIST: If I am really your God and your Lord, have you kept my sacred commandments? Have you fulfilled them?

FIRST LIVING: I have not done so, my God. Pardon me, oh sinner that I am.

CHRIST: There is no more forgiveness now! Go!

(ST. MICHAEL *Places Him On The Other Side, And The Second Dead Kneels Before Christ.*)

CHRIST: Come hither, you who were dead! What did you do while you were living on earth? Did you do my work? Did you serve me while on earth? Answer me!

SECOND DEAD: Not in any way. Forgive me, my Lord, my Master, my God!

CHRIST: There is no forgiveness on the day of judgment! Go!

(ST. MICHAEL *Shoves The Dead Away. The Devils Drag Him Off To One Side.* LUCIA, *The Second Living, Kneels.*)

CHRIST: Come hither, you living. Have you kept my sacred commandments, the ten? Have you loved your neighbors and your father and mother?

SECOND LIVING: (LUCIA) Certainly! First of all, I loved You! And after You, My God, my father and my mother.

CHRIST: If I am really your God and you loved me first of all, and after me your father and your mother, have you kept my commandments and those of my dear and honored Mother concerning the seventh Sacrament, Holy Matrimony? Have you remained pure while on earth? What have you done for a living?

The Final Judgment

LUCIA: No, Lord I have not served You! Nor have I recognized your dear Mother. Forgive me, my God, my Lord!

CHRIST: Never up until now—never while on earth has your heart honestly addressed itself to us. You served only your own lasciviousness. Go away! You are condemned never to forget and to be the slave of your evil life. Well you know that you may expect nothing from heaven, oh unfortunate that you are! You never wanted to be married while on earth. You have won for yourself a dwelling place in the nethermost hell. Go to those whom you have served, for I do not know you!

(*He Pushes Her Toward The Devils.*)

CHRIST: Come here you living who are yet on earth. What was occupying your attentions? Was it, by chance, my Divine Word? Were you constantly calling out to me when sleeping and awake?

THIRD LIVING: I never forgot You, in my eating or drinking, asleep or awake, my dear Master!

CHRIST: You have served me well, my creature. And as I have always remembered you, I am saving for you a flowery garland.

(ST. MICHAEL *Sends Him Over With The Righteous.*)

CHRIST: Come, oh dwellers in hell! Take away your servants to the nethermost regions. Put this wicked woman into a bath of fire and torture her there.

SECOND DEVIL: Our Lord, you have done us a favor. We knew about and were only awaiting your coming! We are happy that You have graciously granted that we may secure your creatures. Go quickly and bring the fiery chain and the fiery rod with which we shall beat them. And tell our lord Lucifer that we are taking his servants down there; and to send the iron fire seat in haste to where we are taking his servants.

(*Exit* SATAN *Who Goes To Bring The Iron Fire Seat.*)

SATAN: Here I bring along everything with which we may chain (bind) them so that they cannot escape from our hands.

(*The Condemned Speak:*)

THE CONDEMNED: Now we have what is coming to us (our water and our food, e.g. the ration idea) here in the nethermost hell.

SATAN *Speaks:*

SATAN: We have all used our power so that they might fall into our hands, these servants of ours!

(*They All Shout:* Oh Lord Help Us!)

CHRIST: You have nothing more to hope for. You may be sure of that. You will be ceaselessly tormented down there in the nethermost hell!

(*Again They All Shout:* Oh Lord, Save Us Sinners That We Are! *Then They All Run Out. There Are Fireworks. They (The Damned) Go Out Shouting. To The Righteous They Give Garlands Of Flowers And Palms. Christ Ascends To Heaven. Halfway Up The Stairs He Speaks.*[10]

CHRIST: Oh my servants, climb up here that you might get what I am keeping for you: happiness, everlasting and without end.

(*There Is A Sound Of Trumpets. Angels, Christ, And The Righteous Climb Up.* LUCIA *Is Brought Out. Flames Are Her Adornment. A Serpent Is Her Necklace, And With One (A Serpent) They Bind Her. She Comes Out Shouting And The Devils Answer Her.*)

FIRST DEVIL: March, oh wicked woman! Do you not remember what you did on earth? Now we are going to reward you down here in the nethermost hell. March! Get along!

LUCIA: It is all over! Oh a thousand times unfortunate that I am! I am a great sinner deserving of hell.

SATAN: So you have just been shouting, wicked woman! Now we shall give you pleasure in the nethermost hell. Down

The Final Judgment

there we shall marry you in our palace, since you were never married on earth. March! Get along! For your lord Lucifer is awaiting you.

LUCIA: Oh! Oh! It is all over, unfortunate sinner that I am! I deserve and have won the sufferings of hell. Would that I had not been born on earth! Oh! Oh! Accursed be the earth and the time when I was born! Accursed be the mother who bore me! A curse on the milk that nourished me and all that I ate and drank on earth. Oh! Accursed be the land I trod upon, and all the clothes I wore there. Everything has turned to fire and is burning me fearfully. Flames are all about my ears. They symbolize the ornaments with which I used to beautify myself. And wound around my neck is a fearsome fire-snake which symbolizes the necklaces I used to wear. What I have wound around my waist, a horrible fire-snake—the heart of the house of hell— is that which symbolizes the pleasures with which I enjoyed myself on earth. Oh! Oh! Would that I had become married! Oh! It is all over. Oh unfortunate that I am!"[11]

SECOND DEVIL: Now you are going to suffer and to pay for all the inattention you gave to the (advice) of your relatives while on earth.

(They Scourge Her.)

SATAN: Get along, you wicked woman! So now you remember that you should have been married? How is it that you did not remember this while you were still living on earth? Well, you are going to pay for all your wickedness now! March! Get along!

(They Scourge Her As They Drive Her Out. There Are Fireworks. The Devils Go Along Blowing Horns. The PRIEST *Enters.)*

PRIEST: My dear children! Christians, children of God! Now you have seen this fearful miracle! It is true for it is **written in the Holy Book. Be awakened! Be advised!**

See yourselves (as you are) so that what befalls your neighbors may not befall you. This is a symbol, an example which our Lord God gives you. The day of judgment is coming soon (tomorrow or the day after). Pray to our Lord Jesus Christ and to the Virgin Mary, that she may entreat her beloved Son Jesus Christ that you might merit and deserve the joy of Heaven—that is eternal glory! Amen.

Ave Maria!

Commentary

Much commentary about this play is unnecessary. The lessons to be learned are apparent. The main interest of the clergy who presented the play was to enforce the sacrament of marriage. To enforce Church marriages was a problem in the sixteenth century as it is today in many parts of Mexico. As previously mentioned, the custom of sexual liaison unblessed by any church has had a long tradition in Mexico. The scarcity of qualified priests and the relative isolation of rural and mountain villages which seldom had (or have) resident clergy made the ecclesiastical control of marriage difficult. The zealous desire of the priests to enforce the seventh sacrament accounts in part for the frightening picture of hell as a locale of eternal castigation by primitive torture apparatuses such as chains of fire and iron fire seats. Echoes of the medieval penchant for torture chambers are also apparent here.

Finally, the usual theme of obedience to the elders and those of authority figures in *"The Final Judgment."* The Scriptures have amply warned of the imminence of the time of judgment, and man's God-given sense of time daily reminds him of his fleeting mortality. Priests are the comforters and the advisors as are one's family and elders. They are all to be heeded. There are undertones of Augustinian theology in the emphasis upon time as a normative experience with axiological implications.

The concept of the guardian angel is also used here. It again seems to be a sort of spiritual double who both protects and acts as one's conscience, and who can testify for one before God (intercede) if not weakened overmuch by the evil deeds of the individual concerned.

The Antichrist was undoubtedly a handy symbol to use as a reminder that clever pretenders to the position of religious authority are to be avoided. The Prehispanic religion was eclipsed by Christianity in what seems to us to be a record time. That there were undercurrents and outbreaks of the "diabolical practices of their gentility" among the Indians is evidenced by the many passages in the chronicles which refer to this omnipresent danger. The cortège of hell had to be inflected through a kind of hierarchy of evil including Lucifer, Satan, and myriad devils. The Prehispanic spiritual world had been liberally populated by diabolical and evil spirits also, and it would have seemed a great impoverishment to think of evil as due to only one depersonalized cause.

The dramatic presentation of the subject matter through the use of fireworks and song, the stylized appearance of God, and the thread of comic relief in spite of the seriousness of the plot all contrive to make this play an important one of impressive proportions to an indigenous audience.

VII

How The Blessed St. Helen Found The Holy Cross

Introduction

The Nahuatl manuscript of this play bears the Spanish title *"Invención de la Santa Cruz por Santa Elena."* The whereabouts of the original manuscript of this play are unknown since its disappearance from the National Museum of Mexico City in the nineteenth century. The play is listed in the manuscript notes of Paso y Troncoso (in the collection of Frederico Gómez) as among those presented during the sixteenth century. There are no microfilm or photostatic copies of the original available to the author's knowledge. Pimentel, in his bibliography, mentions a copy from the eighteenth century owned by a Dr. Nicolás León of Morelia. There are two publications of this play in Spanish: one by Francisco Paso y Troncoso, and another by José Rojas Garciduañas.[1] The translation included here was made by Byron McAfee, and the manuscript was secured from his private collection of translations from Nahuatl into English. This translation bears the following notation in the prologue:

> *"Dialogue of How the Blessed St. Helen Found the precious holy Cross."* It was put in order and written by Bachelor Don Manuel de los Santos y Salazar, Priest by appointment of his Majesty, Vicar and Ecclesiastical Judge, in the town of Santa Cruz Cozcacuauh, on the top of the *barranca,* and at the edge of the water, of the city of Tlaxcala.[2]

This copy was therefore made by Santos y Salazar in May of 1714. As usual, we do not have an original manuscript, but rather a later copy of an earlier play which was probably still presented for the occasion of *Corpus Christi* as late as the eighteenth century.

The plot concerns the Emperor Constantine, who was converted to Christianity largely through a vision, and makes his subsequent military victories under the aegis of the cross. He then sends his mother, the blessed Helen, to Jerusalem to find the cross, whose veracity was then ascertained through a miracle which it subsequently performs.

The play is typical of the kind often chosen for presentation on Corpus Christi, as it teaches a bit of history and instills into the minds of the audience a reverence for the Christian relics and the miraculous powers they possess. The historical background of the events of the play are rooted in fact. Constantine did defeat Maxentius in 312 A.D. Helen was sent to Jerusalem at the behest of her son the Emperor and subsequently found the "true cross."

The cast of characters includes both natural and supernatural personages; and music and dance play an important part in the setting. The play seems to represent a battle of powers: the spiritual power of the holy Cross and the Christian God, versus the power of Evil as embodied by the devil and the necromancers. Political and military power are delineated as dependent upon the proper religious incentive and support for their real value and efficacy, e.g., the first speech of Constantine. The transitoriness of life and worldly splendor is opposed to the imperishable happiness of knowledge and faith in God.

I have not seen the Nahuatl manuscript of this play, and can therefore assume that the only reason for attributing it to the sixteenth century refers to the literary style of Nahuatl, as well as to the content of the action.

How The Blessed St. Helen Found The Holy Cross

CHARACTERS:

St. Helen	Theodora
St. Sylvester	Soldiers
Bishop Macarios	Musicians
An Angel	The Devil
Emperor Constantine	Two Wizards
Emperor Maxentius	
Licinius, a Private	

Captain Leoncius
Captain Faustus
Lorenzo, a Servant
Captain Tharon
Victorillo, a Servant
Theodoricus, a Servant
Clavela, St. Helen's Servant
Queen Fausta, wife of Constantine

Not Mentioned In The Manuscript But Included In The Play Are The Following Characters:

A Company of Jews
Judas, a Jew
A Corpse
A Sick Woman

(There Is A Sound Of Drums. CONSTANTINE *Enters. He Sits Down On A Chair.)*

CONSTANTINE: Oh Power and Authority, how much you trouble, how much you torment me! Oh royal golden crown, all your glory and splendor do not make up for the thorn which is constantly tormenting my heart with its suffering and trouble and suffering. On the outside you are all right; you shine, you glow with splendor, but under your flowery splendor are bitterness, rudeness, and roughness.

(He Sleeps, His Cheek On His Hand. There Is A Sound Of Drums, And Singing Is Heard.)

MUSICIANS: Power truly is the belief in God, our Creator, Lord of the Universe.

(The EMPEROR *Awakes And He Says)*

CONTANTINE: It is true that power here on earth is transient, perishable as we see every day. Only the knowledge of the ever true God—Who made and created us—will continue to rule the world, will never terminate, and will never come to an end. Him shall we seek! Alas! Would that some one had revealed Him to us! But how?

(He Sleeps Again, And There Is Singing.)

MUSICIANS: His beloved, honored Son
Our Lord Jesus Christ,
Has come to declare
His sacred Sacraments!

CONSTANTINE: Am I dreaming? Am I seeing things in my sleep? What do I hear? Is my memory only mocking me? Does our Lord Jesus Christ really exist? Would that somebody had shown me where He is enthroned and what His sacred Commandments are, which He came to earth to declare. Where shall I find some one who will tell me, give me knowledge of Him? Alas! Unfortunate that I am! Although I desire knowledge of Him, I cannot find anyone to satisfy my desire.

(ST. HELEN And An ANGEL Come Out On The Right. On The Left A DEVIL Enters.)

ST. HELEN: Master of all creatures, Lord God, may the many possessors of heavenly bliss and all of the creatures of the earth glorify You forever! You wished to give us light that we might know You and Your beloved Son, Jesus Christ, whom You sent here to earth. He came to show us the road to Heaven, and to save us through His death. May it not be Your desire that Your creature, conceived and born of my womb, should forever remain in the darkness of idolatry. May You give him light that he might be saved!

(The ANGEL Beside Her Speaks.)

ANGEL: You may be sure that God—the Possessor of all things—will give him light, if you will but teach Constantine knowledge of Him.

(The DEVIL Speaks Aside In An Evil Manner [Disrespectfully].)

DEVIL: She will not get her wish, for I already oppose the desire of the mother! For I have already stirred up his brother Maxentius to make war upon him. Here comes his war chief, Leoncius, to tell him about it now.

ST. HELEN: Now is a good time! I shall find him alone. I shall tell him what has been in my heart for such a long time. I hope you are well, my dear son!

CONSTANTINE: My dear mother, my heart is very happy whenever I see you! All the afflicting sadness which troubles me leaves me immediately when I see you. Noble Queen, be seated!

(Enter LEONCIUS.)

LEONCIUS: All joy to you, powerful lord, at whose feet lies all the world! You ought to know that your elder brother Maxentius surpasses the stars in the heavens, the sands on the shores of the seas throughout the world, and the leaves of all the trees, in the number of soldiers he has gathered together. With these he wishes to destroy you in battle. But here am I, your servant, your dependent, I shall shed my blood and sacrifice my life for you, as will all your subjects.

(The EMPEROR Is Troubled.)

CONSTANTINE: My dear Captain, you are the support of my kingdom. You sustain my crown. I thank you very much for what you have just said. Beat the war drum, sound the bugle to assemble our war leaders and our battalions; but first let offerings be made to our gods that they may aid us.

LEONCIUS: I shall go at once to carry out your royal command.

(Exit LEONCIUS.)

CONSTANTINE: Queenly mother, let us go! I shall think upon how I shall defend the crown.

ST. HELEN: May God, the Lord of the Universe, give you strength that you may mock your enemies. Let us go, my dear son.

(They Both Exit.)

DEVIL: Oh, how my will has been done! Whenever his mother should wish to make Jesus Christ known to her son, I shall stop it! Just as I have done up until now!

(*The* DEVIL *Exits. There Is A Sound Of Trumpets And The Beating Of Drums. Enter* VICTORILLO *And* THEODORICUS *Who are Servants.*)

VICTORILLO: Now, Theodoricus, my bread and butter proposition is solved. I wish that they were killing one another right now, so that I could cut out their tripes and eat them. I might cut the throats and drink the blood of others, and some I would skin and dress myself in their hides.[3]

THEODORICUS: What are they? Are they lambs or suckling pigs? Or are they chickens? May I hunt there with you, for I have a hankering after meat?

VICTORILLO: You don't know what you're talking about! I shall kill people just as we soldiers do!

THEODORICUS: And you know that you might be killed in the war!

VICTORILLO: But you never see me, Theodoricus! I am very strong! I kill 60,000 to 70,000 in a day!

THEODORCUS: Tell me what they are! Are they haws or *tacos?*[4] Don't you ever get indigestion from them? I see you always over the cookstove, looking at it! Now I believe in your strength!

VICTORILLO: Leave me alone, Theodoricus! My blood has begun to boil, and my bile has become bitter. Now you will see my valor!

(*He Takes Out A Sword. He Makes Thrusts With It Everywhere.* THEODORICUS *Continues Dodging And Keeping Away From Him. Trumpets Blow And The Drums Beat. The Emperor Enters, And With Him Captains* LEONCIUS, FAUSTUS, *And Some Soldiers.*)

LEONCIUS: The soldiers are all assembled, and your officers lead them. Constantine's standard-bearers have already unfolded their banners, even though the soldiers of Maxentius surpass them in numbers.

FAUSTUS: My lord, your army is not so great in size. It would be well for you to determine what is to be done, so that

How St. Helen Found the Holy Cross

we may not be destroyed or wiped out.

CONSTANTINE: Leave me alone! I am going to think about it.

(*He Sits Down On A Chair And Goes To Sleep Talking.*)

CONSTANTINE: If my soldiers are few, and my enemy Maxentius has more than I, what shall I do? If I throw myself on him, he will destroy me. If I retreat, I shall cover myself with shame. What shall I do? This heartache (worry) makes me sleepy.

(*He Sleeps. There Is The Sound Of A Harp. Up Above, The Holy Cross Appears. There Is Singing. They Sing:*)

MUSICIANS: In this sign,
Constantine, you will conquer,
And through it you will be taken
Into the presence of God.

CONSTANTINE: Oh, lucky, oh fortunate that I am in what heaven permits me to see! I shall obey! Ho, officers, come here!

(*Enter* LEONCIUS, FAUSTUS, *And* SOLDIERS.)

CONSTANTINE: Put a Cross on all my banners at once, for it will always be their symbol! Beat the drums and blow the horns, for with it (the Cross) I shall conquer and destroy my enemy Maxentius.

LEONCIUS: Your commands shall be obeyed.

FAUSTUS: We shall do what you order at once!

(*They Exit.*)

CONSTANTINE: Oh heaven, I am going to do at once what you have ordered me.

(*He Exits. Enter* MAXENTIUS, LORENZO, *Soldiers And* THARON.)

MAXENTIUS: Oh a thousand times unfortunate that you are, Constantine! Now you are going to see your kingdom overthrown and in the dust. All the world will know that I am its master!

LORENZO: My lord, the soldiers he is bring here are a joke! They are so few that we shall crush them like flies!

MAXENTIUS: Now that I think of it, call the enchanters here

—the destroyers—who will blow an enchantment upon them. Go, Tharon, and bring them to me.[5]

(THARON *Exits*.)

MAXENTIUS: There is no need of our dirtying our hands with the plebeian blood of our enemies. What I order is that you shall take Constantine alone, so that I may make my footstool out of him.

LORENZO: I shall do so. Give the necessary orders.

(THARON *Enters, Bringing With Him The Two Wizards*.)

MAXENTIUS: I order you to destroy my enemy Constantine and all his followers with various enchantments.

FIRST
WIZARD: Not even one will remain! With water, air, fire, and earth I shall blow them evil, fill them with worms![6]

SECOND
WIZARD: With my breath alone, I shall weaken them! I shall stop them! I shall fill them with fear.

MAXENTIUS: I shall pay you for what you do. Go and bring together all those who know your science. Let us go!

(*They Exit. Drums Are Sounded. Enter* ST. HELEN, FAUSTA, CLAVELA, *And* THEODORA, *Her Servants*.)

ST. HELEN: Let us go and see the great lord Bishop, he who guides us spiritually, that he may pray to God for my son, although he is not a believer. And that he may order that the Holy Church everywhere pray for him so that he may be helped.

FAUSTA: Let us all prostrate ourselves before him and pray to him; for he is the representative of our Lord Jesus Christ.

ST. HELEN: Clavela, go and see if anyone is coming.

CLAVELA: The bell is already ringing to announce that he (the Bishop) will present himself to the people.

THEODORA: There he shows himself! Draw near, noble Queen!

(ST. SYLVESTER *Appears, Sits Down On His Throne With A Mitre And Cross In His Hands. They All Kneel Down*.)

ST. HELEN: All happiness to you, the head of our Church, the regent and image of our Lord Jesus Christ.

ST. SYLVESTER: May the grace of the Lord God of the Universe be with you always, noble ladies, my dear daughters. And may my blessing be with you.

ST. HELEN: You know, holy father, that my boy—although he does not yet know the true God—is at war. Would you and all the Holy Church pray for him, that he come out successfully?

FAUSTA: He very much needs your prayers, for his army does not equal that which his enemy Maxentius is bringing.

ST. SYLVESTER: The mercy of God shall look upon your boy Constantine. He will conquer his enemies and put them under his feet. He will know him (God), you may be sure of that. Be glad therefore! And may He keep you always!

(*The Holy Father Suddenly Disappears.*)

THEODORA: The representative of our Lord Jesus Christ is worthy of all honor and respect.

CLAVELA: From his mouth come the words of the Holy Spirit.

ST. HELEN: Let us go and pray to the merciful God and wait for (whatever) He sends to us.

FAUSTA: Let us go, my lady.

(*They Exit. There Is The Sound Of Drums. When The Music Stops, Inside Is Heard A Loud Commotion And Shouting. There Are Fireworks. After This Continues For Some Time, Two Wizards Enter. They Come Destroying Things (Practicing Their Enchantments). One Evil One Brings In His Hands Fire, Earth, Air, And Water, Which He Scatters About. The Other Goes About Blowing.*)

FIRST WIZARD: Be strong!

SECOND WIZARD: Be courageous!

BOTH
WIZARDS: Lend us a hand, lord of hell, for we can do no more!
DEVIL: Here I am! I never leave you! Be courageous, my servants.

(*Enter Warriors. They Bring A Flag On Which Is The Holy Cross. The Devil And The Two Wizards, Crackling Like Fire, Run Away From It.*)

DEVIL: We cannot do any more! From over there comes that which is destroying us (the Cross). Run away from it!
FIRST
WIZARD: I became weak as soon as I saw the Cross shining on the flag.
SECOND
WIZARD: Just as the mist melts away when the sun comes out, so all of my accomplishments are undone in the presence of that which comes there on the flag.
DEVIL: We have not accomplished anything, companions, for that death-tree, the Cross, has taken from me all my power.

(*Enter* VICTORILLO *And* THEODORICUS. *The Latter Has A Sword In His Hand. He Chases* VICTORILLO.)

THEODORICUS: Now you will see, setting hen! Now I shall eat your tripes! I shall drink your blood and dress myself in your skin!
VICTORILLO: See here, Theodoricus! I am Victorillo. Don't kill me!
THEODORICUS: Promise me what you will give me.
VICTORILLO: I shall give you three bags of chestnuts.
THEODORICUS: I don't want them.
VICTORILLO: I shall give you twenty bags of haws.
THEODORICUS: I won't have them! Now you are going to die, and I shall roast you and turn *you* into haws!
VICTORILLO: For the sake of your father's leg!
THEODORICUS: I don't want it.
VICTORILLO: For the sake of your mother's liver and bile.

How St. Helen Found the Holy Cross

THEODORICUS: Now I shall carry your head hanging from my hand like a gourd!

(VICTORILLO *Goes Out.* THEODORICUS *Follows, And They Disappear. There Is A Sound Of Trumpets. Enter The Emperor* CONSTANTINE *And His Officers. Some (Of Them) Bring Prisoners With Their Hands Tied. From The Other Side Enter* ST. HELEN, FAUSTA, *And The Servants. There Is Song And Music.*)

1. Constantine is not conquered
   For he honors his gods.
   With the help of the Almighty
   He defies his enemies.

2. May he be praised everywhere,
   Constantine the stout.
   Worthy and deserving,
   Of being looked upon with fear everywhere.

3. His gods are powerful.
   Under his feet they have placed
   All his enemies,
   Who hated him greatly!

4. He has already learned to know
   The precious Son of God.
   And he has received
   His baptism!

CONSTANTINE: Now once more, my brave men, you have placed the crown on my head and the golden scepter of authority in my hand through your bravery.

LEONCIUS: For you, like the sun, warmed us with your speeches and your words.

CONSTANTINE: Welcome, my dear mother.

ST. HELEN: I do not know how to salute you, my dear son. I hope that you have come back successful!

FAUSTA: My dear husband, you have had a hard time!

(She Embraces Him)

CONSTANTINE: Leoncius, tell in detail all that has happened so that my mother and my wife may hear it.

LEONCIUS: I obey your order, my lord. When you and Bicinius joined forces against the drunken good-for-nothing Maxentius, who had taken possession of the city of Rome and the government, as we arrived there our army was not so large as his, which was countless. It was not prudent for us to go against all of them. You ordered us to put the Cross on your banners. At once great courage and valor came over us. We no longer looked at anything, and as soon as the battle began, fear came upon them and they began to run! They had placed a wooden span in the stone bridge which is over the River Tiber, which was not strong. They had thought that when we began to run away, we would try to cross the bridge and it would fall in with us. But it did not happen that way. Instead, it engulfed them with all their leaders and soldiers.[1] They all became frightened. All the wizards and skilled necromancers whom they had brought together that they might destroy us by their witchcraft could not help them! And now these people here, all the lords and nobles of Rome, receive you with great joy since you have saved them and your city and kingdom from the temerity of Maxentius.

ST. HELEN: The Lord God performed a great miracle in your behalf.

FAUSTA: His mercy is without end.

ST. HELEN: And yet I wonder very greatly how you thought of putting the blessed sign of the Cross on your flag?

CONSTANTINE: You must know that when my heart was oppressed by the great weight of the government, I suddenly fell asleep; and exactly three times it was told me that here is an altogether True God, that He sent His beloved Son here, and that His true name was Jesus Christ. And daily I meditated upon this; and when it was time to go against my enemy Maxentius, I saw that my soldiers were not as many as those he was bringing. I fell asleep in sadness, and in my sleep I saw, against the heavens yonder, a Cross shining like the color of the dawn—gleaming, and altogether dazzling were the rays it gave forth. I heard a loud voice which said: "In this sign you will conquer." And when I heard this, I engraved it on my heart. Right then I ordered that it (the Cross) be put on all my banners, and this was done. Is there any one of you who knows Jesus Christ and His blessed symbol, the Cross? If so, tell me in order that I might know and thank Him for what He has done for me.

ST. HELEN: The power of God is truly wonderful!

FAUSTA: His mercy is never ending!

ST. HELEN: And now you must learn about that blessed sign which you took as your symbol and which helped you. Let us go and give thanks to God Almighty and to his Vicar, who will make Him known to you.

(There Is The Sound Of A Bugle. They Exit. ST. SYVESTER *And Two Priests Appear, And From The Other Side All Those Who Had Previously Gone Out.)*

ST. SYLVESTER: May Almighty God and His beloved honored Son —our Saviour Jesus Christ—be praised. For now begins, sprouts forth, and bursts into flower His faith everywhere here on earth.

PRIESTS: Amen!

(They All Draw Near And Kneel Down.)

ST. HELEN: You, oh image and representative of our Lord Jesus Christ—true God and true Man—at your feet we have come to give thanks for His mercy.

ST. SYLVESTER: You, oh mighty lord Emperor, and you noble ladies, let us all praise Him for His mercy! Be seated!

ST. HELEN: It is better that we remain at your feet.

CONSTANTINE: We obey you!

(They All Sit Down.)

ST.
SYLVESTER: Know now, oh mighty Kings, and you lords, princes, and Roman people, that there is one true God Who made the heaven and the earth and all that is seen and unseen. But, furthermore, know that there is only one true God in three: and that the second divine person, the Son, descended here on earth for our salvation. He was born of a Virgin called Holy Mary, who did not lose her virginity; and this beloved Son of God we call Jesus Christ. Through His teaching, He has shown us the road to heaven. For our salvation, the Jews took Him, scoffed at Him, slapped His face, spit in His face, scourged Him with ropes, put a crown of thorns on His head, and put a thorny reed in His hand for a scepter. Afterwards, on the Cross, they pierced His hands and feet with iron nails. He died, was buried, and on the third day He arose from the dead, ascended into heaven, and went to seat Himself on the right hand of God, the Father Almighty. And when the world will end, He will come to judge the good and the bad. To the good, He will give everlasting happiness, and to the bad never-ending, never-ceasing torment. This is the real true faith. He who wishes to receive it, must first receive baptism that he may be saved, and so that he may deserve and merit the everlasting joy of heaven.[8]

CONSTANTINE: Your beloved word has quickened my heart! The light has dawned upon me!

(He Kneels Before St. Sylvester.)

CONSTANTINE: You, oh image of our beloved Son of God, our Lord Jesus Christ, take pity on me and baptize me. I hate the darkness in which idolatry has kept me; and with all my soul I confess the faith.

ST.
SYLVESTER: May your creatures in heaven and earth bless You forever, oh Lord God. Let us go and you will have your wish!

St. Helen: Before You oh Lord God, I cast myself on the ground! I beseech You in Your mercy not to abandon your creatures.

(*All Exit. There Is The Sound Of Trumpets.*)
(*Enter* Victorillo.)

Victorillo: The whole city of Rome is agitated with joy because his Majesty the Emperor has just been baptized.

Theodoricus: His Majesty the Emperor has just become a Christian! Now I shall quit work. Let us go and look at those dancers coming there.

(*The Dancers Enter. They Dance For Some Time. When They Have Finished, Enter The* Emperor, St. Helen, Fausta, Licinius, Captain Leoncius, Victorillo *And* Theodoricus.)

Constantine: Dear mother, dear wife, and soldiers! I cannot find the words with which to express my happiness, as I have come to know the true God! I am under the banner of His beloved, honored Son, our Saviour Jesus Christ, through baptism. And now, dear mother, my heart longs to see the Tree of Salvation, the precious Holy Cross on which He died. It is fitting that you yourself go to Jerusalem and take my soldiers with you to try and find out where it is.

St. Helen: Many thanks, my dear son, for your happy wish. I shall carry it out.

Constantine: Licinius, Leoncius, and Faustus, go immediately with my mother. Take all the soldiers.

Licinius: I shall obey your order!

Leoncius: Your will will be done!

Faustus: My obedience is always at your feet.

(*They All Exit Except* Victorillo *And* Theodoricus.)

Victorillo: Theodoricus, I am going too. Let me get ready.

Theodoricus: You are not going! I'm going.

Victorillo: I am!

Theodoricus: I am! As for you, you are probably going to see some of your relatives there.[9]

(*They Begin To Fight At Once. The* Emperor *Enters Alone.*)

CONSTANTINE: Oh Lord God, may You bring my mother safely to Jerusalem! May my good desire please You!

(*Enter* LORENZO. *There Is A Time Lapse Here Of Uncertain Duration.*)

LORENZO: Hail to you, all-powerful Emperor! Let your heart rejoice! Your dear mother is travelling well. She is taking many of your subjects with her.

CONSTANTINE: I am very glad. When will they reach Jerusalem?

LORENZO: She will enter there tomorrow.

CONSTANTINE: I am very pleased. Now go and rest.

(*They Exit. The Scene Apparently Shifts To Jerusalem. Enter* BISHOP MACARIOS *On One Side, And From The Other Side* ST. HELEN, *And All Who Went With Her.*)

BISHOP: You have had a hard trip, my Queen! You have travelled a long way.

ST. HELEN: All health to you, spiritual governor. Know that my son, the Emperor, has sent me here to hunt for the Holy Cross on which our Lord Jesus Christ, the beloved Son of God, died. Do you know where it is?

BISHOP: No. I do not know where his enemies the Jews hid it. Go and get their sons, for they must know. Their fathers must have told them.

ST. HELEN: Go, Licinius and Faustus! Go and get them; we shall make them speak!

(*They Exit. And Then Return.* LICINIUS *And* FAUSTUS *Return With The* JEWS.)

ST. HELEN: Confess where your fathers hid the Holy Cross!

JUDAS: I do not know. That was two hundred years ago!

SECOND JEW: I have never heard where it is.

ST. HELEN: Shut them all up until they tell; and torture them!

(*They All Exit. There Is A Sound Of Trumpets. Six Jews Enter.*)

How St. Helen Found the Holy Cross

FIRST JEW: Friends, what shall we do? Queen Helen has come to hunt for the Cross on which Jesus of Nazareth was crucified. Say whether we shall tell her where it is!

SECOND JEW: If we reveal it, then immediately the established customs of our fathers will terminate!

THIRD JEW: Let us not tell, even though we are killed!

FOURTH JEW: Judas is being tortured in a dungeon. Six days ago he said that he had heard his father say that his grandfather told him where they had hidden the Cross.

FIFTH JEW: Let us strengthen his resolution so that he will not tell.

SIXTH JEW: May you put all your soul into your words!

(They All Exit. Enter St. Helen. Bishop Macarios, And Others. From The Other Side They Bring In Judas, Who Comes Tied.)

LICINIUS: We shut this fellow, Judas, up in the dungeon six days ago. While he was in there he promised to reveal where the Holy Cross for which we have come is hidden.

ST. HELEN: May he tell here in my presence how he knows this.

(Judas Kneels Before Her.)

JUDAS: Know, oh Queen, that my father, whose name was Simon, told me that his father—my grandfather named Zaccheus—told him where they had hidden, had buried the Cross, in order that it might not be found and worshipped by the Christians. And he further told me that if at any time I should be questioned, I should tell where it was so that I might not be tortured, as I see now myself. And now let us (go?) and let me dig where he showed me.

ST. HELEN: Let us all go!

(They Go Over To The Corner Of The Stage (?). There He Digs. Music Is Heard From Behind The Stage. He Takes Out First One Cross.)

ST. HELEN: How are we going to tell on which of them our Saviour died? For we find here three crosses.

BISHOP: Through a miracle it will appear. Let us try a corpse on it.

FAUSTUS: They are bringing a corpse from over there. Let it be tried on it.

ST. HELEN: Let them bring it here.

(*They Bring The Corpse Before Her.*)

ST. HELEN: Macarios, put it on one of the crosses.

(*He Puts The Corpse On It.*)

BISHOP: It does not move at all.

ST. HELEN: Put it on another one!

BISHOP: Still it does not move!

ST. HELEN: There is only one more. That must be the one!

BISHOP: What a great miracle! It has come to life!

(*The* CORPSE *Sits Up And Speaks.*)

CORPSE: Hail, beloved and honored Tree of Life!

CLAVELA: It is a very great miracle!

JUDAS: There is another poor woman who has been sick for a long time. She is now on the point of death.

ST. HELEN: Let them bring her here too.

FAUSTUS: Here she is now!

(*The Sick Woman Appears.* MACARIOS *Puts Her On The* HOLY CROSS.)

SICK WOMAN: I praise You, oh Lord God above all! Through Your Holy Cross, the great sickness from which I have suffered so long has left me.

(ST. HELEN *And All The Others Kneel Before The* HOLY CROSS.)

ST. HELEN: Oh You glorious Cross! You are the veritable Tree of Life! On You was effected the salvation of the people of the world. Now my heart remains with the joy of peace. May all the creatures of the Lord God of all things bless and exalt Thee forever. May the angels in heaven gladden You with sweet songs, and every heavenly thing bless You! The water in the heavens, you, oh sun; You, oh moon; you, oh stars; you, oh rain; you, oh dew of the night; you, oh cold; you, oh ice; you, oh snow; you, oh night; you, oh day; you, oh light; you, oh earth; you, oh mountains and hills; may all of you glorify the precious Tree of Salvation! And you, oh fountains; and you, oh ocean; and you, oh river; all you great fish who live in the water; you various many-colored birds who go about flying in the air; you four-footed beasts, may you all glorify it (the Cross) and give thanks to the Lord God of mercy who has permitted us to see here on earth the Tree of Life by which we have been redeemed. And now, dear father Macarios, take it to the church and let them look for the nails. Perhaps they too are still there.

(JUDAS *Goes Into The Grave And Looks For The Nails. He Brings Them Out And Gives Them To* ST. HELEN, *Who Kisses Them And Says:*)

ST. HELEN: Oh happy, oh fortunate that I am! There have come into my hands the nails that pierced the blessed hands and feet of our Lord God!

(*They All Kiss Them.*)

ST. HELEN: May my son, the Emperor, be informed that we have found the blessed Holy Cross, so that everywhere throughout the world there may be rejoicing!

(*They Exit. Enter The* EMPEROR *From One Side And* LEONCIUS *From The Other.*)

LEONCIUS: Joy to you, oh great King! Your mother, the Queen, has sent me here to inform you that we have been happy and fortunate in that the precious Tree of Salvation was found on the third day of the month of May.

CONSTANTINE: Sound the trumpets! May there be rejoicing everywhere in the world!

(*He Kneels.*)

CONSTANTINE: Oh Lord God, we are fortunate! We have been dignified in that You have helped us to find the precious Holy Cross, and therefore we are highly pleased!

(*He Rises From His Knees.*)

CONSTANTINE: Leoncius, send a circular letter out everwhere that thanks be given with rejoicing to God, our Creator, for His great mercy!

LEONCIUS: Your orders will be obeyed, my King.

(*They Exit. There is A Sound Of Drums. Enter* MACARIOS, ST. HELEN, *And Others.*)

ST. HELEN: My dear father, God, the Possessor of all things, has granted that our wish has been realized. We have found the precious Cross, and now my desire is that it be divided: one half going to the great city of Rome, and one half remaining here in Jerusalem in a golden box. Here the people of the earth may come to wonder at it, and worship it. Of the three nails, I shall take one and put it in the crown of my son, the Emperor Constantine; another one I shall make into a bit for the animal on which he goes forth to war, that he may conquer his enemies, and the third one, I shall throw into the sea where it is the most fearful, so that it may become calm and peaceful and will not rise. These are my orders. May God, the Owner of the world, give you peace!

BISHOP: Oh Queen, all that you have ordered will be done. I am very sorry that you are going away. May God, the Creator, sustain you always.

CLAVELA: This is the true story of how the beloved and precious Holy Cross was found, as it is written in the annals. May we be aided against our enemies for its sake while we are living on earth, and may we afterwards deserve the Kingdom of Heaven.

FINIS

Finished on *Corpus Christi* Day, May 31, 1714.

Commentary

One of the unique elements of *"How the Blessed St. Helen Found the Holy Cross"* is that it contains the best developed comic motif of which we have an extant example. The figures of Victorillo and Theodoricus furnish comic and ironic relief in an otherwise serious plot. Their function is not only to amuse, however, for they also teach, through dramatic satire, the negative value of human sacrifice, ritual warfare (for non-Christian purposes), and cannibalism. The figures of Victorillo and Theodoricus are foolish in their presumptions, their ideals, and their clearly aimless activity.

"*How the Blessed St. Helen Found the Holy Cross*" does not incorporate a Mass, but it does involve a rather developed sermon, the themes of which are the essentials of the *Apostles' Creed*. This play also contrives to teach a certain amount of history, albeit it is never mentioned that Maxentius, the archvillain, is in fact the brother of Emperor Constantine. Familial insurrection among heroic figures would be poor didactic drama.

According to historical records, Maxentius preceded Constantine as Emperor of Rome, and ruled from 306 until 312 A.D. He was defeated by Constantine at Saxa Rubra, and died in that battle. Actually, Constantine died in 337, and was baptized only shortly before by Eusebius.

This play also focuses mainly upon instilling into the audience a religious respect for the relics instead of for the sacraments, as is true for the majority of the other dramas. Baptism is the only sacrament even mentioned in this play. Visionary knowledge, the broken powers of the necromancers, miracles performed by the relics and faith, and the inevitable transience of all human existence and power not based in Christian ideals, are the foci of actions. The main characters, although powerful and lordly in their own right, bow to the will and power of the Almighty God whom they have come to know through visions and miracles.

A certain amount of information about the Church *per se* is treated in *"How the Blessed St. Helen Found the Holy Cross."* The power and the authority of the Bishop, who is Christ's Vicar on earth, is depicted; and it is made doubly clear that salvation is impossible except through the medium of the Church on earth.

VIII
"THE DESTRUCTION OF JERUSALEM"

INTRODUCTION

The *"Destrucción de Jerusalén"* was first translated from Nahuatl into Spanish and presented as a paper to the Fourteenth International Congress of Orientalists by Francisco Paso y Troncoso in 1905. A limited edition of the translation was later published in 1907.[1] It is from the latter publication that this translation was made.

Paso y Troncoso sought the origins and precedents of this drama and was able to establish the following. In the *Biblioteca de Autores Españoles* in the National Library of Madrid is a list of ninety-five works defining the orgins of the Spanish theater by Moratín, the thirtieth of which is entitled *"Auto de la Destrucción de Jerusalén."*[2] This *auto* included the following as a cast: Vespasian, two Pages, a Chamberlain, a Jew, the woman Veronica, Pilate, King Archelaus, a Servant, Clement, two noble Widows, and some Soldiers.

The Spanish version as compared to the Nahuatl lacks the characters of Titus, Jaffel, and the Viennese; it therefore also lacks the episodes in which these characters are involved. Paso y Troncoso found yet another version of this play in Latin, entitled *"Destruccio de Hierusalem,"* which seems to have been an earlier version and which included the enlarged cast, lacking only the Viennese interlude. Paso y Troncoso further traced the *lemosin* copies of this drama and concluded that one or more copies of this early drama had reached Mexico either through the Padres of Montserrat, or the religious Order of Mercy, which had placed in charge of its *Colegio do Belén* in Mexico a titular head named S. Pedro Pascual. This same Pascual was the author or editor of the Latin *lemosin* version of *"The Destruction of Jerusalem"*, which Paso y Troncoso had seen in Spain.

181

According to the handwriting, the Nahuatl manuscript of the play seems to date from the seventeenth century. It is quite probable that the content of the play dates back to the sixteenth century and was first presented then. It is anonymous, its only mark of identification being certain formalized lines of writing on the last folio including the name of the city Tlaxcala. The written formula used on this folio was a standard one employed by the scribes of the seventeeth century on official records and documents. Paso y Troncoso concluded that the author or adaptor-translator of the *"Destrucción"* was an Indian, probably a minor goverment official or scribe in the area of Tlaxcala. Certain juridical expressions and phrases in the text as well as neologisms from the Spanish reinforce this conclusion.

Several awkward repetitive phrases and tortuous passages suggest that the translation might have been made directly from the Latin and transposed by the author; in other words, there was no other intermediate Nahuatl copy.

That the author was an Indian, possibly a *mestizo*, who knew Nahuatl well, is clear because of the alterations which were made in certain historical names: *Archareo* for *Arquelao, Cain* for *Caio, Berbasiano* for *Vespasiano,* and *Tidos* for *Titus,* among others. The fact that Veronica is presented as a mute was possibly because the Indians who saw her in processions of the Passion thought her a saint, and therefore believed it would be disrespectful of her to speak so freely to humans.

Certain crudities in the Nahuatl are also apparent: the absence of many initial and final letters and the interpolation of unnecessary letters and phrases, as well as the replacement of correct letters with incorrect ones of similar sound. Certain Nahuatl anachronisms, archaic expressions, and verbal terminations are also marked.[3]

In summary, the author was probably an Indian or *mestizo* of fair education from Tlaxcala, but whose language was at the same time crude and antiquated. He was very likely a minor official in the government.

This drama was not creatively translated or transposed by

the "author." The interludes follow one another in a helter-skelter manner with little attention or sensitivity to organic dramatic action. Entrances and exits are poorly conceived and indicated, nor are the scenes and the time sequences divided with care.

Certain interludes in the Latin version are not included in the Nahuatl form of the play. Notably, there is a scene in which the women of Jerusalem weep and bemoan the death of their children, and ultimately eat them to assuage their starved bodies. An indigenous author would naturally want to suppress the presentation of such a scene to an audience of people who had practiced ritual cannibalism in the Prehispanic period of their history. The Church had, of course, labored incessantly to destroy this uncomfortable and un-Christian custom.

Finally, Paso y Troncoso states that there is no good reference as to the time or place of the presentation of this drama. His translations, he states, are close and literal translations of the Nahuatl text.[4] The author in turn has maintained a sometimes uncomfortable and awkward proximity to the original language in the hope that the closeness of phraseology might give a more authentic feeling of the original style.

A few notes have been added where it seemed advisable to clarify the more oblique references to lesser known Prehispanic or colonial customs.

The Destruction of Jerusalem

CHARACTERS WHO DO NOT SPEAK:
Veronica
CHARACTERS WHO SPEAK:
Vespasian, the Emperor
Titus, his son
Caius, the Chamberlain
Clement, a disciple of Christ
Roman Nobles
A Buffoon
Nobles from Vienna

A guard
Pilate, the Governor
Archelaus, the King
Monques, a Noble
Jaffel, a Noble from Jappa
Jacob, a guest of Caius
Jewish Noblemen
Jewish Commoners
A Jewish Slave

Here is presented the life of the Apostle St. James; how it happened that Vespasian, battling against the great city of Jerusalem as well as the Jews and Pilate, completely destroyed it. Here is the beginning of the discourse of Caius, that which he deigned to say to Pilate when he (Caius) was sent with a letter to him; and of the manner in which he left the great city of Rome and passed from it to Jerusalem, that is, near to Pilate.[5]

EMPEROR: It has now been three years that we have been in Rome; it is certainly necessary to write to Pilate about this.

(Apparently PILATE *Has Not Been Communicating With The Emperor Of Rome. The Scene Shifts To Jerusalem As The "Letter" Travels To* PILATE *With* CAIUS.*) When The* EMPEROR *Has Said This To Them,* Caius *Enters Into The Presence Of* PILATE. *He Gives The Letter To King* ARCHELAUS, *Who In Turn Gives It To* PILATE, *Who Then Looks At It.)*

PILATE: How shall we compose a response to this? How can we answer it?

(First KING ARCHELAUS *Speaks, Then The Others.)*

ARCHELAUS: Oh great lord, oh Pilate! Truly it is clearly seen that the Emperor Vespasian is very angry with you. For this reason he threatens you. Oh lord, you hold and rule over your city, your vassals, and your people here, while he (Vespasian) dwells far away in that place (Rome).[6] Here we have many valiant men, and moreover the whole band of the Eagle (warriors) is gathered together inasmuch as it is your servant.[7] If the Emperor should want to do something (harmful) to you, he probably won't be able to. What then will he do? They cannot easily come to your city; and if, in spite of this, they should come, it will be in vain. Even though he should come and encircle the city, he could not hold it for much time. How would he have water? Where would it come from? His warriors would have to go to the Reservoir of the Devil to drink water, and that is far away! Perhaps they could sustain their afflictions, but not only would the brave soldiers be irritated, they would perhaps abandon the siege quickly. Oh lord, if it were I, I wouldn't answer the message. I would only ask how it is that he doesn't care for *his* city, Rome, as we do for *our* city, Jerusalem. For truly we do care for it, thusly. And in case our message should go directly into his hands, in order that we all be not so bent down (oppressed) with tribute, let him now be advised that we shall no longer give it; that we do not recognize him!

(*Then The Other Subjects Speak.*)

JEWISH
NOBLEMEN: How is this? Oh lord, that which King Archelaus has deigned to counsel you is true! What more shall we say than this? How good that he said this to you, as it is also what our heart desires!

(*Here* PILATE *Moves Forward (Nearer). He Sits Down And Then Calls To* CAIUS *And To King* ARCHELAUS.) [8]

PILATE: Oh Caius, you must go! Please return to Rome and tell Vespasian that I acknowledge no one as my lord; that I alone guard my city, as I am the Lord of Jerusalem. Further, he should guard well his city of Rome; as well perchance as he will do this, so shall I also do likewise with the city of Jerusalem.

(*Then* CAIUS *Speaks.*)

CAIUS: Oh lord, oh Pilate, how can we say this? How can I go and tell such a thing to the Emperor? He who persuaded you (to do this) did a wrong thing. For it is certainly not good what he constrained you to do; it is nothing other than a corruption! Cure yourself! What are you about to do? Surely if you but send your tribute with another and by this (action) be a little tolerant, then the anger of the Emperor will be calmed.

(Here PILATE *Stands Up And Looks With Anger At* CAIUS. *He Then Seizes Him By His Neckpiece.)*

PILATE: Truly we are most certainly able to speak in this manner! How good it is that we are in agreement among ourselves. Go! Leave! Don't detain yourselves here but rather in some other place! For I know what *you* are doing!

(The Scene Apparently Shifts To Rome.) CAIUS *Exits. He Reappears And Brings With Him* VERONICA. *He Arrives, And Salutes The* EMPEROR, *And Kisses His Hand There In Rome. Afterwards He Speaks To Him (Apparently The* EMPEROR *Has An Infirmity Heretofore Unmentioned.)*

CAIUS: Oh great lord! Truly I went there where you sent me, and gladden yourself as I brought back a good woman; her name (is) Veronica, and she will surely cure you. She has carried with her here a linen cloth to dry the face which is painted with the likeness of the Holy Prophet of that place. Truly in other places they have cured many with this. Oh great lord, in order that you really believe what I say to you, deign to do some merciful act, and in the reality of truth it will cure you. Certainly I shall help you to know this tomorrow.
(As CAIUS *Goes Closer, He Speaks To* VERONICA.*)*

CAIUS: Oh Veronica, tomorrow you will surely cure the face of the Emperor, and then you will see a person who feels inside the same way as we do. Speak to him. Give him that which you keep (the linen cloth) to wipe his face; for truly you two (the cloth and Veronica) will cure the Emperor.

(Then He Encounters CLEMENT, *As Yet Unreceived, And They All Go Into The Presence Of The* EMPEROR. *Then* CAIUS *Speaks To Him.)*

CAIUS: Oh great lord, here is Veronica! She came through love of the Holy Prophet and truly for your sake. Actually she abandoned everything there in Jerusalem. Here also is Clement who was a disciple of the Holy Prophet and who knows much about his life, and how with many lying words and calumnies they finally killed him. Truly, Clement saw when he underwent tribulation and where they hanged him on the cross with his arms outstretched, and even where they interred him.

*(*CLEMENT *And* VERONICA *Salute The* EMPEROR. *Then* CLEMENT *Speaks.)*

CLEMENT: Oh great lord, deign to hear me! Truly place your faith firmly in the Prophet, Who alone is the unique and true Lord and God. He is indeed also truly Man, as he is Father, Son, and the Holy Spirit, which is one God only. And this same One was pleased to create heaven and earth. Truly He is the Lord of all of us! They killed this same One in Jerusalem. But believe, oh lord, that even if men as numerous as the grains of sand from the depths of the sea had been there they could have done nothing; since it was the case that He died freely of his own will. Could we change this? Certainly not! Why did they kill him and punish him? Because it was necessary that all the world know of his death. By the love of Him whose precious image is here (painted) would that you be cured! And thus we (are able) to accomplish this, as He was kind enough to desire it. Because you have occupied yourself with spiritual things, and prayed and believed strongly in God, so He turns to you in order that He might heal you!

(When CLEMENT *Brings The Linen Cloth To Wipe The Face Closer To The* EMPEROR's *Visage, He Speaks.)*

EMPEROR: Oh Clement, wait yet for a little while! Bring out my sword and my imperial crown.

(*Having Kneeled, The* EMPEROR *Says:*)

EMPEROR: I swear truly by my imperial crown and my sword that when I shall have carefully purified myself, then immediately I shall arrange to depart for Jerusalem where I shall alleviate my anger for the death of the Prophet. Furthermore, I shall punish them! I swear that I shall destroy them—those wicked ones who acted thusly!

(*Here As His Discourse Concludes, They Take Out His Sword And His Crown, And He Speaks.*)

EMPEROR: Oh Clement, would that you deign to place over me, and lay upon me by your own hand your precious image of the Holy Prophet. This is my wish.

(*Here The Two Of Them Pass The Holy Image Over His Face And Move It Quickly About. Then The* EMPEROR *Kisses* VERONICA's *Linen Cloth.* CLEMENT *And* VERONICA *Kneel. The* EMPEROR *Says To Them:*)

EMPEROR: What thing do you desire? Speak! Ask yourselves! Truly whatever you might wish, I shall grant it! Speak! Perhaps you desire cities, or perchance gold, fine gems, or precious objects?

(*Then* CLEMENT *Answers Him; He Says*):

CLEMENT: Oh Vespasian, oh Emperor! In truth we desire no rewards, be they precious objects, gold, or cities; for you know what we ultimately value over these. In the last analysis these are only earth, for they neither delight or give much pleasure for a long time. They do no more than pass away quickly, here below in your water and mountains (territories) [9]. We are saddened for another cause. Would that you hungered for baptism, and that you would embrace Jesus Christ with your faith; that same One who was merciful enough to redeem you, and Who vouchsafed to die on the cross. And would that you might persuade all of your subjects that they too should hunger for this!

(*The* EMPEROR *Speaks.*)

EMPEROR: What you have said is certainly very good. Let it be done in this manner: that you agree to preach in all parts of my land, and that you be kind enough to teach them (my subjects) and to baptize them.

(*Then He Calls To Caius.*)

EMPEROR: Let everyone prepare themselves for war—for all must go to Jerusalem!

(*Now* CAIUS *Speaks To Him*):

CAIUS: Oh lord, oh Emperor! Because you were worse, and because of your illness at that time, I said nothing to you of what Pilate sent back from Jerusalem (in answer) to your command. When I was there, that is, when you were pleased to send me there for the tribute, then Pilate was truly angered. Deign to hear, oh lord, that he has really united the city of Jerusalem and has done (likewise) with his province. When I disturbed him he said: 'Say to Vespasian that we do not recognize him, and that as *he* guards the city of Rome, so do *we* watch the city of Jerusalem!' And oh, my precious lord, if some of his nobles had not pleaded with him for my life, he would certainly have killed me.

(*The* EMPEROR *Speaks To Him*):

EMPEROR: Indeed then, my heart resolves this: I shall punish them for the death of the Holy Prophet. Truly I have condemned them and I shall in truth destroy them! Let all prepare themselves for war! The valiant soldiers will go out to do battle against Jerusalem. They will conquer and decimate it. Hasten! Our arms and our insignias are already gathered into the ships.

(*A Sound Of Trumpets And Drums Is Heard.*[10] *Then They Arrive In Jaffa. As* Vespasian *Prepares Himself, They Conduct*

(JAFFEL *And* ARCHELAUS) *Into His Presence.* JAFFEL *Kneels And Speaks To Him.*)

JAFFEL: Oh Emperor, oh great lord! Would that you have compassion upon us. Would that you not surround and kill us, and would that you alone govern here in your home, Jaffa! Truly, in a little while we shall inform you so that you might come out well in your enterprise against the city of Jerusalem.

(After The EMPEROR *Listens To Him, He Speaks To Him.)*

EMPEROR: This is good, for truly my heart longs for this.

(Then As He Leaves, He Takes Them With Him From Jaffa. [This Is Unclear. The Sense Is Probably That JAFFEL *And* ARCHELAUS *Return To* PILATE *In Jerusalem After Seeking To Betray Him To* VESPASIAN.] ARCHELAUS *Then Speaks To* PILATE.)

ARCHELAUS: Oh great lord, strengthen yourself, and let us all strengthen ourselves in order that Vespasian be not able to tarry long here.

(Then PILATE *Climbs Upon The Wall. A Noble Subject Speaks To Him.)*

JEWISH
NOBLEMAN: Oh great lord, certainly that one with the scepter in his hand is the Emperor.

(After He Hears This, PILATE *Speaks):*

PILATE: Truly who is this one whose insignias we are asking about?

(PILATE *And* VESPASIAN *Are Apparently Close Enough To Call Out To One Another.) The* EMPEROR *Says To Him)*:

EMPEROR: Oh, it is you! I left you here guarding my house, the city of Jerusalem, and I ordered you to pay tribute annually. Not only did you do evil in this (respect), but moreover in addition to this, you wanted to kill my head Chamberlain whom I sent here. Worse than this, you returned my message saying that I should guard my own city as well as you alone guard the city of Jerusalem. Now for all these important reasons, open the gates of the walls immediately and give up! Moreover, if you don't do this at once, I shall proceed as my heart desires and shall truly vanquish you by whatever method (is possible).

(*Then* PILATE *Steps Aside. He Consults With His Subjects. Then He Leaves Them To Come Again Into The Presence Of The* EMPEROR. *He Speaks To Him.*)

PILATE: Vespasian, truly we do not recognize you! Where have you come from to raise yourself up here? For I alone am overseer of my city and have right of judgment and power. Therefore, (act) in whatever manner you should desire, but truly our hands will bear up under adversities against the enemy. Therefore, take great care of your warriors, Vespasian, for I shall do likewise with my valiant soldiers and with my city. Truly I in person, I, Pilate, have answered with a verbal declaration to the proposition of the Emperor Vespasian.

(*He Concludes. After* PILATE *Speaks, The* EMPEROR *Replies To Him.*)

EMPEROR: In truth, here is my imperial crown, and in my hand is my imperial sword. Because of a love of them, then, let no one have mercy upon you (Pilate)! Let no one have compassion on you!

(*At This Point The* EMPEROR *Goes Apart From Where He Is; Then He Returns Again. Then Some (Soldiers) Battle With Others.* PILATE *Goes To Battle Another Time. The* EMPEROR *Is Very Sad.* JAFFEL *As He Also Departs Says:*)

JAFFEL: Oh great lord, truly you did well to come for this. Certainly you have come to subdue the city with which you battle. Jerusalem lives in abundance. The people possess goods therein, and all the necessary provisions for food have been gathered. Further, they are securely encircled with walls, so that the inhabitants are strengthened. Most assuredly I think that you will not do well because of hunger if you don't take the city quickly. On the other hand, if you have come (prepared) to stand guard for a long time, then in some other way your valiant men and soldiers might encircle it (Jerusalem) and perhaps fell it without combat. Then truly you should not suffer much more labor, nor shall you undergo ill. For this reason hear me as I express myself here. This is my opinion, and I want to do you a service. If you should deign to take my counsel, you will really judge wisely that which you hear from me. Moreover, you will most assuredly conquer the city.

(Here The EMPEROR *Says To Him:)*

EMPEROR: Oh, Jaffel, it is true that because of the blockade we are nearly dead of thirst. Because of this, I suffer greatly for my warriors. Therefore, we shall greatly rejoice if some one counsels us how we might be able to accomplish now what we have planned for, and how we shall return to Rome and extend our glory.
(Thus The EMPEROR *Speaks. Then* JAFFEL *Speaks.)*

JAFFEL: Oh lord, truly you have many of those great deer (animals), horses by name, as well as bulls from your land. Let them (the men) kill them, and take off and clean their hides. And when they have done this, let them bring them here. Then let them go to the little valley with the (skins); and when they have done this, make a covenant with them that (live there) so that the valley be filled by pouring water into it. That is, that the men go to take water from the waterhole whose name is 'the devil.' In fifteen days they will fill the little valley and then you, as well as your valiant warriors, will be able to drink of it. Then truly you will be greatly pleased; you will feel even as in Rome. You will easily encircle the city and perhaps the beseiged will not suffer this a long time, but will be obedient to you.

[*The Time Lapse Is Uncertain Here. The Direction Is Un-*

The Destruction of Jerusalem

clear And The Action Moves Back And Forth Without Careful Indication.]

(JAFFEL *Concludes His Discourse.* PILATE *Feels His Heart Moved And Speaks.)*

PILATE: Indeed, it is as Jaffel said before many times when we consulted about a war which was threatened here. He told me the same thing. For this reason I should have killed him (unclear). Why didn't I act accordingly? Surely death would have been well-employed in this case —for him who being a vassal gives advice about what can be done to harm his master!

(Apparently JAFFEL's *Fanciful Scheme Has Been Successfully Carried Out According To The Sense Of These Speeches.) Then They Go To Call King* ARCHELAUS *With The Idea That He Will Send Them Into The Presence Of The* EMPEROR. PILATE *Says to Them:)*

PILATE: Oh, Archelaus, since we are in such a state, what remedy is there for us? Would that you might go into the presence of the Emperor to beseech him not to surround us by his hand, so that the people of Jerusalem should not die in such a fashion. Then truly I shall place the city into his hands, in order that we might not be blockaded by him and that he not punish us.

(Then ARCHELAUS *And Others Go Into The Presence Of The* EMPEROR. *They Kneel Before Him and Speak.)*

ARCHELAUS: Oh Emperor, would that you might deign to make us happy! Pilate sends us here into your presence that he might place the city and the people of Jerusalem into your hands. He places it at your feet. Vouchsafe to accept it in such a manner so as not to despoil us, nor kill and castigate us. In order that we might live some days more by your grace, judge it good to agree to this. Deign to give us mercy, oh lord!

(The EMPEROR *Simply Answers Him With Anger. He Says:)*

EMPEROR: Go and speak with Pilate. Tell him that I do not

consent! He shall place the city into my hands without conditions. I have come here for nothing other than this.

(ARCHELAUS *Is Saddened. He Turns And Leaves. With Reserve (Quietly) He Departs From His Friends. He Pushes His Sword Upright Into The Earth, Its Sharp Edge Exposed, And Casts Himself Upon It. It Comes Out The Other Side Of His Body, And With This He Dies. His Warriors Who Had Lost Sight Of Him Go To See Him, But He Is Already Dead, As He Died Immediately When He Cast Himself Upon His Sword. They Carry Him Into Pilate's Presence And Place Him Upon The Floor. They Weep And Speak To* PILATE.)

MONQUES: Oh lord, oh Pilate, truly we went to see the Emperor! We stated our grievance to him and he repulsed it saying that he would show us no mercy, and further that he will destroy all of us in combat.

(*Then Another* NOBLE *Speaks To Him.*)

JEWISH
NOBLEMAN: Oh noble lord, when we had gone there, Archelaus left us quietly. Truly we were plotting destruction. Now perhaps he (Pilate? Unclear.) will be ashamed. And when we hadn't seen him for quite a while, we went to look for him. He was already dead upon the ground, cast upon his sword, as one kills oneself because of grief.

(PILATE *Weeps And Then Speaks.*)

PILATE: Oh my friends, surely our spirit is no longer the same! Indeed, now we shall not die as good (men). Since this is most important and in order that we should not die as yet, let us go in to the Emperor. Let us go and weep before him, pleading that we shall deliver over the city into his hands. Perhaps his heart will concede to this! Moreover, before we go, every precious metal, every fine stone—like emeralds and pearls—are all to be gathered together to be ground up and drunk (as a potion). Thus if we actually fall into the hands of our enemies, they will not rejoice the more because they are made rich with our fortune, our wealth. And when this has been done, we will place the city of Jerusalem into his hands.

(*At This Point The* JEWS *Speak To* PILATE.)

JEWS: Oh Pilate, what have you forced us to do? Truly you yourself constrained us! Oh what have we done, oh Pilate? By now it is already evident that it would have been better if, exerting ourselves, we had died at the hands of the Emperor when we went in to meet him, oh Pilate! We greatly doubt that he will extend us even a little mercy now!

(*Then* PILATE *Speaks To Them.*)

PILATE: Oh my lords, don't die because of sadness; gladden yourselves! For soon I myself shall go into the presence of Vespasian; for I myself have something to ask of him. Surely he will have mercy on us! Although I myself am lost, most assuredly he will extend mercy to you, oh my nobles!

(*At This Point The* JEWS *Draw Back A Little. They Then Go Before* PILATE *Another Time And Say To Him*):

JEWS: That which you told us (to do) has been done. What remains for us to do? Help us! For already we die of hunger!

(*Then* PILATE *Speaks To Them.*)

PILATE: Oh my friends, truly I admit my crime which is an ugly thing. My repentance is most genuine. It is entirely because of me that you suffer such trials. What remedy is there now? How disgraced I am!

JEWS: Oh great lord, it is most evident in your expression that we move you most deeply to compassion. Truly in our company you have come to suffer great labors, and with us now as surely as our life is to be lost, so shall your dominion, your nobility, and your greatness be lost. You shall go about useless where once you resounded (were important); and likewise it shall come to pass with your city Jerusalem. Indeed, together with us, all shall be destroyed! (All this) is because of you, as you yourself have said, since you were the cause of the evil.

For really what else can happen to us now? So let us all go into the presence of the Emperor and prostrate ourselves. Let us go and weep before him! (We shall ask), 'How can you wish this to happen to us? Will this all perhaps be in vain? Will you have compassion? Will you view us with pity?'

(PILATE *Weeps And Guides His Subjects To Where The Emperor Is. Then He Signals To* TITUS *With His Hand, And Speaks To Him.*)

TITUS: Who is calling us with his hand like a mute?

(*A Nobleman Speaks To Him.*)

MONQUES: Oh great lord, truly it is that same one Pilate who implores you. He desires counsel.

TITUS: Let us go and see what thing Pilate wishes to tell me.

(*Then* PILATE *And His Subjects Kneel Down.* PILATE, *Before* TITUS, *Weeps And Speaks To Him.*)

PILATE: Oh sir, oh great lord Titus! You surely know that I have not accomplished my duty well. If someone is to blame, then I, unworthy one, confess my guilt: that I, miserable one, have greatly sinned; that I vile thing, was so stupid; and that I lived in such a way as to offend the person of the great lord, of the monarch and emperor. Truly I, despicable one, confess my guilt! Furthermore, I, undeserving and miserable one, took possession of his property, his goods, and the revenue of his city. I stole from his tribute gathered together from year to year as the people came to give it. And in addition to this, I appropriated for myself his sovereignty, the right of dominion of the Emperor.

Because of this, Oh I have come to weep in your presence. I have come to pay for my guilt, as I, unworthy one, have sinned—as I was so wicked! I, despicable one, shall place the city at your feet. Would that you know all this. Here truly is a miserable man, afflicted in vain! Would that you have mercy upon me, so that we all might live still a few more days by the grace of your (mercy).

(No Sooner Does PILATE *Finish With His Supplication When* TITUS *Speaks To Him.)*

TITUS: Oh Pilate, truly I have heard your weeping and your sadness; but I must first seek counsel and implore something (mercy) for you from my father, from the lord Emperor. Now truly I shall speak in supplication before him in your favor, and I shall lament.

*(*PILATE *Turns Away.* TITUS *Goes To The Presence Of The Emperor. He Arrives, Salutes Him, And He Speaks To Him.)*

TITUS: Oh great lord, let it please you to know that your vassal Pilate has come, that he came to salute us, and he has truly wept. I was moved with compassion by his sad words, for he indeed confessed his guilt as he—ruinous one—has truly offended you. I have come into your presence to prostrate myself, and also your nobles do likewise. Surely he comes to deliver the city of Jerusalem into your hands. He no longer is afraid for his life, that is, that you might shorten it at some time. Nor did he come into my presence only to weep; he came to lament in order that because of some affection for him, I might appease you, oh lord, oh great lord, oh Emperor.

(The EMPEROR *Answers Him.)*

EMPEROR: Oh Titus, no longer shall I show compassion for him, for his nobles, or for the city. Indeed, for the (reason) that I came here to vent my anger for the death of the Holy Prophet. Further, you know how much I esteemed all of them (in Jerusalem), and of my affection for him—a man of nothing—who aggrandized himself at my expense and over me; he offended my very presence. And besides, how many of my valiant soldiers, my nobles, have I lost, as well as things which I prized? I am most indignant against them for this. Furthermore, you know that when I sent my aged Chamberlain Caius here, he received him with great anger, and that he held my message in no honor, and would have killed Caius if some one had not interceded for him.

Not only that, but when I came here—even though he did not appear—I still thought that perhaps he would greet us and receive us, since he is the magistrate.

Moreover, I admonished the two of them, also King Archelaus, that they make restitution of my things, and they answered that they would not submit to my jurisdiction. (They asked) why we had come here since I no longer had charge of Jerusalem. (He said) that we should desist, and that as we would do thus so he also would do with the city of Jerusalem, that my jurisdiction is *there* (in Rome) and that he would no longer place the city in my hands. For naught will he come to fall down before me! Because of all this then, he must know that as I wish it (the destruction of Jerusalem) to happen, thus must it occur. Let the rest have compassion for him, but with reserve—oh my son—for certainly you know that I have many times manifested it (compassion) through my imperial crown. As I am the Emperor Vespasian, so should I make manifest my belief. I would assuage my anger for the death of the Holy Prophet whom they killed there.[11] Speak thusly with Pilate, for I shall no longer pardon him. And as I wish, so must it be.

(With This The Emperor Finishes Speaking. TITUS *Goes To The Presence of* PILATE *And Says To Him):*

TITUS: Oh Pilate, I have truly spoken to the Emperor, my father. Thus it was done. I pleaded for you as much as it was in my power; but actually he only agrees that you must place the city in his hands, and further that you will prostrate yourself before him no more!

(TITUS *Turns Away and* PILATE *Speaks To The Jews*)

PILATE: Oh my friends, surely now you see how we are (ploys) in the hands of our gods! Certainly you have now heard that both Titus and I myself went to exculpate ourselves in the presence of the Emperor, and that it was impossible to do. What do you say? Speak! What can be done?

(*Then* MONQUES *Speaks.*)

MONQUES: Oh great lord, how then can we deliver ourselves? As there are no longer even two rations of food, we cannot defend ourselves for much time. As he (the Emperor) wishes, so shall it be. Let us all go into the presence of the Emperor as he wishes; let us go into his presence and weep. Perhaps he will be compassionate with us without reason (if) he wishes; although we were not merciful when his Chamberlain Caius came here, and you simply denied him with anger when he said, 'Deign to hear my message.' Perhaps now nothing can come of it.

JEWISH NOBLES: What he says is good. Let us do it!

(*They Go To Overtake The Valiant Men Of The Emperor.* PILATE *Salutes Then And Says To Them:*)

PILATE: Oh my noble lords, I implore you as in the presence of the Emperor! I have come to place the city at your feet.

(*They Go To Tell This To The* EMPEROR.)

CAIUS: Pilate has now come! He has come into your presence to entreat you!

EMPEROR: When he comes, let him bring along only two of his nobles.

TITUS: Enter, oh Pilate, for the Emperor summons you.

JEWS: Oh Titus, may your heart have whatever it desires! For truly you have humbled the great pride of Pilate.

(*He* (PILATE) *Goes Closer To The* EMPEROR. *He Comes To* TITUS *Who Says To Him):*

TITUS: Bring your sword here, as you are not to carry it into the presence of the Emperor.

(PILATE *Then Says To Him*):

PILATE: Oh great lord, I beseech you that I bear it no longer (in warfare? Uncertain).

(TITUS *Says To Him*):

TITUS: So will it be, Pilate.

(PILATE *Goes Before The Emperor. Then He Kneels Down And Raises His Macana.*)[12]

PILATE: Oh very great lord, oh Emperor! Truly I, the undeserving Pilate, your vassal, have come into your presence. Into your presence I, despicable one, have come. And thus I lay down my sword and the city before you. At your feet I place everything. Whatever you should wish to do, let it be done accordingly. Truly I, miserable one, declare my guilt; that I, ruinous one, rose up against you; and that I, unworthy one, aggrandized myself at your expense; and further that in the same way (spirit) I deserve the stone and the cudgel (to be punished).[13] In whatever manner you might do this, indeed so let it be; for the power of government belongs to the Emperor, whereas I only guarded and ruled by the favor of another.[14] Would that I had placed all these things here into your hand, and had recognized you as the lord, oh worthless one that I am! How wicked I was! Perhaps you will extend me mercy, and perhaps your heart will go out to me? Would that it be not in vain! Deign to look with compassion upon these men, my friends, who are here.

EMPEROR: Rise, oh Pilate!

(PILATE *Arises. He Wishes To Kiss The Hand Of The Em-*

The Destruction of Jerusalem

peror, But He Remains Ignored To One Side. The EMPEROR
Says To Him:)

EMPEROR: Oh Pilate, indeed through many things (acts) you have created evil among others, thus perverting them. Because of this, I shall show you no mercy. And hear this as it will relate to you:

The first thing—by your sentence and with great evil they killed the Holy Prophet here on the cross; His name was Jesus the Nazarene. You understood this well, for they confessed and knew that his life was good, and that only you slandered and hated him. Indeed, we now see that because you are as you are, you cared not to pray to Him, nor did you care to be thankful to Him although it would have been good for you (to have done so). For when you were suddenly ill, he would surely have cured you; and if you had died suddenly, he would have given you life. For such a thing then—and hear well—for His death I have really come to punish you.

And here is the second thing—because you usurped that which belonged to the Emperor, his seat and his domain, you did not recognize my true jurisdiction here as Emperor, nor did you obey me. Instead, you aggrandized yourself at my expense, and appropriated from the yearly tribute which had been gathered for me. When I sent my aged Chamberlain Caius here, you chided him when he warned you about the tribute. Furthermore, you plotted to kill him secretly, even as he bore my message. You return my command in this manner! What a thing you have done, Pilate, and *how* you did it! Yet you sinned not only in this.

The third thing—when I came here, I came only in the proximity of your little town, and it was an ugly thing which you arranged for them to do to me there. It was not good that you came forth and fought against me. Truly my heart cried out at this. You held me as nothing. Further, while I am still here, how many more will your soldiers kill? How many more of my men will perhaps fall into their hands? When you had power you strengthened your corruption. Moreover, do not forget that when I came here you were upon the wall, and you had sent a message to King Archelaus. You were with your company of soldiers, and when I approached the wall I said to you, 'Recognize the Emperor! Humble yourself as I am your lord and your master and open the gates of the city at once!' But you replied, 'As we (my nobles) have not yet talked, they will first consult with me.' And then you said, 'Guard your life likewise as we guard the city.' After this I left.

Who am I that *you* rule and command in Jerusalem? Oh Pilate, because of these things, and the other things which I won't mention again—as I have repeatedly said —I warned you there upon the wall that I would not have pity upon you. I told you there that you would see something frightful, and not only you alone but all your nobles and those of the city as well. You will indeed find that the warning will fall back upon you.

(PILATE *Says To Him:*)

PILATE: Oh my noble lord, is there perchance anyone who still lives in Jerusalem? For truly, I have brought them all here.

(*Then The* EMPEROR *Seizes A Rope And Binds Pilate. The* EMPEROR *Speaks.*)

EMPEROR: Here are the Jews whom Pilate brought. Sell them all publicly so that they become slaves and captives.

(CAIUS *Seizes Jacob By The Hand. He Takes Him Into The Presence Of The Emperor, And* CAIUS *Says To Him*)

CAIUS: Oh great lord, truly this man lodged me in his house when you chose to send me here. Indeed, he also took me to see Veronica. Actually he served me greatly here, and because of this—oh my sovereign lord—will you not show him mercy so that he doesn't fall under the stone and cudgel with the others? Moreover, it is for the love of you that I have said this, as it pleased me consummately when Veronica cured you.

EMPEROR: Oh Jacob, how many of them are there of your family still in the high city (Jerusalem)? Inform them that I shall show mercy only to them.

(JACOB *Speaks:*)

JACOB: Oh great lord, your heart has conceded much! Who is there left in Jerusalem perchance? Truly they are all here. Would that we might live yet many days by your grace!

(The EMPEROR *Says:)*

EMPEROR: Oh valiant soldiers! Certainly you see that the city of Jerusalem is already in our hands! Yet you do not know that Herod is not far away; that he is a great king and lord and that he is our enemy. Furthermore, if we leave the city abandoned, even if we leave someone established as our guardian to protect the city—the seat of the government— (while we are gone), when we might come back Herod would be angry because of this, and would seize the city as Pilate did. Shall we perhaps not do what seems good to me at the moment? That we raze it, that we destroy it completely, so that not one stone remains standing in it? And so not only do we punish it, but we also honor our Divinity in this!

BUFFOON: Oh Emperor, oh my beloved sovereign! Why is it that all the Jews whom we have killed excrete only precious metal?

(Another NOBLE *Subject:)*

A NOBLE: Oh my beloved lord, what he says to you is true. Please listen!

(The EMPEROR *Speaks:)*

EMPEROR: Is it not evident? I surely believe it as he (Pilate) is so evil! But we *are* going to enjoy his goods for he certainly merits this.

[*Apparently* The Emperor *Understood The Plot Of The Jews To Destroy All Available Wealth.*] (*They Take* Pilate *Away, Accompanying Him. Then* Clement *Speaks.*)

CLEMENT: Oh my Emperor, my lord, surely our Lord has favored you! Would that because of this you might pray that you would accept for yourself the worship of his Divinity, and that you be baptized. Furthermore, that along with this you see fit to command every person to do the same thing.

(*The* Emperor *Speaks To Him:*)

EMPEROR: Oh Clement, truly you acted well for me, and I most assuredly rejoice and feel pleasure. With my heart —with all of my heart—I do believe everything which you teach me.

(*Those From Vienna Kneel Down In The Presence Of The* Emperor.)

VIENNESE: We, your vassals, who guard your property in your house in Vienna, have come into your presence. Oh you, our beloved monarch, strengthen yourself greatly! Truly you know that in your city of Vienna—which not recently but rather a long time ago received the mercy and gift of your sovereignty—assuredly if there were anyone there who ever offended the presence of the Emperor, he would be given the stone and the cudgel. That is, they would punish him with death. And now that Pilate, who governed your hills and your waters, has offended you in your presence, so that proper punishment be not lacking and that you dispose of things as you wish, should you perhaps not lash him? We shall take him to your dominion there in Vienna, where he will be our prisoner according to your sentence. Truly, Vienna will be honored with this duty. Would that you deign to hear and to indulge this (petition), oh great lord!

(*The* Emperor *Answers Them.*)

EMPEROR: Oh gentlemen, oh wise men, oh magistrates! Indeed, I am honored with your discourse. Truly this one speech is already payment for my mercy. What you say is good. Certainly I myself ought to seize Pilate! How many, oh august ones, died while I was in battle with this haughty person? Consequently, he will forever have to undergo the sentence of his life in Rome. It is therefore with this statement that I answer your discourse.

A VIENNESE: In order that you be no further irritated, in one word you shall hear my speech. May it please you to listen, oh my lord! We are now here—we who rule your hills and water (province) in Vienna—in order that no one will slander us, and so that your heirs to your city here will not murmur tomorrow or in the future that you gave us our state of sovereignty uselessly; nor will they talk of you in like manner. Is it perhaps not in your power to act as did the Emperors who were here before (you) and who are now dead? Incline your heart! Concede that we take Pilate away and that he will be our prisoner. And however you will decide it, so indeed shall it be done there in Vienna.

(The EMPEROR *Speaks.)*

EMPEROR: Oh learned ones, you do me honor! I have already gathered together my nobles. What will be the outcome of all this?

(Then CAIUS *Speaks To Him.)*

CAIUS: Oh my esteemed lord, let it be thus! They did you a service in what they proposed to you. Fail not to concede to them the privileges of their city!

(At This Point The EMPEROR *Says To Them:)*

EMPEROR: Oh my gentlemen, as your heart wishes it, so let it finally be! I concede Pilate to you.

(Then The Learned Ones [The Viennese] Enter (Closer?) Into The Presence Of The Emperor.)

EMPEROR: Come! Truly it will not harm me that my people (the Viennese) will see my mercy, for you know well that he (Pilate) offended my person and my presence. But first you must leave guarantees of your good faith; for if you should perhaps free Pilate, then my heart will be placated with the hostages.

(Then The Old Men Speak To Him.)

A VIENNESE: Oh my esteemed lord, your words have gratified us. We shall bear Pilate away. You do us a great kindness.

(Then They Bring PILATE *Out. The* EMPEROR *Speaks.)*

EMPEROR: Into your hands I place him, you lords who are present, the lords of Vienna, that you take him away!

(The Scene Shifts.) Then He [PILATE] *Is There In Vienna. A Dog Howls And* PILATE *Asks Of Some One:*

PILATE: Oh my lord, oh valiant man, whose dog is this who howls and barks near here every day?

(He Whom Pilate Has Asked Says To Him)

GUARDS: Oh my lord, truly it is your dog which has come here from Rome. He has traced you here by his sense of smell. When they brought you here, indeed he also came; so it is that he searches for you.

*(*PILATE *Then Says:)*

PILATE: Would it be possible that I might profit by the grace of the magistrate and that they might permit him in here?

GUARD: It is not possible to do what you ask.

PILATE: Oh my beloved friend, is there then no remedy? I have been disgraced in vain! Would that you do what I beg you to do, that is, at least to carry the dog away, so that I won't hear him any more. For truly he makes my heart weep greatly, and makes me feel profound pity.

(The Scene Apparently Shifts Again.) A SLAVE *Speaks In The Presence Of The Elders Of Vienna.*

SLAVE: Oh our lords, indeed I am but a slave, but I say that Pilate *cannot* die. Do me the favor and allow me to inform you, and I shall tell you why Pilate is unable to die. For perhaps he dies without reason. (Unclear)

(The ELDERS Say To Him:)

VIENNESE: Certainly we give you permission. Tell us how this can be.

(Here The SLAVE Says To Them:)

SLAVE: Oh my lords, please hear me! Truly when they killed the Holy Prophet who was Jesus Christ and when they raised him on the cross, indeed it was done in my presence as I was there. Now please listen carefully! When they had hanged him on the cross by verbal order of the magistrate, first they disrobed him; and he who was able to took a little cape which was truly a very beautiful and fine thing. Then as the Jews seized it, they say a great miracle happened to whoever took it in their hands. In the same manner, Pilate searched for it, took it, and guarded it with great love. And wherever he went, before he left he went carrying it with him. He was very happy. It didn't occur to him to offer it to God. Perhaps he is still carrying it! Go and see if it is true that he still bears it, and then may it please you to offer it to God.

(At This Point The ELDERS Go To Look. They Go To Make Certain About The Little Cape. When They Are Certain (That Pilate Has It), They Take It Away From Him.)

PILATE: Oh misfortune! I am disgraced! Who told you about this?

(Then Finally, He [Pilate] Too Falls Because Of This And Dies. The Elders Run About And Go Back And Forth And Look Upon Pilate To See If Perhaps He Really Died Because of This.)

Commentary

We can only wonder if a round of applause or other commendation followed such a smashing curtan line. At any rate, the reasons why *"The Destruction of Jerusalem"* seemed a likely vehicle for the teaching of Christianity are several. The whole play emphasizes a respect, albeit militant, for the figure of Christ, or the Holy Prophet as he is styled. The drama does convey a certain amount of information about the Crucifixion, albeit the surrounding circumstances are fanciful. In addition to a respect for Christianity, *"The Destruction of Jerusalem"* teaches a pointed respect for authority, both political and religious. All subjects bow to the will of the Emperor and God, or nemesis overtakes them; and, finally, even the Emperor bows to the will of his spiritual advisors and acts in the hope of avenging the death of Christ. The cherishing of religious relics, such as Veronica's veil and Christ's tunic or cape and investing them with miraculous curative or life-preserving powers, taught additional reverence for the trappings of Christianity in a way that was meaningful to the recently converted Indian of the sixteenth century.

Although we do not know the dates and places at which this drama was produced, if Motolinía's description of the lavishness of settings can be applied to this play, we can well imagine that the total effect was impressive. It is likely that it was presented in Tlaxcala, as were the plays Motolinía described. The battle scenes, the ramparts of Jerusalem, the elders of Vienna, the miraculous curing of the Emperor, the dramatic touch of the howling dog, Pilate's abject defeat at the hands of the Emperor, all of these combined to make what was probably an effective and perhaps very successful *fiesta* interlude.

It might be mentioned that the historical detail of the drama is woefully incorrect, and that more than poetic license was taken with the personages and their roles in history.

Pilate, the procurator of Judea, was in power until 26 A.D. Vespasian, the Roman Emperor, came to Rome as the supreme ruler in 70 A.D., and left his son Titus in Judea at that time to continue the war against the Jews. Archelaus was actually the son of Herod the Great, and was appointed by his father as his successor as ethnarch in Judea, Samaria, and Idumea. Augustus banished him to Vienna in Gaul in 7 A.D. for his tyrannical misuse of power, and he subsequently died there.[15]

In *"The Destruction of Jerusalem"* it seems as if the historical personages and actions of Pilate and Archelaus are confused. The roles of Vespasian and Augustus (who in fact banished Archelaus to Vienna and not Pilate) are also transposed.

Pilate is as usual portrayed as a complete villian, in spite of his rather bland and unwilling delivery and sentencing of Christ as pictured in the New Testament. The role of Herod as an omnipresent threat to the power of Rome must have referred to Herod Antipas, who held power in Galilee and Peraea, while his brother, Archelaus, was in power in Judea. Christ was said to have been brought to an audience before Herod Antipas in Jerusalem by Pilate, who was the Roman Procurator. Herod Antipas was more rightfully thought the "king of the Jews."[16] But the message of the play is forcefully presented although the facts on which it is based are historically inaccurate.

IX

SOULS AND TESTAMENTARY EXECUTORS

INTRODUCTION

The original of this drama is in Nahuatl, and the manuscript from which this translation was made is extant in the Archives of the *Museo Nacional de Antropología e Historia* in Mexico City. It is bound with manuscripts of *"La Adoración de los Reyes"* and *"El Sacrificio de Isaác."* The Nahuatl title of the play is *"In Animastin Ihuan Alvaceasme,"* which is best translated as *"Souls and Testamentary Executors."*

This drama has never before been published. There are in libraries one or two microfilm copies of the original manuscript, a translation from the Nahuatl to Spanish by Chimalpopoca dated 1855, paleographic copies made by Byron McAfee and John H. Cornyn, and finally the translation presented here, made by McAfee and Cornyn in 1931. Byron McAfee has authorized the publication of this translation from his personal collection, and has extended editing privileges to the author.

Nothing is known of the provenance of this drama; the manuscript bears the date 1760, but it is clear from the internal evidence of the play that it originated in the sixteenth century.

The English translation secured from Byron McAfee contains a few notes relevant to the original Nahuatl of the drama. The annotations were made by Cornyn and McAfee when they worked with the original manuscript, and include the following evaluations. The Nahuatl itself contains many errors, which probably means that it had been previously copied many times. Occasionally it appears that older, more classical phrases have been replaced by more modern terms to accommodate the content to the understanding of the audience. Although the manuscript is composed in the trochaic meter of the older Nahuatl poetic tradition, no tendency to divide the paragraph into poetic lines as one finds in later, more studied dramas, was noted.

Apart from the peculiarities mentioned, which may also be due in part to the scribe, the Nahuatl of the text is excellent, and not as eclectic or corrupted as that found in the plays composed after approximately the first quarter of the seventeenth century.

Angel Garibay concludes that, since the subject matter of *"Souls and Testamentary Executors"* concerns the duty of honoring the dead with masses and prayers in order to extricate those souls remaining in Purgatory, it was probably presented about the time of the First Ecclesiastical Council of 1555; this Council too dealt with respect and sacramental care for the souls of the dead.[1] It is interesting to compare the content of the aforementioned *"Tlacahuapahualiztli"* with that of this play. There are obvious similarities of theme and treatment.

Footnotes and annotations have been included with the appropriate passages in the text of the play in order to make obscure symbols and references more readily comprehensible.

The message and action of the play are direct and self-explanatory. Terrestrial and celestial characters, together with several demons, Lucifer, and a handful of tortured but vocal souls in Purgatory all contrive to make the cast typical of those used in didactic drama during the sixteenth century. At the end of the play, Christ, through his Archangel St. Michael, orders the condemned souls to be placed upon a wheel of fire and turned about like animals on a spit, confined to the house of smoke that has no chimney, and put in the mansion of liquid fire, of never-ending suffering. This sentence was apparently carried out onstage with a kind of vivid and realistic dramatization and scenario which must have terrified yet delighted the indigenous beholder.

The theme of the play is basically an exhortation to respect the souls of the dead; however, the Ten Commandments as well as a plea for the keeping of religious holidays, are added to the judgment scene, thus enlarging the theme to that of a more generalized imperative to practice the Sacraments and to obey all the teachings of the Church.

The use of music and dancing is again typical as an invariable component of the early Spanish dramas in Mexico as it was of the Prehispanic indigenous ceremonies.

Souls and Testamentary Executors

Cast of Characters

Guardian Angel of the Widow
Widow
Two Executors
Don Pedro
Wife of Don Pedro
Lucifer
Five Devils
Souls in Purgatory
Angels Who Watch over the Souls on Earth
Priest
Virgin Mary
Jesus Christ

(Enter Don Pedro *And* Wife. *Music Of Drums And Flutes.)*[2]

Don Pedro: Come, my dear wife! I have been greatly troubled and have been meditating, in the presence of God, about the dead who have been delivered over to God, the Guardian of souls. They have been called to Him to account for their deeds; and many have been condemned because of their various sins. If they could return again to earth, they would undoubtedly tell us that they were justly sentenced. But perhaps they have not since received all the help which should have been given to their souls. As you very well know, we have been aiding them for a long time with masses and prayers intended for the dead. My heart is ever filled with deep compassion whenever I think of where the Lord our God has sent them. Who can know all the mystery there is behind this, my beloved wife? We ourselves are now suffering trials and deprivations. Even our daily food does not come regularly. How then can we aid the souls of the dead? Give me your advice of these things, my dear wife.

WIFE: Dear husband, this is what I think should be done to aid the souls of the dead who are still suffering in the other world. Let us sell the little house which we have over there, and with what we get for it we shall have masses said for the dead. God will take care of us. Are not those whom we are about to help also His creatures? Since the Lord has not given us a child who is dependent on us, let what I have just proposed be done while we are still living so that we shall not have to look in vain, in the near future, for someone to come to our spiritual aid when the Lord God will have ended our lives.

DON PEDRO: All that you say is quite true, dear wife. Let us go to the church now and offer up our prayers to the Lord God. The mass is about to begin. Let us say a prayer for the souls suffering in Purgatory, so that God may look upon them with pity down there where they have fallen.

WIFE: Yes, let us do that, dear husband. Let us go there immediately.

(They Both Exit. The Devils Enter.)

LUCIFER:

(to the devils): What are you doing? What have you been attending to that you have not been looking after the people of the earth? Don't leave them for a single day! Keep right on the heels of those to whom the dead have left their property. Go and see to it that they squander all the wealth willed for the salvation of souls, so that those in Purgatory may not slip through our hands. See that my orders are obeyed at once!

SECOND
DEVIL: Don't worry about that, your majesty! We are going at once to lead them into the way of perdition.

THIRD
DEVIL: Come, let us go and see our subjects and our companions. Let us be off at once.

(The Devils Go And Sit Under A Table. They Begin Writing. Enter The Executors Carrying The Will To Be Read.) [3]

FIRST
EXECUTOR: Here is the scheme which I have thought out. You take one half of the property for yourself, and I'll take the other half. Let us divide it evenly between us. I shall change everything, blotting this out and keeping this until we are satisfied with the will.[4] Later we can help the souls of the dead. Do you suppose that they know anything about it anyway? Are they making inquiries about it? No! They are dead.

SECOND
EXECUTOR: That suits me all right. Let us do it! If we should lose the money, who will say anything about it? Is there anyone of their blood and color likely to be concerned enough for them to make trouble for us? Don't let that worry us, brother. Let us enjoy ourselves! Come on! All the wealth and property now belong to us, for when the dead took their departure there was no one present except you and me.

FIRST
EXECUTOR: What you have just said is quite true. So let us go and have a good time, dear companion!

(They Both Exit. They Meet The Widow Who Is Dressed In Black Mourning Garments. She Is Accompanied By The Devils Who Come Behind Her.)

WIDOW: Lords and companions, where are you going? May I have the pleasure of listening to your conversation?

FIRST
EXECUTOR: My dear Lady, we have just come precisely to

meet you! For today is Sunday and we are out enjoying ourselves. And you? Where are you going? May we follow along with you?

WIDOW: I am going to the house of our Holy Mother, the Church, to hear mass.

FIRST
DEVIL: Don't go there! What are you talking about? The mass? Leave all that and go and have a good time with your lovers.

SECOND
EXECUTOR: Come here, my lady. Sit down with us and let us have a good time together!

(The Two Executors Take Her By The Hand And They Sit Down With Her.)

WIDOW: My dear young men, I'm going right now to pass time with my friends who are in the church, for all last night in my dreams I saw my husband suffering in Purgatory. I want to have a mass said for his soul. This will be the second one, although it is only a short time since he died. I do not want him to continue suffering.

FIRST
EXECUTOR: Forget all that, my lady! For the wise men say, he who wants to go to church let him go; and he who wants to enjoy himself while on earth, let him do so. Let us be merry, for tomorrow we die. Don't forget this! This much is true and certain. So let us have a good time while we may![5]

WIDOW: What you have said is quite true, young man. Let us make the best of our time.

(There Is Music. A Bell Tolls For The Dead. Prayers For The Dead Are Being Chanted In The Church.)

SECOND
EXECUTOR: Who could have arranged for this mass? They are tolling the death bell. And we? What are we doing? What action are we taking to counteract this?

WIDOW: It is our neighbors who are doing this. If this pleases them, well why not let them spend their money in this way? It is theirs; and besides, it flatters their vanity. As for us, why should all this bother us?

SECOND
EXECUTOR: What you have done the honor of telling me is quite true. The mass is no concern of ours. If we should die tomorrow, would we come back to earth? Let us have a good time while we may!

SECOND
DEVIL: That is a very nicely put thought of yours. Forget the souls of the dead. Eat, drink, and send out invitations to a feast! Be sociable! Come together with wine and let there be no restraint!

WIDOW: Well, my dear young men, let me take the money left to me by the deed, and together we'll have a good time with it.

FIRST
EXECUTOR: All right. Come on and let us go.

(The Devils Take The WIDOW *Away. Enter* DON PEDRO *And His* WIFE.*)*

DON PEDRO: We are contented to have been to the mass for the souls of the dead. And now I pray you never to forget those who are suffering in Purgatory; for they cannot help themselves, nor can they save themselves. It is the command of the Lord our God that Christians still living on earth should help the souls of the dead, spiritually to aid with penitence and the making of offerings, so that they may thus be saved from their sufferings. Will they perhaps return again to earth to do penance? Certainly not! For the Lord our God has shut them forever in their prison. We who are still on earth must make offerings for them. Perhaps the Lord may take pity on them and perhaps not. He alone knows what is to be. He is the Lord God. And now I must rest my body— which is as ashes and dust—for I am very tired.

WIFE: Dear husband, there is great understanding in your heart. I shall take a good example from you. May you stimulate and instruct me, your wife. For I am like a child and will do all that you teach me. Be stout of heart and put all your strength in what you are doing. Let us go.

(They Both Exit. Enter The EXECUTORS, *The* WIDOW, *And The* THIRD DEVIL*).*

WIDOW: I am very happy and contented, my dear young men. Here is part of the money which the dead left to me. Take it and have a good time with it so long as it lasts. Does it come from the sweat of our brows? Certainly not!

FIRST EXECUTOR: Put it away over there. Let us take from it what we need to have a good time.

SECOND EXECUTOR: But there is something which we must do first, elder brother. Let us go and hear the sermon for it is about to begin. Come, dear friends, let us go!

THIRD DEVIL: Don't talk about sermons! No one is thinking about them now, so shut up about them.

FIRST EXECUTOR: Leave us alone! Don't bother us now for we are having a most pleasant time. We are finding our pleasure right here. Is the sermon any of our business? Get out! Leave us! Go away! It is none of your affair what we are doing here.

(The Sound Of Wind Instruments. Enter DON PEDRO *And His* WIFE.*)*

DON PEDRO: Dear wife, let us stroll along slowly. Let us go to the church. I am to partake of the precious body of our Lord and Saviour, Jesus Christ. Oh, unfortunate that I am! Into what am I throwing myself? Into pleasure? Into scoffing? Oh, my Lord! Oh, my Master! Look upon me with pity and help me! Do not forget me—I am but human! I am a very great sinner! Have pity on me with Thy boundless compassion! Wash me thoroughly in many places! Wash from me all that is not good and proper, all that is black and filthy.[6] Cleanse me of all the iniquity which pollutes me, that makes me so vile! My sins weigh upon me, a great burden pressing me down like a too heavy load on my back, threatening to crush me into the earth. Have pity on me for I am a great sinner, oh my Lord![7]

(Here He Cries Out.)

WIFE: Dear husband, be strong of heart! Leave yourself all together in the hands of God our Creator. Let us go then to church.

(They Both Exit. A Soul Of The Dead Enters. Flames Of Fire Curl Upward Around It. The PECCATA Is Sung. The Soul Answers. NULLA EST RESPONSIO.)

THIRD SOUL: Alas for me! Oh, Lord God, all pitying, all merciful! Have compassion on me with Thy great pity! My heart and soul are sorely afflicted because of the things which I have done to Thy compassionate heart. It is because of this that I am crying out. I have offended Thee, my God, my Sovereign Lord, You who are worthy above all to be loved! Have mercy on me, for no one on earth pities me! You are my beloved Father; You have created me—have given me life! You are my helper and defender. While I lived on earth I gave my wealth and property that I might be helped with it in the afterlife. Unfortunate sinner that I am! My relatives still living on earth have forgotten me. All this You know.

(The Soul Exits. They Chant The Prayer For The Souls Of The Dead. A Woman In Mourning Carrying A Candle And Fruit To Offer At Mass Enters. An Angel Leads Her.)

WOMAN: Lord God, it is all finished! Oh unfortunate that I am! You have left me alone, for my husband is dead!

May my life on earth not be long. I am going to the church to hear mass to help the souls of the dead.

FIRST
ANGEL: Courage! Do all that you are able to do! Don't stop! Go and make your offering that it may help someone in Purgatory.

(She Meets The SECOND DEVIL.)

SECOND
DEVIL: Where do you intend to go? What are you going to do in the church? What will you do there? Will you perhaps find what *you* need there? Of course not! Will you be able to make a living there? If you keep on going to the church, you will die of hunger. Don't go there!

WOMAN: I can't do that now, my dear young man; leave me alone! It is the command of God that I should hear Mass.

SECOND
DEVIL: Have you not heard, my lady, that there is no mass? And that there are no priests in the church? I have just come from there this very moment. So turn back, for what I am telling you is true. Go home. Don't be out seducing your neighbors. Go on away! Leave here!

FIRST
ANGEL: Leave her alone, Devil! Do not say anything to her, for she is the servant of God. Go away! You are not allowed to lead her astray; for here am I, her guardian, ever protecting her. Leave her! She is God's creature.

(The Devil Is Sent To The Underworld, And He Shouts Back From The Gates Of Hell.)

SECOND
DEVIL: Do you not hear me speaking to you, woman? Turn back! If you come with me, I shall give you everything —all the wealth and possessions with which to enjoy yourself on earth.

FIRST
ANGEL: Leave her alone! She is God's creature!

(They All Exit. There Are Prayers For The Souls Of The Dead, At the Conclusion of Which Enter A Priest And The Woman.)

PRIEST: My dear daughter, for the love of God remember always and forever those who have preceded you in death. May those who have died before you stir you to pity! May you excite compassion for them in the presence of God, for they are suffering greatly down there in the Place of the Cleansing of Sins, called Purgatory. They are imploring you to have masses said for them and to help them here on earth with prayers and offerings—are those who are over there! It is still possible to do something to help them. They are waiting, expecting help from others that they may be saved. When pity is shown them they are grateful, very thankful for the aid given them. As for what you have told me of your not being able to sleep well or breakfast well, do not let that trouble you, my dear daughter. Do not abandon the souls of the dead for that reason. Rather plead to God with prayers and supplications, that He may serve them and that He may lessen their sufferings that they remain not long in Purgatory. Then, when your earthly life will have ended, they will plead to God for you that He may have pity on you, that you may deserve the joy of heaven, which is life eternal.

WOMAN: Dear and reverend father, your heart has understood! I thank you for what you have done for me. With your permission I shall leave you now, but I shall return again. I am going to look for something with which you may help the souls of the dead. With your permission I must go now.

PRIEST: May the Lord our God be with you! I shall expect you, my dear daughter.

(They Both Exit. Enter The EXECUTORS *And The* WIDOW.*)*

FIRST EXECUTOR: We ought to be very happy today since there is nothing to trouble us. As for me, here is my portion of the money which we are going to spend in having a good time. Friends, are we perhaps going to remain on earth forever?

WIDOW: And here, my dear young men, is my part of the expenses which is fifteen *pesos*. With the rest I bought clothes. Could I go out among people the way I was?

SECOND DEVIL: That's right! That's fine! All this is very necessary. Are the property and wealth not yours? Squander them! Be merry and have a good time.

FIRST EXECUTOR: Here I am back again! And here is something with which to make our lives merry. Let us have music and singing! What are you doing, companions?

(There Is The Sound Of Music And Drums. The Widow Drinks The Wine, And Wipes Her Mouth On The Mourning Garment. Then She Takes It Off And Throws It On The Table Where There Is Fruit. There Is Singing And A Wild Celebration. Bells Toll For The Dead. Enter The Souls.)

FIRST SOUL: Alas! Remember us, friends who are still living on earth. Do not forget us in the presence of God our Lord. You, our relatives still living on earth, for the love of God please say a *Pater Noster* or an *Ave Maria* for us.

WIDOW: Dear me! Good lord, what is that? Let us go in. Let us go home, for it is very late.

SECOND DEVIL: Don't be disturbed, for it is merely the voice of time with which the night passes. It is no sickness; it hurts no one. Go on with the party!

SECOND EXECUTOR: Let him (Time) shout! Is it any of our business? We are having a good time.

(There Is Music. The Soul Cries Out Again. He Speaks Twice To The Cross. The Heavens Open And Other Souls Kneel In The Presence of God [8]*)*

SECOND SOUL: Alas! Unfortunate that I am! Lord God, look on me with pity! You who are our Creator and ever seated on the right hand of God, your beloved and honored Father. We are crying out to you because of your creatures who still live upon the earth. They never forget us, in your presence, not even for a day. They make offerings and prayers with which to remember us. May the time not come yet to end their lives upon the earth. Still continue to look upon them with pity. Have mercy on them!

(There Sounds The Tolling Of Bells For The Dead.)

THIRD SOUL: Alas! Oh, most High, our Saviour Jesus Christ! In your sovereign presence we beseech you humbly to listen to us. Because of your great mercy have pity on all those who remember us upon earth; on those who took out a holy bull for us, and offer prayers and masses for the dead in your presence. For if You should bring them to judgment tomorrow or the day after, Lord God, who will aid us? Who will look upon us with pity? For then there would be no Christians upon earth to make offerings for us in your presence. Extend the time for all the people upon the earth!

(Bells Toll For The Dead.)

FOURTH SOUL: Oh You, ever merciful, ever compassionate, for the sake of your most Blessed Mother, Holy Mary, who gave birth to you and nourished you with her milk, look with pity on those whom I left behind and who interceded for me! My dear relatives do this for me most devoutly; monthly they receive Holy Communion in mourning garments. Have pity on them too!

FIFTH SOUL: Oh, have mercy on me, unfortunate that I am, Lord God! How can I bring people to have pity upon me? How can I make them cry out for me? No one remembers me! Oh, a thousand times unfortunate that I am![9] For no one on earth recognizes me! Perhaps my father, my mother, my elder brother, my younger brother, my elder sister, and my near family are standing aloof from me. Oh unfortunate that I am! Oh, my Creator, because of your mercy, look with pity upon me! And you, ever blessed Virgin, remember us, your creatures whom no one remembers! For the sake of your Rosary and the prayers said to You. For, while I still lived upon the earth, I never forgot you! Help me for I am suffering! I left my wife behind me on earth and she no longer remembers me. I have not been able to excite her pity. There is no longer anyone there who helps me in your presence. Would that she remember me with a mass or a prayer! She is squandering in vices all that I left to be used to help me down here. She has disgraced her mourning garments, which she wears constantly to get drunk in and to go about with her illicit lovers, thus also dishonoring them. Let this all end! Cut short her earthly life, for she has already lived too long this way in your presence.[10]

(The Sky Opens, And MARY *Speaks.)*

VIRGIN MARY: Oh my beloved and reverend only Son, Jesus Christ, I prostrate myself before you in behalf of your creatures who are suffering in the Place of the Cleansing of Sins by Fire called Purgatory. Look upon them with pity! Have mercy upon them, beloved and honored Son. Have God listen to my pitiful sobs and supplications, and look upon my tears for those still living upon earth. My beloved, honored Son, may He who has never forgotten You remember that they have always followed You, and have remembered the sufferings by which You saved them.

JESUS CHRIST: Ever pure Virgin, beloved Mother, do not mourn for your servants! For while they still lived upon earth, they always trusted in me. They always had faith in me that they would be helped; that they would be saved through my protection. They know my beloved Father, God. When they cry to me, I will hear their supplications. When they become repentant, cleansing their hearts through divine grace and losing their pride, I shall comfort them. I shall honor them. I shall glorify them and set them up in the high places. They will live forever and be happy. I shall bestow upon them my eternal felicity in the Home of the Blessed.

VIRGIN MARY: Look with pity on them, oh beloved Son, for they are crying out to Thee! Listen to them! They are suffering, these creatures you have created!

(There Is The Sound Of Drums, Followed By The Tolling Of The Bells For The Dead.)

THIRD SOUL: Alas! The end has come, oh unfortunate that I am! Remember us you who still live upon the earth! You, our friends, do not desert us in the presence of God our Lord. Alas! Alas! If all people were to suffer, burn, and be in torture as we, then they would have pity on us. Should you—our families—forget us? Don't cease for a moment to think of us! Keep us always and constantly in mind; for if you don't who will have pity on us? We are suffering intensely! Alas! Oh God, judge those whom we have left behind us on earth to be our intercessors before your sovereignty quickly. They do not remember us! They are squandering what we left in their keeping in eating and drinking. Will it so that they appear here in your presence, oh Lord Jesus Christ!

JESUS CHRIST: Archangel, Saint Michael, order the earthly people to present themselves here.

ST. MICHAEL: Your sovereign command shall be obeyed. Come forth from Hell, you accursed! The just Dispensor of Justice, the Judge, orders you to appear before Him, and to bring with you a statement of accounting for the property of the dead. They have squandered the wealth and possessions of the souls of the departed who are now suffering in the Place of Fire-Cleansing called Purgatory. For no one remembers them any longer!

(Enter LUCIFER And The Other Devils.)

LUCIFER: Your heart has granted it. We thank you. Let us go. Let us be on the march, companions!

THIRD DEVIL: Let us quickly gather together our servants and our companions, for thus our Lord God has ordered it.

(*They All Go Into The House. They Seize The Condemned. The Widow Is Dressed In Black. They All Cry Out. There Are Brilliant Fireworks When The Executors Enter. Bells Toll For The Dead.*)

FIRST EXECUTOR: Alas, it is finished at last! Oh, unfortunate that I am! Alas, alas, alas! The end has come! Oh, unfortunate sinners that we are!

SECOND EXECUTOR: It is your fault that we are in torment here, that we are suffering! For I told you that the wealth and property of the dead should go to the church that they might thus be helped. And now this is what it happening to us!

FIRST EXECUTOR: Devil of a woman! It is your fault that we squandered the wealth and property of others! You are to blame for all we are now suffering.

WIDOW: The end has come! Oh unfortunate that I am! Would that we had never been born! Then this horror, this frightful thing would not have happened to us!

LUCIFER: Go quickly! Do you not remember your own sins? It is all over now! You are now our property and possessions!

(*They Present Themselves Before* JESUS CHRIST. *There They Stretch Out Their Hands And Open Their Papers.* LUCIFER *And The Other Devils Kneel Down.*)

LUCIFER: Oh You, the altogether Just One, the Judge! You who pass judgment on all! We have brought before You here great sinners who have not obeyed You, who have not kept Your commandments—although You redeemed them with Your precious blood. Wicked in their deeds and evil of heart they have never remembered You. Pass judgment on them. They belong to us since they are forever cursed. They have hated all things holy. In no way have they attended to your service. Here are their sins. Behold their deeds! Read their iniquities, oh angel!

St. Michael: Here are the commandments of the one and only God; they number ten. The first three treat of the honor which is due to God; the remaining seven of the love which is due to the people of the earth by one another. The first says that you shall love the Lord God alone with all your heart.

Lucifer: Certainly those who are here have never loved You. They have never worshipped You.

St. Michael: The second is that you shall never take the name of the Lord your God in vain.

Lucifer: They were always swearing. They constantly took your name in vain during their pleasures and sinful debauches.

St. Michael: The third is that you shall not do any work on Sundays or feast days; but that you shall give your time to spiritual things.

Lucifer: Never did they pray to You all the time they lived upon earth. Never did they remember You. They worked on feast days and committed carnal sins.

St. Michael: The fourth is that you shall honor your father and mother.

Lucifer: How could they honor them? You have given them all that is right and just. You died for them on the cross. Yet they have never honored You. They always lived unheedingly in your presence. And their fathers themselves too became leaders of their sons—taking them to the pulque shops and wine taverns, thus breaking your commandments, oh my Lord.

ST. MICHAEL: That no living soul shall die by your hand is the fifth commandment.

LUCIFER: How could no one die by their hands? They have destroyed the souls of men by leading them to commit sins while they were upon earth. Further, they have often wished the death of those who were leading good lives.

ST. MICHAEL: The sixth commandment is that you shall not commit adultery on earth.

LUCIFER: This very day they were caught in this forbidden pleasure, in the sin of adultery.

ST. MICHAEL: The seventh is that you shall not steal or covet the property of others.

LUCIFER: And yet they have just been taken, been caught in the houses of others. We are not accusing them falsely.

ST. MICHAEL: The eighth is that you shall not accuse others falsely or put the blame on them.

LUCIFER: They certainly have falsely accused their neighbors; and they have blamed others for their faults.

ST. MICHAEL: The ninth is that you shall not covet the wife or husband of another.

LUCIFER: Those who have dishonored many with their pleasant flattering words and their adulteries are here. They have never looked upon You with fear; they have never respected your Commandments. All they have done is to laugh at them. They have treated the day of the last judgment with mockery, although they have to give an account of their sins and they wish to save themselves from them (the sins) here in your sovereign presence.

ST. MICHAEL: The tenth is that you shall not covet the wealth and property of others.

LUCIFER: How is it possible that they should not covet them? They have gathered to themselves all the wealth and property of the dead. They have not procured a papal Bull for them. Nor have they had a mass said or prayers for the dead, or said rosaries with which to aid them after death. None of these things have they done. And when the bells tolled, calling people to remember the dead, all they did was to go on living in their adulteries. Never once did they remember those who had gone on before them. Pass judgment on them now!

ST. MICHAEL: Here are the sacred commandments of our Holy Mother the Church. There are five of them. The first is that on Sundays and feast days you shall attend at least one mass.

LUCIFER: Never willingly have they heard mass. Daily they congregated in the taverns. They never occupied themselves with spiritual things in your sovereign presence.

ST. MICHAEL: The second commandment is that you shall confess at the time set apart for penitence in the Lenten season.

LUCIFER: They certainly never confessed when they lived on earth; nor did they ever have a desire to repent.

ST. MICHAEL: The third commandment is that you shall receive the sacred body of Jesus Chirst our Lord during the Lenten season.

LUCIFER: They have never willingly received Communion. They have aways partaken of your sacrament in sin. And if at times they did receive Communion, they went at once into the streets to enjoy themselves arrogantly, and to pass their time in pleasures and lusts. They act only with pride and a desire to make themselves attractive.

ST. MICHAEL: The fourth commandment is that you shall fast when the the Holy Church commands it.

LUCIFER: How could they fast when they were daily eating and drinking, sending out invitations to the feasts where they met together and squandered the property of the dead?

ST. MICHAEL: The fifth commandment is that tithes shall be given when the Holy Church commands it.

LUCIFER: They have certainly not done anything that was good! How then could they give anything or make any offerings? Although they received proper instructions in the sermons, all they did was to laugh at the priests. And they said: "Is this really true, or are they only trying to frighten us?" Nor have these supreme idiots ever respected mourning garments! They were always in the taverns gossiping in courtly words and committing their adulteries. They went about with their heads in the air as if they didn't know that they were giving incentives to adultery.

You are, oh just Judge, always keeping watch over them. We are in no way bearing false witness against them, for there are still more of their sins written down here. So deliver them over to us at once! May these sinners no longer be permitted to remain in your presence!

JESUS CHRIST: I keep constant watch over all of my creatures. Never do I leave them! I am ever keeping an eye on sinners. When transgressors commit offenses, I am ever measuring their acts so that I may punish them. I seize them and chastise them with torment. And as for them—how have they dared to squander, in their sinful pleasures, the wealth and property of others? How have you ruined your souls, your spirits? I created and formed you so that you might remain near to me, close to me, in my house! So that you might ever continue to serve me there. And you have delivered them into the hands of the eternal tormentors where they will suffer torture forever. You will be burned down there in the nethermost Hell; in the House-of-Smoke-without-a-Chimney, where you have thrown yourselves! What have you done with the property left in your charge by the dead who are now suffering down there in Purgatory? Why have you not helped them? Answer me! Take them away at once! May those for whom they have worked pay them! Dwellers in Hell—away with them! For they ever served you well.

FIRST
DEVIL: Your dear heart has done us a favor! You have heard our request; we thank You! Let us take them immediately down to the nethermost Hell! Oh unfortunate and accursed that you are! Let us be off to our eternal dwelling place. Hurry up! Our lord Lucifer is waiting for you!

ST. MICHAEL: Our Lord Jesus Christ has ordered you to put them on the wheel of fire. He commands that you deliver them to the House of Flames; that you put them into the Firebath-Place; that you destroy them with suffering! Take them away at once and see that the sentence pronounced on them is carried out.[11]

(They Are Taken Away. The Heavens Then Close.)

FIRST
EXECUTOR: Alas! Alas! Alas! The end has come, oh unfortunate that we are! Would that we had returned the wealth and property of those who are now dead. Alas! Alas! Alas! The end has come! Oh unfortunate that we are. Would that we had not been born! Where are you, devil of a father? Would that you had not brought me on the earth!

WIDOW: This is the end! Oh unfortunate that I am! What have my lustful pleasures brought me? Where are you who helped me to squander the money together? Come and help us! Come and save us!

THIRD
DEVIL: The time for crying is past. How will you be able to meet those from whom you took the money left in your care when they died? Come, let us be getting along. You are detaining us. Get on the march, you sinners!

(They All Go Out. Immediately They Place The Souls Of The Dead On The Fire-Wheel In The Shape Of Dummies Or Effigies. The Condemned Cry Out From Inside. They Turn Them Around [as on a spit, I assume]. Firecrackers Explode. They

Take Them Out Again And March Them Around In Procession. There Is The Sound Of A Cow Horn (a horn trumpet).)

SECOND
EXECUTOR: Alas! Alas! Alas! Hell-house, swallow us at once! Let us not behold you whose mother is the devil. And you, devils, tear us to pieces this moment. Alas! Unfortunate that we are! Take an example from us, you people who still live on earth, and return the wealth and property of others, so that what has happened to us will not happen to you!

WIDOW: Alas! Alas! Alas! You who wear mourning garments, do not give yourselves up to pleasures and mockery! You must know that you are commanded to receive Communion with penitence and prayer as well as fasting every month, when you wear them. As I have not done this, I am suffering my just punishment now. May all people take warning from me! You—women—do not act as I have done! Oh, oh, oh, oh!

THIRD
DEVIL: Companions, come, let us get them on the march. There is no way out of this now! So it doesn't matter what you condemned ones say. Get in here at once! You will soon see what will happen to you, now!

Commentary

The focus upon the cult of the dead is the essential mark of this last play. Few people are aware of the extent to which this facet of Catholicism is important in Mexico. Even today in small churches of the *pueblos* one almost invariably finds a sculptured figure or head representing the dead with hands clasped and eyes rolled heavenward, and with flames licking about the base of a slotted box to receive money for Masses for the souls of the dead. There is a surprising amount of attention directed to this, and burnt-out candles are in evidence on the altar for the dead.[12]

Purgatory was clearly styled as the place of suffering, the

Place of the Cleansing by Fire; and a spiritual working-relationship between the living and the dead was nurtured on the theory that the dead depended largely on the living to help ameliorate their suffering. Since at some future time each individual would suffer death, an effort to tie the yet-living to the Church and its sacraments was accomplished through dramatic presentation of the possible sufferings of purgatory, and much worse those of hell.

Both this play and *"The Merchant"* serve as a warning to the ordinary "citizen" to conduct his affairs with prudence. Doubtless there was a liberal amount of cheating and avaricious taking-advantage of the indigenous person whose Prehispanic legal system and customs were distinct from those he was experiencing during the early colonial period. From *"The Merchant"* we know that the imprisonment and the selling of debtors into bondage were constant threats. Consequently, the people were urged to be careful with respect to this possibility, and to invest any accumulated wealth in sacred rather than in secular activities as a kind of spiritual life insurance.

It is notable that in contemporary Mexico indigenous people rarely spend money on extra-ritual activities. The bulk of all accumulated wealth—limted as it may be—is dispensed in the ritual cycle through the *compadrinazgo* system and Saints' Days, and no particular importance is attached to wealth *per se*.[13]

In conclusion then, both in *"Wills and Testamentary Executors"* and in *"The Final Judgment"* a woman is chosen as the protagonist, the foolish one who has lived without regard for the teachings of the Church. We can only assume that women were judged to be more regularly disobedient in these respects, or that it was easier to attack a problem by using a female as a symbol of negative values than to attack the male directly. The fear of God and divine retribution is traditionally more easily instilled into women than men. The villains of the dramas such as Herod, the Jews, the insurgent kings, and the corrupt lawyers, etc. were necessarily male because of their offices or roles in the society. That the woman has a certain responsibility in directing activities of child-training and the religious sanctity of the home is suggested by the chastisements dealt to the figures of Lucia *("The Final Judgment")*, the Widow *("Wills and Testamentary Executors")*, and Hagar *("The Sacrifice of Isaac")*, when they neglected precisely these duties.

X
Epilogue

In all of these dramas, the didactic methods are clear-cut. Negative and positive values are represented by villains and spiritual-heroes. Good and evil are well-defined categories, free of theological subtleties, and the path to glory is straight—carefully marked by the Creed and the Sacraments, *fiestas* and priestly exhortations, the relics of the Christian martyrs, the symbols of Jesus, the Virgin Mary, and above all, the Saints. These all stand ready to help; they may also stand ready to condemn and torture, as do St. Helen *("How the Blessed St. Helen Found the Holy Cross")*, and the Emperor Vespasian *("The Destruction of Jerusalem")*, or Abraham *("The Sacrifice of Isaac")*. The judgment of God toward wrongdoers is, of course, invariable and total, as in *"The Final Judgment," "The Merchant,"* and *"Wills and Testamentary Executors."*

It must also be noted that a certain amount of anti-Semitic feeling is apparent in at least three of these plays: in *"The Destruction of Jerusalem," "The Adoration of the Kings,"* and most clearly in *"How the Blessed St. Helen Found the Holy Cross."* Mexico shared in the dark days of the Inquisition, and the figure of the Jew as the idealized One-who-killed-Jesus-Christ stands behind these presentations as a personalized threat to the canons of Christianity.

The total purpose of religious drama cannot be defined by the content of the small sampling which we posses of what must have been a very large corpus of literature. Certain conclusions of a preliminary nature can be drawn due to the almost invariable patterning of the extant dramas. The various values endorsed cluster heavily into several gestalts. The dramatic interludes were obviously meant to bolster up and incite desired behavior patterns. Perhaps the most basic of these values was to inculcate the beholder with a fearful respect for authority. This attitude was in agreement with rather than at odds with Prehispanic custom. In both cultures, religious and secular authority were interrelated. This respect for authority pattern is apparent in each of the dramas included in this study. A second value-gestalt is reflected in the endorsed attitudes of the individual to his church; this includes: the clarification of the role of the priest as educator and as undisputed counsellor of the right act; the theological and social necessity of complying with the fulfilment of the sacraments as defined by the Church; and the obligation of destroying whatever vestige of Prehispanic non-Christian behavior was discovered, or of adapting it sufficiently to Christian standards as to change its context and meaning: A third important value-gestalt defines behavior in the area of human interrelationships and of economic relevance. This includes modifying the structure of the family to Christian specifications, and of defining the proper expenditure of wealth through the Church and its sacraments.

However crude in language and structure these missionary dramas might be, their richness and value as a teaching-technique cannot be denied. The music, dance, colorful costumes, occasional interludes of humor, repeated idealizations, and especially the beloved saints all helped to bridge the experiential gap between the highly inflected Prehispanic religion and the new Christian ethos. They marked Mexican Roman Catholicism with the rich pattern of the *fiesta*; they permitted the cult of the saints to provide the personal and daily contact between individuals and that otherwise vague abstraction, the Church.

Schismatic fragments of the early plays still adorn the *fiestas* as dances, interludes, and brief tableaux, the original significance and context of which have often been forgotten; but they are repeated yearly by indigenous groups who carefully learn their familiar roles, and who cherish the colorful costumes and props which belong to their well-known dramatic characters.

The *Passion* has replaced the *flor y canto* of the Aztecs, and the road to Golgotha is complete. Processions of *Penitentes* and worshipfuls bearing their beloved images to the *Calvario* have long since replaced the geometry of the skull-rack beside the pyramid. The early *padres* fought their spiritual battle well and effected an essential victory. But the mountain tops are not free of spirits; now they are saints.

Notes To The Prologue
(Pages _____ — _____)

Copyright © 1969 by
The Catholic University of America Press, Inc.
All Rights Reserved

[1] The concept of "flowers" or "flowers and song" was most important in Prehispanic Indian culture. "Flower and song" represented an offering, but more precisely the best verbal offering of poetic inspiration which one could give. Since the wisdom and philosophy of the Aztecs were couched in poetic words, "flower and song" further designated the offering of inspired wisdom in esthetic terms, or poetry. Whenever the phrase "flower and song" is encountered, these connotations should be kept in mind.

[2] The "red and black" colors refer to wisdom and by metonymy to those who keep and disperse wisdom through the medium of the codices.

[3] The image of the wise man or teacher as one who places a mirror (*espejo*) before others is most important. The Aztecs had a highly developed system of education and a philosophy which supported it. The mirror which is placed before one entails the idea of measuring one's configuration or visage with that of the ideal or well-formed personality. Furthermore, the teacher himself can be considered as acting as if *he were* the mirror, thus attempting both to be and to symbolize the ideal type image. This fits in with the concept of *"rostro y corazon"* or "visage and heart." This phrase refers to the total personality or development of an individual, which is reflected in the mirror placed before one by a teacher or wise man. Shortcomings and lack of development are easily recognized and apparent.

[4] Both of these poems were taken from the *libreta* of a record entitled *Poesia nahuatl*, pp. 4-5. These poems were translated from the Nahuatl to Spanish and edited by Miguel León-Portilla The record and text were published under the direction of the National Autonomous University of Mexico (Mexico: 1962).

[5] For a brief study of this see Alfonso Caso "Importancia y caracteristicas de la religión," as well as, "Organización sacerdotal," in *México prehispanico* (Mexico: Impreso por Rafael Loera y Chavez para la Editorial Emma Hurtado, 1946), pp. 343-354, *passim.*

[6] The problem of which group, the Mayans or the Toltecs, first developed the calendar system is beyond the scope of this study. It is generally agreed, however, that the Aztecs as latecomers to the valley of Mexico did not invent or develop the calendar but rather "inherited" it from their progenitors. Rémi Siméon, *Annales de Domingo Francisco de San Anton Munon CHIMALPAHIN QUAUHTLEHUANITZIN, Sixième et Septème Relations (1258-1612Q* (Paris: Maisonneuve et Ch. Leclerc. 1889), pp. 22-29. See also Alfonso Caso's "Mecanismo del calendario azteca," *México prehispanico, op. cit.,* pp. 394-399 *passim.*

[7] Eduardo Noguera, "Huitzilopochtli," *México prehispanico, op. cit.,* pp. 454-457.

[8] Miguel León-Portilla, "Tres formas de pensamiento nahuatl," *Cuadernos del Seminario de Problemas Cientificos y Filosóficos,* No. 14, Second Series (Mexico: National Autonomous University of Mexico, 1959), pp. 50-60 *passim.*

[9] *Ibid.,* pp. 44-45. This poem was translated from Spanish into English by the author. The original in Nahuatl is from the *Informantes de Sahagún, Códice Matritense* of the Academia de la Historia, 1907. The phrase "wild signs" refers to those days the characteristics of which could not be systematically calculated. These days of the "wild sign" had a surd quality, an enigmatic and uncontrollable essence.

[10] *Ibid.,* pp. 61-62. For a more exhaustive treatment of number symbolism and cosmology see Jacques Soustelle, *La Pensée cosmologique des anciens mexicains* (Paris: Hermann et Cíe, 1940), pp. 66-85, and *passim.*

[11] León-Portilla, *op. cit.*, p. 67.

[12] *Ibid.*, p. 66.

[13] *Ibid.*

[14] It is important to know that in Nahuatl the suffix *"que"* denotes the idea of possession and closeness. For this reason, the author has chosen to translate *Tloque Nahuaque* as the Lord of the *Near* and *Far* instead of the Lord of *Everywhere*. The latter translation is essentially correct but sacrifices the concreteness of the "near" and the "far," which is directive and seems to have the self as the center of personal reference and the universe as the opposite pole of reference.

[15] León-Portilla, *op. cit.*, p. 46.

[16] The language spoken by the Aztecs is variously referred to as *nahuatl*, *mexicano*, and *azteca*. The Nahuatl language is one of many members of the larger linguistic family designated as *Uto-Aztecan*. Languages included in this family were spoken in areas throughout central, coastal (eastern), and northern Mexico, as well as in some areas now the southwestern part of the United States.

It is estimated that there are still perhaps 700,000 speakers of a somewhat changed form of *Nahuatl*, who live primarily in the highland areas surrounding the central valley of Mexico.

[17] Bernardino de Sahagún, *Florentine Codex*, trans. by Arthur J. O. Anderson and Charles E. Dibble (Santa Fe: The School of American Research and the University of Utah), Bk. II, "The Ceremonies," 1951, p. 9.

[18] *Ibid.* p. 13.

[19] *Ibid.* pp. 46 and 50.

[20] José Rojas Garcideuñas, *El teatro de Nueva Epaña en el siglo XVI* (Mexico: 1935), p. 22.

[21] Angel María Garibay, *Historia de la literatura nahautl* (Mexico: Editorial Porrua, 1953), I, 343.

[22] Gerónimo de Mendieta, *Historia eclesiastica indiana* (Mexico: Editorial Salvador Chavez Hayhoe, 1945). In Volume I, p. 153, of this work, Mendieta makes the following statement: " . . . in each village every lord had in his home a little chapel with singers, and composers of dances and songs; these sought to be most ingenious. . . ."

[23] The *teponaztli* was a wooden percussion instrument or drum made in the form of an "H," with one or two "tongues" which produced up to four sounds. It was played with rubber tipped sticks. One rarely finds a place in contemporary Mexico where this instrument is still used. Detailed descriptions of the instruments used in Prehispanic Mexico are included in Samuel Marti's, *Canto, danza, y música precortesianos* (Mexico: Fondo de Cultura Económica, 1961). For information about the *teponaztli*, see p. 335.

[24] The *huehuetl* was a large upright drum made of the trunk of a tree covered with a single or double parchment head. *Ibid.*, p. 335.

[25] Garibay, *op. cit.*, p. 352.

[26] Sahagún, *Florentine Codex, op .cit.*, VIII (Santa Fe: 1954), No. 14, Part 9, 45.

[27] Garibay, *op. cit.*, p. 353, and *passim*.

[28] *Ibid.*, pp. 346-350. Also see Miguel León-Portilla, *Aztec Thought and Culture*, trans. by Jack Emory Davis (Norman: University of Oklahoma Press, 1963), pp. 4-5, and *passim*.

[29] *Nacxitl* is another name of one of the many forms of Quetzalcoatl, especially when he is being designated as a traveler. It is nearly impossible to untangle the many names, titles, and aspects of Quetzalcoatl. The best explanation that one can offer for their variety is that "Quetzalcoatl" indicates a whole class of historic and mythological phenomena and events. Some of these refer to a deity, a priesthood, a specific priest and/or famous culture hero, or probably even to a lineage of rulers. To the Maya speakers in the South, "Kulkulcan" had a similar repertory of meanings. In the myth or poem cited in the text here, it is likely that the culture-hero-priest figure is meant. For example see León-

Portilla, *Aztec Thought and Culture, op. cit.,* pp. 19-20, 29, 43-45, 98-99, 106-112.

[30] *Tlapala* is a mythological land in the east to which Quetzalcoatl is said to have disappeared (*"La tierra del rojo,"* or "the land of the red"). Angel María Garibay, *Llave del nahuatl* (Mexico: Editorial Porrua, 1961), p. 310.

[31] Garibay, *Historia de la literatura nahuatl, op. cit.,* pp. 359-361, *passim.*

[32] Miguel León-Portilla, "Teatro nahuatl prehispanico," *La Palabra y el hombre,* February-March, 1959. No. 9 (Jalapa: Univeridad de Vera Cruz) pp. 13-15.

[33] Some of the preceding information was presented in a lecture by Miguel León-Portilla on August 22, 1961, entitled "Comedia y drama precolombinos," in the Teatro de la Universidad Nacional Autómona de México, under the auspices of the Dirección Generál de Difusión Cultural and the Teatro Estudiantil de la Universidad de México.

[34] This manuscript is folio no 75 from a collection entitled the *Cantares mexicanos.* These *cantares* are for the most part still untranslated and the unpublished manuscripts are kept in the Archives of the National Library in Mexico City. The poems included in the *cantares* were said to have been collected by Sahagún from an area near Tenochtitlan (now near the center of Mexico City). See Garibay, *Llave del nahuatl, op. cit.,* p. 120.

[35] Gerónimo de Mendieta, *Historia eclesiástica indiana* (Mexico: Editorial Salvador Chavez Hayhoe, 1945), I, 156

[36] Bernardino de Sahagún, *Informantes de Sahagún,* trans. from the Nahuatl to Spanish by Angel María Garibay and included in *Revista Tlalocan,* II, No. 3 (1947), 235. The translation into English is the author's.

[37] *Ibid.,* pp. 236-237.

[38] The dance, which was a principal element of Aztec dramatic rituals, is variously referred to by the chroniclers and other writers as the *mitote* and *arieto. Mitote* would be the more correct reference since it is derived directly from the *Nahuatl* word for dance *"mitotl." "Arieto"* is a word from the Antilles and is derived from the Arawak term *"aririn,"* meaning "to speak" or "to recite." In South America the word *"taqui"* is frequent. This derives from the Quechua *taki,* meaning "song or recitative." José Juan Arrom, *El teatro de Hispanoamérica en la epoca colonial* (Havana: Anuario Bibliográfico Cubano, 1956), p. 36.

[39] *Codex Ramirez,* entitled *Relación del origen de los indios que habitan esta Nueva Epaña, según sus historias* (Mexico: Editorial Leyenda, 1944), p. 158.

[40] "*Momoztli*" probably refers to a small house-like structure of stuccoed and painted adobe in which idols, urns, and other items used in rituals were placed. These were built within temple compounds as well as along roads. See Cecilio A. Robelo, *Diccionario de Aztequismos* (Mexico: Ediciones Fuente Cultural, 3rd ed., no date), pp. 424-425.

[41] They appearently fired upon their "game" with a sort of peashooter. It is interesting to note that many similarities between the Prehispanic ritual celebrations and contemporary Christian commemorations by the indigenous population still exist. They still practice for long periods before their religious presentations; they often use flowers and boughs to decorate their settings; the processions of the gods in their regalia are similar to the processions of the saints on their day of *fiesta.* Near Coyomeapan, Puebla, Nahua-speaking Indians still build a house of boughs and flowers in which is presented the Last Supper (the roles enacted by men) each Easter season. Figures with masks and occasionally animal skins still portray the roles of animals and spirits in certain religious celebrations.

[42] Diego F. Durán, *Historia de las Indias de Nueva España* (Mexico: Editorial Nacional, 1951), II, 231.

[43] *Ibid.,* pp. 231-232.

Vestiges of these two farcical traditions exist in the more indigenous areas of Mexico. A dramatic dance *"Los Viejitos"* like the one described is still presented in, for example, Patzcuaro, Michoacan. Similarly, the *"Guëguënce"* exemplifies the second humorous device of changed words and meanings, and subsequent deliberate misunderstanding. We have one version of this play in the Nahuatl-Spanish dialect of Nicaragua.

A similar passage is recorded by Padre José de Acosta, in the *Historia natural y moral de las Indias* (Seville: Casa de Juan de León, 1590) ; see Bk. V., pp. 391-392.

For the "Guëguënce" see *Brinton's Library of Aboriginal American Literature* (Philadelphia: 1883), No. III.

[44] Hernán Cortés, *Cartas de la relación de la conquista de Méjico* (Madrid: Espasa-Calpe, 1942), II, 37.

[45] For other details, see Ignacio Martinez Espinosa, "La estética y el significado de las pirámides." *Boletín Bibliográfico de la Secretaria de Hacienda y Crédito Público*, No. 272, Year 9, June 1, 1963.

[46] *Teatro indigena prehispanico (Rabinal Achi)* (Mexico City: Edicones de la Universidad Nacional Autónoma de México, 1955), pp. 9-91, *passim*. See also Antonio Magaña Esquivel and Ruth S. Lamb, *Breve historia del teatro mexicano*, (Mexico: Ediciones de Andrea), Manuales Studium No. 8, 1958, pp. 12-13.

[47] Pedro Sánchez de Aguilar, *Informe contra idolorum cultores del obispado de Yucatan* (Merida: E. G. Triay y Hijos, 1937), pp. 66 and 149.

[48] Other authors say that this did not develop until the twelfth century. See José Rojas Garcidueñas, *Autos y coloquios del siglo XVI* (Mexico: Ediciones de la Universidad Nacionál Autónoma, 1939), p. 8 of the introduction. Agapito Rey, *Cultura y costumbres del siglo XVI en la peninsula ibérica y en la Nueva España* (Mexico: Edicones Mensaje, 1944), p. 39.

[49] Rex Ballinger, *Orígines del teatro español y sus primeras manifestaciones en la Nueva España*, (unpublished thesis in the National Autonomous University of Mexico Library), pp. 11-12.

[50] *Ibid.*, p. 13.

[51] *Ibid.*, pp. 17-18.

[52] *The Catholic Encyclopedia* (New York: The McGraw-Hill Co., 1967), Vol. IV, pp. 345-347.

[53] Alfonso Reyes, "Los autos sacramentales en España y en América," *Boletín de la Academia de Letras*, V (Buenos Aires, 1937), 350-352.

[54] According to the Royal Academy of Spain, an *auto* is a "dramatic presentation of brief dimension in which Biblical or allegorical characters take part. Such a composition may be called sacramental when it is written for the purpose of praising the mystery of the Eucharist." This is a quotation from C. E. Castaneda, "The First American Play," *Preliminary Studies of the Texas Catholic Historical Society* (Austin: St. Edward's University), III, No. 1 (January, 1936), 7.

[55] Gil Vincente, Lope de Vega, and Calderón are perhaps the best known and most creative of the writers who consistently used the *auto sacramental* as a medium. In this study we shall not be concerned with this literary or humanistic theater except as it is related to the didactic or missionary theater of the early colonial period.

[56] Marianne Oeste de Bopp, *Influencia de los misterios y autos europeos en los de México* (unpublished thesis of the Faculty of Philosophy and Letters of the National Autonomous University of Mexico, 1952), pp. 98-100.

[57] Bernal Díaz del Castillo, *The Discovery and Conquest of Mexico* (New York: Farrar, Strauss, and Cudahy, 1956), pp. 76 and 63.

[58] Joaquin Garcia Icazbalceta, "La instrucción pública en México durante el siglo XVI," *Obras, opúsculos varios* (Mexico: Imprenta de V. Agüeros, 1896), I, 163-170, *passim*.

[59] Torquemada went to Mexico as a child, and subsequently entered the convent of San Francisco in 1579. He acted as guardian of the convent of Tulancingo in 1602, and of Tlaxcala in 1612, and later also of Tlaltelolco. In 1614 he was elected Superior of the Province of the Holy Gospel. He was more important politically than Sahagún, but not as important for the information he gathered.

Sahagún worked with a select group of Indian informants for many years and was the most careful and adept chronicler of them all.

⁶⁰ Juan de Torquemada, *Monarquía indiana*, (Mexico: Editorial Salvador Chavez Hayhoe, 1944), III, Bk. 15, c. 13, p. 31.

⁶¹ Male children were dedicated shortly after birth to the school which they were later to attend. These schools were of two kinds, the *calmecac* and the *telpochcalli*. In the *calmecac*, students were trained for the priesthood and for adult positions of religious and political authority. The curriculum included the religious and historical traditions of the Aztecs, their knowledge of nature, and especially of astronomy, the calendar, the painting and reading of the codices, and in general the intellectual tradition of the Nahuatl speakers. In the *telpochcalli*, the youth were trained in their religious and historical heritage, but with a special emphasis on warfare; they became the military bulwark of their culture.

Female students were dedicated to special schools for training in religion and ritual practices; some ultimately became priestesses.

Discipline was rigorous in all the Aztec educational institutions and included not only enforced study but also religious and devotional activities such as fasting, dancing, acts of penitence, and rote learning of the complex rituals.

It was the pattern for sons of the *señores* to be dedicated to the *calmecac*, but this possibility was open to children of the commoners or *macehuales* as well, if their parents dedicated them to this type of school at the birth ceremonies.

⁶² García Icazbalceta, *op. cit.*, pp. 165-170, *passim*.

⁶³ García Icazbalceta, "Representaciones religiosas de México en el siglo XVI," *Obras, opúsculos varios, op. cit.* II, 311.

⁶⁴ Joaquin García Icazbalceta, *Bibliografía mexicana del siglo XVI, Catálogo razonado de libros impresos en México de* 1539 *a* 1600 (Mexico: Fondo de Cultura Económica, 1954), pp. 94-95.

⁶⁵ *Ibid.*, p. 64.

⁶⁶ Gerónimo de Mendieta, *Vidas franciscanas*, (Mexico: Imprenta Universitaria, 1945), pp. 43-48.

⁶⁷ *Ibid.*, pp. 44-45.

⁶⁸ García Icazbalceta, *Bibliografía, mexicana, op cit.*, p. 96.

⁶⁹ *Ibid.*, p. 103.

⁷⁰ The question of the propriety of extending the sacraments to an indigenous and basically uneducated populace was a thorny and complex one. Ricard presents the most succinct and comprehensive discussion of this matter. Robert Ricard, *La conquête spirituelle du mexique, op. cit., trans.* by Lesley Byrd Simpson, pp. 104-109; *The Spiritual Conquest of Mexico* (Berkley and Los Angeles: University of California Press) 1966.

⁷¹ This work was discovered in 1924 and published by Poú and Marti as *El libro de las platicas o Coloquios de los doce primeros misioneros de México, Miscellanea Francesco*, Ehrle III (Rome: 1924), 281-333.

⁷² They then proceeded to explain about the God whose sole representative upon earth is the Pope, the Scripture, and the Church. To a people whose culture had supported a traditional ritual of role-playing of gods and spirits, this was an important point to be understood.

⁷³ Robert Ricard, *op. cit.*, p. 108.

⁷⁴ *Codice franciscano*, (Mexico: Editorial Salvador Chavez Hayhoe, 1941), p. 55.

⁷⁵ *Ibid.*, pp. 29-54, *passim*.

⁷⁶ Marianne Oeste de Bopp, "Autos mexicanos del siglo XVI" *Historia Mexicana*, III, No. 9 (July-August, 1953), 112-116.

⁷⁷ Francisco A. Icaza, "Orígines del Teatro en México:, *Boletín de la Real Academia Española*, II (1915), 57.

⁷⁸ José de Acosta, *The Naturall and Moral Historie of the East and West Indies*, trans. by Edward Grimstone. (London: Printed by Val Sims for Edward Blount and William Aspley, 1604), II, 445-447.

[79] This translation was made from the French text as given by Ricard, since the author was unable to consult the original source. Ricard, *op. cit.*, p. 247. Bautista's *Confessionatio* was published in Mexico in 1599.

[80] For more information about this, see Garibay, *Historia de la literatura nahuatl, op. cit.*, II, 97. For the text itself see Francisco Lorenzana, *Consilios provinciales* (Mexico: 1769), pp. 146-148.

[81] For most of the basic information in this section concerning early religious poetry, I am indebted to *Padre* Garibay. The translations included here are from his published Spanish texts. The Nahuatl originals are difficult either to consult or decipher. See Garibay, *Historia de la literatura nahuatl, op. cit.*, II, 95-119, *passim*.

[82] *Ibid.*, pp. 103-104.

[83] The original of this poem appears in *Cantares mexicanos, op. cit.* folio 41, lines 30-41.

[84] These lines refer to Herod's order commanding all the newborn male children of Bethlehem be killed, so that whoever might be a threat to his rule would in this way be destroyed. The "precious bracelets" and the "plumage of the quetzal" refer to these children.

[85] *Cantares mexicanos, op. cit.* folio 38, lines 9-25.

[86] *Ibid.*, folio 39, lines 1-10; 2-27.

[87] Garibay judges that this song was presented probably during 1530 or 1531; the manuscript mentions the arrival of the bishop, probably Fuenleal, who was in Mexico City from 1531 until 1535.

[88] *Cantares mexicanos, op. cit.* folio, *op cit.* 48, lines 17 ff.

[89] *Ibid.*, lines 20 ff.

[90] *Ibid.*, folio 47, lines 17 ff. For a reference to the sorrow of the Indians (over the death of Gante, see Mendieta, *Vidas franciscanas, op. cit.*, p. 48.

[91] With reference to this data also see García Icazbalceta, "Representaciones religiosas de México en el siglo XVI", *op. cit.*, p. 343.

[92] As nearly as the author can determine, the Nahuatl manuscript of this play is in the *Archivo* of the *Instituto Nacional de Antropología e Historia* in Mexico City. The library officials were unable to locate it; however, a microfilm of the original is included in the former Benjamin Franklin Library collection of John Cornyn's and Byron MacAfee's manuscripts and paleographic copies, which is now housed in the library of the historical museum in Chapultepec Park, Mexico City.

[93] This quotation was taken from John H. Cornyn's "Aztec Literature", *International Congress of Americanists, Twenty-third Congress* (Mexico: Instituto Nacional de Antropología e Historia, 1947), II, 334.

[94] García Icazbalceta, "Representaciones religiosas de México en el siglo XVI", *op. cit.*, p. 344.

[95] Bernardino de Sahagún, *Historia de las cosas de Nueva España*, edited and annotated by Angel María Garibay (Mexico: Editorial Porrua, 1956), II, Bk. 8, ch. 2, 287.

[96] Garibay, *Historia de la literatura nahuatl, op. cit.*, II, 131.

[97] Rojas Garcidueñas, *El teatro de Nueva España en el siglo XVI, op. cit.*, p. 44.

[98] Mendieta, *Historia eclesiástica indiana, op. cit.*, IV, Bk. V, ch. 33, 94.

[99] Library of Congress Manuscript Division, AC 1139, III, 48-C, 4.

[100] Garibay, *Historia de la literatura nahuatl, op. cit.*, II, 131.

[101] Joaquín García Icazbalceta, *Bibliografía mexicana del siglo XVI* (Catálogo razonado de libros impresos en México de 1539-1600) (Mexico: Librería de Andrade y orales, Sucesores, 1886), pp. 19-20. This source was later republished (Mexico City: Fondo de Cultura Económica, 1954).

[102] Mendieta, *Historia, op. cit.*, IV, Bk. 5, ch. 34, 98. Juan de Torquemada, *Monarquía, op. cit.*, III, ch. 39, 47.

[103] Toribio Motolinía, *History of the Indians of New Spain*, trans. by E. A. Foster; see p. 101, n. 1.

[104] *Ibid.*, pp. 101-102. See, also, Torquemada, *op. cit.*, III, 220 ff.

[105] *Ibid.*, pp. 102-103.

[106] The ability to memorize lengthy passages both well and rapidly is still notable among the Indians of Mexico; they still celebrate their *fiestas* with occasional long drama. The longtime maintenance of a rich oral tradition undoubtedly explains this faculty to memorize and retain long passages of speeches as well as songs.

[107] Note here the similarity of this kind of comical interlude with that previously noted in describing the Güeguënce. Contrast this further with what Durán, *op. cit.*, p. 231, says about the presentation of comical farces.

[108] Motolinía, *History of the Indians of New Spain*, *op. cit.*, p. 109.

[109] Armando María y Campos, *Guia de representaciónes teatrales en la Nueva España*, (Mexico: Costa-Amic, 1959), p. 40. See also Rojas Garcidueñas, *El teatro de Neuva España en el siglo XVI*, *op. cit.*, p. 46, for a paraphrase of this idea.

From Puebla de los Angeles there is a short report from the *cabildo* records of 1538 agreeing that they should back the production on *Corpus Christi* of a *"comedia"* in the cathedral. Since no mention of language or title is given here, we can assume that the drama was in Spanish for a Spanish-speaking audience.

[110] See the Icazbalceta's introduction to Hernán González de Esclava's *Coloquios espirituales y sacramentales y poesías sagradas* (Mexico: Ant. Librería Portal de los Agustinos, No. 3, 1877), pp. 20-21.

[111] Motolinía, *History of the Indians of New Spain*, *op. cit.*, p. 118.

[112] *Ibid.*, pp. 119-120.

[113] José Rojas Garcidueñas, "Los primeros misioneros y el teatro de evangelización", *Divulgacion Historica*, I, No. 11 (September 15, 1940), 52.

[114] Rojas Garcidueñas, *El teatro de Nueva España en el siglo XVI*, *op. cit.*, p. 52.

[115] "Tlacahuapahualiztli", *Tlalocan*, trans. and ed. by John H. Cornyn and Byron McAfee, I, No. 4 (1944), 314-351.

[116] *Ibid.*, p. 351.

[117] *"Hueyhueytlatolli"* means "counsels of the elders". There has been a translation into Spanish and publication of a *"Hueyhueytlatolli"* by Garibay. See *"Hueyhueytlatolli"*, *Tlalocan*, I, No. 2 (1943), 31-53.

Since the language of the "Hueyhueytlatolli" is literary and pure in quality rather than vulgar, we must have a version which was written in the sixteenth century, close to the time of the Conquest. It had been kept in the culture of the Nahuatl speakers before this but, of course, only as a part of the oral tradition.

[118] Garibay, *Historia de la literatura nahuatl*, *op. cit.*, II, 129-130.

[119] A *macana* is a wooden weapon, generally edged with sharp flint, used by the Aztec warriors.

[120] Garibay, *Historia de la literatura nahuatl*, *op cit.*, II, 141.

[121] *Ibid.*, p. 142.

[122] Armando María y Campos, *op. cit.*, p. 54.

[123] The *pallium* is a stole presented by the pope to an archbishop as a mark of special distinction. It is also that which covers the host when it is borne in any procession, more commonly called a pall.

[124] This play has been published in Rojas Garcidueñas, *Autos y coloquios del siglo XVI*, *op. cit.* pp. 41-77. There are extant two manuscript copies of this play: one in the *Biblioteca Naciondl de México*, and another in Spain.

As noted, the play is in Spanish, and many of the speeches and songs conclude with cuplets or are entirely composed in a fairly elementary Latin.

[125] It must be noted, however, that dramas of a purely religious theme and flavor were often designated as *"comedias"*; this classification—correctly or incorrectly in literary terms—seems to have increased in the seventeenth century.

[126] Rojas Garcidueñas, *El teatro de Nueva España en el siglo XVI*, *op. cit.*, p. 98.

[127] *Ibid.*, pp. 50-51; See García Icazbalceta, "Representaciones religiosas de Mexico en el siglo XVI", *op. cit.*, p. 339.

[128] Agustín Dávila Padilla *Historia de la fundación y discurso de la provincia de Santiago de México de la Orden de Predicadores.* (Mexico: 1596), Vol. II, Ch. 28.
[129] Harvey Leroy Johnson, *An Edition of "Triunfo de los Santos",* (Philadelphia: University of Pennsylvania Press, 1941).
[130] See Jose Rojas Garcidueñas, "Fiesta en México en 1578", *Anales del Instituto de Investigaciónes Estéticas, op. cit.,* IX (Mexico: 1942), 33-57, *passim;* Icazbalceta, pp. 353-354 and Harvey Johnson, *op. cit., passim.*
[131] Dávila Padilla, *op. cit.,* pp. 89-94. Holy Week is still commemorated in Mexico, especially among the indigenous peoples, by a *Passion* or a series of dramas depicting the events of Holy Week as described in the New Testament. The following are favorite subjects for dramatization: *"El Gran Concilio del Sanedrin"* ("The Great Trial of the Sanhedrin"); *"La Cena"* ("The Last Supper"); *"El Lavatorio"* ("The Washing of the Disciples by Christ"); *"El Procurador Romano Poncio Pilato"* (The Roman Judge Pontius Pilate"); *"Las Tres Caídas"* ["The Three Falls" (of Christ while bearing the cross)]; *"Camino al Monte Calvario"* ("The Road to Calvary"). The latter usually involves a procession of the *Cristo de los Trabajos* (The Christ of Labors) and *La Soledad* (The Sorrowing Mother) through the streets of the village, and sometimes to a hill nearby dedicated as the *"Calvario".*
[132] Mendieta, *op. cit.,* pp. 83-84. Mendieta also refers to the beauty of the floral decorations and processions organized by the Indians and describes the dances performed by the beautifully costumed children to the tunes of "devout couplets" which "singers chant together with the musicians".
Fray Gerónimo de Mendieta went to Mexico in June of 1554; he studied Nahuatl and soon became proficient in it. In his *Historia* he describes both the history and the customs of the Indians, and also refers at length to the work of the Franciscans.
[133] The indigenous languages of this area are of the Uto-Aztecan linguistic group.
[134] Icazbalceta, "Representaciónes religiosas de México en el siglo XVI", *op. cit.,* pp. 340-341. We know from other sources that the practice of a liturgical and missionary drama was common in the southwestern part of the United States, and, in general, wherever the Roman Catholic Church was established in the Americas. See Sister Joseph Marie, *The Role of the Church and the Folk in the Development of the Early Drama in New Mexico* (Philadelphia, University of Pennsylvania Press, 1948).
[135] Manuel Pazos, "El teatro franciscano en México durante el siglo XVI", *Archivo Iberoamericano* (Madrid), XI, No. 42 (April-June 1951), 142. The work to which we have referred as being written by Motolinía in 1585 is *Relación de la descripción de la Provincia del Santo Evangelio.*
[136] Torquemada, *Monarquía indiana, op cit.,* III, 45.
[137] "Paso" is the name also given to the image carried about in processions during Holy Week. See Rojas Garcidueñas, *El teatro de Nueva España en el siglo XVI, op. cit.,* pp. 52-53.
[138] Pazos, *op. cit.,* p. 144. If any of these manuscripts are still extant, the author has been unable to locate them. Rojas Garcidueñas, *op. cit.,* p. 53.
[139] Chocho-Popoloca is a member of the large family of Oto-Manqueyan languages. The Mixtec language is tonal and very complex; it belongs to the larger language family bearing its name, "Mixtecan".
[140] Estéban Arroyo, *Los dominicos, forjadores de la civilización oajaqueña,* Vol. I, *Los misioneros* (Mexico: Imprenta "Camarena", 1958), pp. 273-279.
[141] The *Invención* is one of the plays included in this study; for this reason, nothing further will be mentioned about it now.
The cast of the *Cuaderno* includes Cortés, Moctezuma, the Malinche, Chimalpopocatzin (Moctezuma's messenger), an archer, and an executioner, Moctezuma's princes, and the soldiers of Cortés. This manuscript has been published with parallel texts in Nahuatl and Spanish in *"Un Cuaderno de Marqueses",* trans. and ed. by Byron McAfee and Robert Barlow, in *El México*

antiquo, VI, Nos. 9-12 (March 1947), 392-404. For a more modern Spanish version on the same theme, see Frances Gillmor, "Spanish Texts of Three Dance Dramas from Mexican Villages". University of Arizona, Humanities Bulletin, XIII, No. 4.

[142] Garibay, *Historia de la literatura nahuatl, op cit.*, pp. 132-133. The title of this play is "La pasion del Domingo de Ramos" ("The Passion of Palm Sunday"). To the author's knowledge, it has never been published, but a microfilm copy of an English translation is contained in the collection of the Historical Library at the Museum in Chapultepec, Mexico City.

[143] The Nahuatl manuscript of the *Coloquio* with notes by Paso y Troncoso is located in the Archives of the National Institute of Anthropology and History in Mexico City. A microfilm of a Spanish translation by Chimalpopoca is in the collection at Chapultepec; the original is supposed to be in the New York Public Library. A microfilm of the Nahuatl version of *"El portento mexicano"* is also in the Chapultepec collection. This latter was made from a manuscript in the Cathedral of Guadalupe collection, with a translation into Spanish by one Ramirez, dated November 12, 1856. There is also a photostatic copy of this play in the Libreta 7 (14) 182 of Paso y Troncoso in the Archives of the National Institute of Anthropology and History.

[144] For example, see *Libreta* 7, the original number of which was changed from 182 to 22; and *Legajo*, No. 25, Paquete 20, of Paso y Troncoso.

[145] Fernando Horcasitas Pimentel, "Piezas teatrales en lengua nahuatl; Bibliografía descriptiva", *Boletin bibliográfico de antropología americana*, XI (Mexico: Instituto Panamericano de Georgrafía e Historia, 1949).

[146] María y Campos, *op. cit.*, p. 51.

[147] Antonio Magana Esquivel, and Ruth S. Lamb, *Breve historia del teatro mexicano* (Mexico: Ediciones de Andrea, 1958), Manuales Studium No. 8, 1958, pp. 17-19.

Alfonso Mendez Plancarte, "Piezas teatrales en Nueva España del XVI", *Abside*, VI, No. 2, (April-June, 1942) 218-224, *passim*. The latter contains information about sixteenth-century dramas not strictly missionary in essence but celebrating ecclesiastical or civil events of note.

[148] Hildburg Schilling, *Teatro profano en la Nueva España* (Mexico: Imprenta Universitaria, 1958), pp. 151-153.

[149] María y Campos, *op. cit.*, p. 151

[150] C. E. Castañeda, "The First American Play", *Preliminary Studies of the Texas Catholic Historical Society* (Austin: St. Edward's University), III, No. 1. (January 1936), 5-14. There is also a Spanish version of this play in Rojas Garcidueñas, *El teatro de Nueva España en el siglo XVI, op. cit.*, pp. 182-221.

[151] Garibay, *Historia de la literatura nahuatl, op. cit.*, II, 157.

[152] Charles Gibson, *Tlaxcala in the Sixteenth Century* (New Haven: Yale University Press, 1952), pp. 89-90.

[153] In 1959 the author interviewed several indigenous individuals living on the skirts of the Malinche (the mountain) in the State of Tlaxcala who knew the names of these last four kings but were unable to name the two former presidents of Mexico.

[154] Robert Ravicz, "La Mixteca en el estudio comparativo del hongo alucinante," *Anales del Instituto Nacional de Antropología e Historia*, XIII, No. 42 (1961), 73-92, *passim*. See also V. P. and R. G. Wasson, *Mushrooms Russia and History* (New York: Pantheon Books, 1957), II, 218-228, and 255-274, *passim*.

[155] Castañeda, *op. cit.*, p. 13.

[156] This translation was made from a quotation in Hildburg Schilling, *op. cit.*, p. 166.

[157] García Icazbalceta, Representaciones religiosas de México en el siglo XVI," *op. cit.*, pp. 349-350.

[158] Pazos, *op. cit.*, p. 137.

[159] *Documentos inéditos muy raros para la historia de México*, ed. by Genaro

García, No. XV, of *El clero de México durante la dominación española,* (Mexico: Librería de la Viuda de Ch. Bouret, 1907), LXXXI, 141.
[160] García Icazbalceta, *Representaciones, op. cit.,* p. 352.
[161] Genaro García, *op. cit.,* II, folio 56; est. 2, caj. 2, leg. 3, p. 245.
[162] *Ibid.,* No. XC, p. 195.
[163] García Icazbalceta, *Representaciones,* p. 353.
[164] *Actas de Cabildo de Puebla,* lib. 12, folio 110. This is also included in Schilling, *op. cit.,* p. 13.
[165] The author has seen an excellent example of the use of the *tablado* method of presentation in the village of Hueyotlipan in Puebla. On that occasion (during the Holy Week celebrations in 1963), the square in front of the cathedral was the area used. The procession came out of the cathedral and moved around the square. At each corner of the square a *tablado* had been constructed. In this way, as the procession including the cast of characters moved around, it stopped at the various *tablados*. The first one was entitled (with a painted sign) "Gran Sanhedrin," and here the trial of Christ was enacted. The procession then moved to another *tablado* where Pilate and his consort were enthroned. Here the final pronouncement and handwashing to free himself of the guilt of Christ's death were enacted by Pilate. The crowd viewing the spectacle both filled the square and followed the procession and cast from *tablado* to *tablado*. Stagee props were simple, but painted drops were used as well as furniture.
[166] William Hutchinson Shoemaker, *The Multiple Stage in Spain during the Fifteenth and Sixteenth Centuries* (Princetons Princeton University Press, 1935), *passim.*

Notes to The Sacrifice of Issac

(Pages _____ — _____)

[1] The problem of the proper education of youth was a serious preoccupation for the indigenous peoples of Mexico. Perhaps this is the principal reason for the rapid and complete adoption of the *compadrinazgo* system early in the colonial period. The main purpose of the *compadrinazgo* (godparent system) was precisely to care for the spiritual education of the children in the absence or default of the parents. Since the *compadrinazo* helped to inculcate accepted Christian values, it grew to have socio-economic and cultural implications in Indian Mexico far beyond those in European Roman Catholicism. See Robert Ravicz, "The Compadrinazgo," *Handbook of Middle American Indians* (Austin: University of Texas Press 1967), VI, 238-252, *passim.*
[2] The kind of metaphor used here is typical of prehispanic Nahuatl poetry. Children were often likened to jewels or gold. They were considered as ornaments worn by and, therefore, beautifying the parent. They were judged as valuable as are all things of beauty.
[3] The staging of this play is problematic. When the word "enter" is used, one is not certain that the character entered into some kind of *cabaña* or stage device which represented the house, or whether, if the drama were presented outside the church, the characters entered the church as they went offstage. The description of the music here is *"música de viento"* in Spanish, which literally means "wind instrument music." Since it is most unlikely that reed instruments were meant here, the most informed guess would be that flutes were used.
[4] That the "angel" could appear either as an old man or as an angel is interesting. In Aztec culture, the *"anciano"* or old man is to be treated with great deference and respect. He is the repository of knowledge and his advice is to be heeded. On the other hand, a genuine "angel" from heaven would also be paid respect and obeisance.

[5] The entirety of this speech is most interesting in relation to indigenous educational practices. It was customary for the father to give advice to his children in this measured and rhetorical manner. The qualities which the beautiful things of nature such as jewels and flowers possess are admirable; thus, the phrase ". . . feel as a precious stone and think as a pearl." The early priests often used this same manner of speech in their homilies. They took the standardized speeches of the *hueyhueytlatolli,* substituted Christian saints and God for the indigenous deities, and continued to use them both in church and in mission schools. Thus such a homiletic message as an interlude between father and son was completely comprehensible to an indigenous audience. The audience also understood the importance of the banquet scene which follows. Abraham had obviously invited his kinsmen to present Isaac to them. For this reason, Isaac's deportment as a young noble had to be impeccable as a reflection of the quality of his rearing.

[6] It is notable that the apparent "villain" of the play is a sunworshipper. He directs his supplications to the sun instead of the Christian God. Since the sun was one of the most important deity-symbols before the conquest, there must have been a constant battle against tendencies to slip back into the old pattern of the Prehispanic beliefs.

[7] The idea that the love of the father for the son is subject to fluctuation with the obedience of the son is a clue to the importance which was placed on obedience, both filial and religious.

[8] Both the Nahuatl and the Spanish texts here use the phrase *"rostro y corazon."* It is also used in the following speech of Abraham's where it is translated as "understanding." The connotation, as was explained in the introduction, is that of designating the whole personality, the individual plus his thoughts and ideas.

[9] It is possible that a small "mountain" of some kind was actually constructed as part of the scenario. We know from the previous references cited from the chroniclers that such elaboration in setting was not uncommon.

Notes to The Merchants

[1] Here again we note the concept of evil or sin which seems to link the physical condition of the body with the spiritual. Mexican Catholicism is more conditioned to this way of thinking then are other subgroups of Roman Catholics. There is in Mexico a greater plethora of miraculous cures incorporating both the magical elements of the Prehispanic and contemporary indigenous curing techniques with flourishes of *Ave Marias* and appeals to the Saints.

[2] Angel María Garibay, *Vida económica de Tenochtitlan. L. Pochtecáyotl (arte de traficar)* (Mexico: Universidad Nacional Antónoma de México, 1961).

[3] Charles Gibson, *The Aztecs under Spanish Rule* (Stanford: Stanford University Press, 1964), pp. 264-267 and 356-360, *passim.*

Notes to the Adoration of Kings

[1] The author translated Ponce's account from the Paso y Troncoso edition of *"Adoración de los Reyes"* (Florence: Salvador Landi, 1899), pp. 69-71. The original is found in Alonso Ponce. *Relación breve y verdadera de algunas cosas de las muchas que sucedieron al padre F. Alonso Ponce en las provincias de la Nueva España* (Madrid: Imprenta de la Viuda a de Calero, 1875) II, 39-45.

[2] The author has seen *paxtli;* this term includes both Spanish moss as well as some of the larger species of ground mosses. *Paxtli* is still referred to and described as that which one places in creches for any presentation or tableau of the manger scene at Christmas time. A secondary use is as a shock-absorber in packing.

³ *Chicuitle* is a carrying basket, probably of small size and woven of plant fibers. See Alonso de Molina, *Colección de incunables americanos, siglo XVI, IV, Vocabulario en lengua castellana y mexicana* (Madrid: Ediciones Cultura Hispanica, 1944), 24. This edition is a fascimile of the original edition printed in Mexico in 1571.

⁴ A literal translation of the Nahuatl would state, "we kiss his hands and his feet four-hundred times." This "four-hundred" is the usual designation meaning "repeatedly," "on and on." This was also a stereotyped greeting designating great respect in Prehispanic times. See *Hueyhueytlatolli*, edited by Garibay, *op. cit.*, pp. 52-90.

⁵ Again the directions give us a hint as to the staging of the play. The "ups" and "downs" designate at the least that Herod is seated on a raised dais. It is most likely that this portion of the play was presented outside the church, probably in the courtyard before the main entry.

⁶ It is interesting to note that the character portrayals of the noble and kingly figures in the play are very much in keeping with the Prehispanic values accruing to social position and wealth. A visiting Aztec lord would also have been made welcome through music, dance, and other marks of respect.

⁷ This latter phrase is a standardized way of referring to and defining a deity in Aztec tradition. This translation is as literal as possible for good sense. The idea is that "godness" is omnipresent, but that the accent is on interiority. See *Hueyhueytlatolli, op. cit.*, pp. 39, 41, 45, 47, 50, 83, 85, 95.

⁸ Such portents were thoroughly familiar to the indigenous peoples of Mexico. They were accustomed to seeing "faces" and "forms" in the heavenly bodies, the most familiar of which was perhaps *"Tochtli,"* the Rabbit god, who was clearly seen in the moon at certain periods.

⁹ The flaying and deep-frying of animal skins for food was, and is, a common practice in Mexico. It was a double insult, one should suppose, to threaten the Jews with turning them into "pork-cracklings." In Mexico, this is called *"chicharrón."*

In Prehispanic Mexico, there was at least one *fiesta* at which captives were literally flayed, and their skins were subsequently donned by the priests. I doubt that this passage has any reference to this practice. This allusion might have been recalled, however, in sarcastic or satirical threats such as these.

¹⁰ The staging of this play becomes clearer as the directions become more detailed. The interludes involving the Kings, Herod, and the Jews obviously occur outside the church, probably in the courtyard. The actual *nacimiento* scenes involving the Holy Family are inside the church, perhaps immediately inside the doorway, and therefore visible to the audience gathered outside. The *capilla abierta* would have adapted itself most admirably to this kind of production.

¹¹ Note the nahuatlisms in the description referring to the Christ Child. The references to a beloved child as "rich plumage" or as a "precious jewel" is typical.

¹² The symbol of the "load" as that which a king must bear on behalf of his ancestors and his subjects was standard in Prehispanic Aztec tradition. In this passage, the sense is that the prophets and earlier kings had received and interpreted the word of God with relation to their people (the Jews) and thus prepared the way for the future birth of the King or "Messiah," whose task in turn was clearly to assume the burden of rule and prophecy as his own role. See *Hueyhueytlatolli, op. cit.*, p. 84. A dead king is referred to as one who has laid down his *cacaxtli* or burden.

¹³ It is the author's opinion that this rather obscure passage refers to the devil and his attempts to walk about destroying the works and preparations of the prophets even in the moment of their apparent actualization.

¹⁴ This passage is undoubtedly couched in this fashion for didactic purposes in an effort to dispel the Prehispanic Aztec cosmological interpretation of the earth as living, a child of divine forces or "parents."

¹⁵ *Copal,* the congealed sap or resin of the ocotl or pine trees is the most

familiar form of incense used during ritual occasions in Mexico. Its use for the same purpose was equally popular in Prehispanic times.

[16] The author assumes that this image refers to the Cross which Christ will take up; that is, not only will Christ assume the burden of his Kingship but he will also have to assume physically that which brings about or is the instrument for his travail and suffering-in-labor.

[17] There are several places in Mexico where single *interludes* from the action of this play are still presented. Few places still produce it in its entirety. For example, as late as 1961 in Tehuacan, Puebla, and surrounding villages, it was the custom for the three kings, costumed and on horseback, to ride about the square and to enter the church to make offerings to the newborn Christ. People, seated in a group near the altar, also enacted the roles of the Holy Family. The *posadas*, or nightly searchings of the Holy Family to find lodgings and refuge for the birth of Christ, are widely practiced. When the people of Tehucan were asked if they planned to continue presenting the interlude of the Three Kings, the response was affirmative, with the qualification that the bishop be absent at this time; he discouraged such theatrical presentations.

[18] Fray Toribio Motolinía, *History of the Indians of New Spain*, translated by E. A. Foster, *op. cit.*, p. 39 ff. See García Icazbalceta, *Bibliografía mexican del siglo XVI, op. cit.*, pp. 19-20. Also see Angel María Garibay, *Historia de la literatura nahuatl, op. cit.*, II, 131.

Notes To The Final Judgment

[1] I have been informed that there is another English copy of this play under the name of John H. Cornyn in the Library of Congress.

[2] The indigenous people of Mexico were not unfamiliar with the idea that the world would come to an end. They had a doctrine in Prehispanic times which propounded the periodic destruction of the world. This doctrine of the "suns" was briefly explained in the introductory part of this study. The Aztecs had no doctrine of personal divine judgment, however. They conceived of "places" to which people might journey or go after their life on earth. Women who died after childbirth went to a place in the sky (roughly corresponding to the Milky Way; and warriors and those who died in battle went to another place; and those who died of anything related to water (drowning, dropsy, hydrocepholitis, etc.) went to *Tlalocan*. No particular joy or repose connected with these places is known; one's fate merely seemed to be completed by this last step in human destiny. They had no highly developed concept of personal sin or guilt. They did, however, have a concept of personal "good" or "evil" although this seemed to be more related to human destiny or fate than to human freedom and individual responsibility. This latter idea is what the Christian missionaries tried to instill. Results of poor deportment seemed to have been primarily avoided because they upset the social pattern and were immediately punished and did not contain the idea of anything like everlasting penance or suffering attributed to an ontological dimension of guilt or expiation.

[3] The Nahuatl here is literally "Oh, four hundred times unfortunate. . . ." Here, as noted before, "four hundred" is the figure used to denote any large number or a profound degree.

[4] Note the severity of this condemnation. The priest hears the confession but is unable to offer help or absolution because of the degree of the serious sin committed by Lucia. A cardinal sin requires a different kind of treatment.

[5] This concept of the termination of the world and time is interesting to note. It implies that God is bringing about the end of the world *because* the people of the earth have "defiled things through their evil deeds." Whether or not this was the conscious view of the priest who composed the drama, it agrees admirably with the old Aztec view that in part the responsibility for the preservation of the world belongs to men.

They apparently believed that the responsibility for the "feeding" of the gods was the ritual counterpart for the conceptual framework which implied that man had a duty with ontological proportions regarding the maintenance of the created world.

[6] These phrases which describe "heaven" are clearly nahuatlisms. Jewels and flowers are the qualifiers of that which is most precious and desirable.

[7] The emphasis here on the fact that the dead are to assemble their bones and resume their bodies in order to be judged is patent. The Prehispanic practice had usually been cremation of the dead, and the Church had a particular battle to fight against this custom.

[8] The stage directions of this play give us clues as to the possible stage devices used. Heaven was probably portrayed on either a raised platform, possibly curtained off, or portrayed on a raised *tablado* or kind of stage within the general area.

[9] Again we note that the stage directions are for the actors to "ascend" to heaven. It is possible that the altar was used as the heaven. The church would have had to be very large, however, both to permit the presence of several characters on the altar at the same time, and to make the use of fireworks not too dangerous. For this latter reason, I believe that this play was presented in the courtyard of the church.

[10] The use of the serpent as a symbol had double connotations to an indigenous audience to whom Christianity was being preached. In the corpus of Christian thought, the serpent has been connected with temptation, evil, and human failing. To the Prehispanic Aztec, however, the serpent was a most powerful symbol of positive value and significance; it was the symbol and embodiment of Quetzalcoatl, among other things, and all that he connoted. It was important for the first missionaries to put the serpent in its proper Christian context, that of evil, and to stop any reverence which might be directed toward it.

Notes To How The Blessed St. Helen Found The Holy Cross

[1] See Francisco Paso y Troncoso, *Invención de la Santa Cruz por Santa Elena* (Coloquio), who states that it was probably composed by Don Manuel de los Santos y Salazar (Mexico: Imprenta del Museo Nacional, 1890).

[2] Among the notes of Paso y Troncoso is the following information about Santos y Salazar. He apparently was descended from a noble or important family, as "Santos y Salazar" had often ruled in Tlaxcala since 1563. Our priest-copyist said his first Mass in October of 1685, in Santa Maria Acuitlapilco, Tlaxcala. He had been in charge of Santa Cruz and died in August of 1715.

[3] The sense of this passage is somewhat obscure. Theodoricus and Victorillo are probably making light of the Prehispanic custom of ritual warfare, followed by religious *fiestas* including ritual cannibalism. They might be mocking ritual warfare and cannibalism by having mere servants boast of their valor. Among the Aztecs of Preconquest Mexico, the noble warrior mystique was the highest value socially and religiously speaking. All reverence and solemnity accompanied the *"guerras floridas."* In this play, buffoons call themselves great warriors, and equate human game with suckling pigs and cakes from which one might get indigestion. Shame as a teaching technique was used in early Colonial Mexico as it is today, in an attempt to accelerate the changing of indigenous customs.

[4] *"Taco"* is the closest we can come to a translation of the Nahuatl word here. The word has the connotation of beans *(within) wrapped around by a tortilla*.

[5] This phrase "to blow an enchantment" is to be understood as literal. As before the Conquest in contemporary Mexico, both cures and hexes are still supposedly effected by blowing *(soplar)* either good or evil air in the direction of the patient or victim.

⁶ It is interesting to note that the four elements which were basic to the old Mexican cosmology are called upon in this manner. Although they were important in European alchemistic circles also, it is clear that they were familiar to the indigenous audience in terms of their own cultural tradition.

⁷ This passage is remarkably correct historically. It is generally accepted that Maxentius died at Saxa Rubra, near Rome. He tried to escape over the Milvian bridge into the city, but perished in the river instead. Maxentius is usually represented as a monster of rapacity and lust. William Smith, *Classical Dictionary of Biography, Mythology, and Geography* (New York: Harper and Brothers, 1884), p. 247.

⁸ This is a dramatized version of the *Apostle's Creed*. All the basic elements of the Christian belief-system are contained in this speech.

⁹ This is the first of a series of clearly anti-semitic allusions and jokes in this play. The Inquisition in Mexico becomes more comprehensible when we read the content of some of the history and religion lessons presented to the people in the process of their Christianization.

Notes To The Destruction Of Jerusalem

¹ *La Destrucción de Jerusalén*, translated and edited by Francisco Paso y Troncoso (Florence: Salvador Landi, 1907).

² *Ibid.*, p. 132.

³ *Ibid.*, p. 136.

⁴ *Ibid.*, p. 139.

⁵ There is no certain explanation as to why the prologue of this play contains the description that it concerns "the life of the Apostle James," for in fact it does not. It is likely that the Indian scribe either made a mistake or described another play which may have been presented immediately before *"The Destruction of Jerusalem,"* and dedicated to St. James on his day.

⁶ The phrase for "holding rule" here literally translated from Nahuatl would be "here are your tail and your wings." This is an example of both a phrase and a literary device often used in Nahautl. This is a kind of metonymy, a defining of one thing in terms of another. Here a domain or territory as ruled is spoken of as the "wings" and "tail" of the possessor or ruler.

⁷ This phrase referring to warriors is clearly taken from the Prehispanic days. Among the Aztecs, the two highest and most valiant military orders were those of the "Order of the Eagle" and the "Order of the Ocelot."

⁸ It is uncertain what is meant by "moves forward" in these directions. It is probable that in fifteenth-century Europe, where portals were often used as a part of the scenario, four columns and a chair represented the place of Herod. See Marianne Oeste de Bopp, *Influencia de los mysterios y autos europeos en los de México, op. cit.*, p. 119.

⁹ Here is another example of a figure of speech so often used in Nahautl, the phrase "your water and your mountains" to mean "your territories."

¹⁰ The author has used the word "trumpets" in the translation. The original says "wind music"; therefore, "flutes" could also be used. Instruments very similar to a valveless trumpet were used in Prehispanic as well as colonial Mexico, so the author has chosen to name this instrument as the more martial of the two.

¹¹ In his notes Paso y Troncoso mentions that the manner in which this particular speech of the Emperor is written is similar to that in which some of the legal documents of the early colonial period were composed. It has a legalistic tenor to it and the "moreovers" and the "therefores" as well as the concluding statement sound convincingly like an official pronouncement. This similarity would also indicate that the author of the play might have been a petty government official accustomed to such terminology.

¹² Apparently he was permitted to proceed with the weapon in hand and then to turn it over to the Emperor as a symbol of surrender.

[13] This mention of the "stone and the cudgel" is the Nahuatl way of describing public punishment and disgrace. Sahagún and others mention public beatings in squares and marketplaces to punish and disgrace wrongdoers. Thus the punishers were assured of an audience and a healthy fear of disobedience among the spectators: See Pomar y Zurita, *Relaciones de Tezcoco* (Mexico: Salvador Chavez Hayhoe, 1891), p. 123.

[14] The Nahuatl phrase states that the power belongs to the "chair" of the Emperor. In the Prehispanic codices, the ruler is often pictured as seated on a raised platform in a special "house" surrounded with other symbols of power. Thus the actual "chair" of the ruler is associated with the concept of the seat of authority.

[15] William Smith, *op. cit.*, pp. 52 and 427.

[16] *Ibid.*, p. 196.

Notes To Souls And Testamentary Executors

[1] Garibay, *Historia de la literatura nahuatl, op. cit.* II, 130.

[2] The combination of drums and a wind instrument such as a flute was the most common Prehispanic practice. It was typical of the basic instrumentation used in the early Post-conquest dramas and processions and is not uncommon in Mexico today.

[3] This stage direction is unclear. Perhaps it refers to some staging device which permits the devils to remain on the stage yet not be a part of the action. In this way, they sit under a table and become inobtrusively conspicuous.

[4] The plan is clearly to change the provisions of the will so they (the Executors) can profit from it.

[5] This speech of the First Executor epitomizes some of the hedonistic principles contained in the indigenous literary oral tradition. The idea of the brevity of life which ought to be enjoyed, therefore, was a familiar ideology to a sixteenth-century indigenous audience; for example:

". . . Perhaps it is only here on earth that fragrant flowers exist,
As well as those songs which are our happiness and joy.
Then enjoy them!
Take pleasure, oh Chichimecan princes, for we must go soon to his mansions;
To the dwelling place of Death, oh Prince Popocatzin. . . ."

Or again:

"Consider this earth only loaned to you, oh friends.
Tomorrow or soon afterwards, oh Giver-of-Life,
By your judgment we must go to your dwelling.
So let us rejoice, oh my companions."

Poesia Indígena, edited and translated by Angel María Garibay (Mexico: Universidad Nacional Autónoma de México, 1962), pp. 106 and 112.

[6] This reference to spiritual cleansing interpreted as ritual washing of the body (in many parts) is comprehensible in the light of the Pre- and Post-Conquest indigenous practice of the same. Sahagún, Landa, and others refer to this custom. It is practiced in contemporary Mexico in the form of a post-baptismal handwashing (*"lavada de manos"*) of the *padrino* and *madrina* (Godparents) and by their respective *compadres*. Other ritual washings include those of corpses, and those before marriage. These rituals are practiced by the indigenous population only. See Robert Ravicz, The Washing of the Hands: A Structural element of indigenous Interpretation of Christian Baptism," *Summa Anthropologica en homenaje a Roberto Weitlaner* (Mexico: Instituto Nacional de Antropología e Historia, 1966), pp. 281-290.

[7] The burden-image refers to a very popular manner of carrying things in Mexico; that is from a tumpline which is suspended from the forehead and

attached to a net *(ayate)* or basket *(tenate)* which rests on the upper back and shoulders.

⁸ Again, the staging of this play is problematic, especially because of the ambiguity of the stage directions. It must be left to our imagination how the heavens opened and how the host of souls was garbed and presented. Apparently heaven was "offstage" to one side and designated by the presence of a cross. Until this point, God has been included in the cast only by implication and reference. We can assume that God and Jesus Christ are the same characters in this drama, thus to avoid at least the Arian heresy.

⁹ The Nahuatl is, "Oh four hundred times unfortunate that I am. . . ." This is the usual usage of "four hundred," which simply means a great number, or repeatedly.

¹⁰ The spiritual investment is made doubly clear here. Those who have masses said for the dead are rewarded in kind by the already dead who naturally wish them long life. The forgotten soul rather vindictively beseeches the heavenly power to shorten the life of the one who has forgotten him.

¹¹ The concept of Hell is most interesting, and rather like that of a torture chamber. A more literal translation of "wheel of fire" is "fire-wood gladiatorial stone"; and for "Fire-bath place," is "fire-smoke-water-place." These descriptions actually reflect some of the punishments used in Prehispanic indigenous Mexico; gladiators were used in ritual ways during *fiestas* as sacrificial victims, and children were sometimes punished by being made to inhale smoke from burning chilis.

¹² In contemporary Mexico, the celebration of the festival of *Todos Santos* (All Saints' Day) is one of the most highly inflected celebrations of the year. In the more indigenous areas, the following elements are usually included in the *fiesta*, which lasts from three to six days: the making of household altars of food and floral offerings to the souls of the familial dead; floral arrangements, including petal-pathways, usually of marigolds *(cempoalzochitl)*, outside the houses to direct the spirits of the dead to their residences and proper altars; all night encampments in the cemeteries with portable altars decorated with flowers, fruit, bread, etc., for the nourishment of the souls of the departed: refurbishing of the graves, including new markers, crosses, or the repainting of old decorations; the use of *fiesta* foods including *mole,* special breads, candy skulls (with the name of the commemorated in frosting), candy animals; the giving of toys in the form of skeletons, funeral-processions, grinning *papier mâché* skulls brightly painted, and miniature orchestras of skeletons. The basic idea here seems to be one of *remembrance* of the souls of the dead, and, in the case of the toys, a tongue-in-cheek reminder of the transitoriness of life. Masses are said daily for the alleviation of whatever sufferings the souls of the dead might be undergoing. See Octavio Paz, "Todos Santos, dia de muertos," *Evergreen Review,* November, 1959, pp. 22-37, *passim.*

¹³ Ravicz, *"The Compadrinazgo," op. cit., passim.*

Bibliography

Acosta, José de, S. . *Historia natural y moral de las Indias.* Seville: Casa de Juan de Leon, 1590.

———. *The Naturall and Moral Historie of the East and West Indies.* London: Printed by Val Sims for Edward Blount and William Aspley, 1604.

Arrom, José Juan. *El teatro de hispanoamérica en la época colonial.* Havana: Anuario Bibliograficao Cubano, 1956.

———. "Raíces indígenas del teatro americano," *Selected Papers of the XXIXth International Congress of Americanists.* Chicago: University of Chicago Press, 1952, pp. 299-305.

Arroyo, Estéban. *Los dominicos forjadores de la civilización oajaqueña, los misioneros.* Mexico: Imprenta "Camarena," 1958, Vol. I.

Ballinger, Rex E. *"Origenes del teatro español y sus primeros manifestaciónes en la Nueva España."* Unpublished thesis from the National Autonomous University of Mexico Library, 1951.

Brinton, David G. *Ancient Nahuatl Poetry, Containing the Nahuatl Texts of XXVII Ancient Mexican Poems.* (Library of Aboriginal American Literature, No. VII) Philadelphia, 1887.

———. *The Güegüence, A Comedy Ballet in the Nahuatl Spanish Dialect of Nicaragua.* (Library of Aboriginal American Literature, No. III) Philadelphia, 1883.

Caso, Alfonso. "Importancia y caracaterísticas de la religión," *México prehispanico.* Mexico: Impreso por Rafael Loera y Chavez para la Editorial Emma Hurtado, 1946, pp. 343-347.

———. "Mecanismo del calendario azteca," *México prehispanico.* Mexico: Impreso por Rafael Loera y Chavez para la Editorial Emma Hurtado, 1946, pp. 394-399.

———. "Organización sacerdotal," *México prehispanico.* Mexico: Impreso por Rafael Loera y Chavez para la Editorial Emma Hurtado, 1946, pp. 348-354.

Castañeda, C. E. "The First American Play," *Preliminary Studies of the Texas Catholic Historical Society.* Austin: St. Edward's University. Vol. III, No. 1 (January, 1936). (This was also published in *The Catholic World,* January, 1932).

Cornyn, John H. "Aztec Literature," *International Congress of Americanists.* Mexico: Instituto Nacional de Antropología e Historia, 1947, pp. 322-336.

———. and McAfee. Byron. Translated and edited. "Tlacahuapahualiztli," *Tlalocan,* I, No. 4 (1944), 314-351.

Cortés, Hernán. *Cartas de relación de la conquista de Méjico.* Vol. II. Madrid: Espasa-Calpe, 1942.

Dávila Padilla, Agustín. *Historia de la fundación y discurso de la provincia de Santiago de México de la Orden de Predicadores.* Mexico: Editorial Academia Literaria, 1955.

Diaz del Castillo, Bernal. *The Discovery and Conquest of Mexico.* New York: Farrar, Straus, and Cudahy, 1956.

Durán, Diego, O. P. *Historia de las Indias de Nueva España.* Mexico: Editorial Nacional, 1951.

García, Genaro. *Documentos inéditos o muy raros para la historia de México, El clero de México durante la dominación española.* Vol. XV. Mexico: Librería de la Vda. de Ch. Bouret, 1907.

García Icazbalceta J. *Bibliografía mexicana de siglo XVI, catálogo razonado de*

libros impresos en México de 1539 á 1600. Mexicos Fondo de Cultura Económica, 1954.
─────. Introduction to Hernán González de Esclava. *Coloquios espirituales y sacramentales y poesías sagradas.* No. 3. Mexico: Antigua Librería Portal de los Agustinos, 1877.
─────. "La instrucción pública en México durante el siglo XVI," *Obras, opúsculos varios,* I, 163-270. Mexico: Imprenta de V. Agüeros, 1896.
─────. "Representaciones religiosas de México en el siglo XVI," *Obras, opúsculos varios,* II, 307-368. Mexico: Imprenta de V. Agüeros, 1896.
Garibay, Angel María. *Historia de la literatura nahuatl,* Vols. I and II. Mexico: Editorial Porrua, 1953.
─────. Translated and edited. "Hueyhueytlatolli," *Tlalocan,* I, No. 2 (1943), 31-53.
─────. *Llave del Nahuatl.* Mexico: Editorial Porrua, 1961.
─────. (Translated and edited), *Poesía indigena.* Mexico: Universidad Nacional Autónoma, 1962.
─────. *Vida económica de Tenochtitlan. L. pochtecáyotl (arte de traficar).* Mexico: Universidad Nacional Autónoma de México, 1961.
Gibson, Charles. *The Aztecs under Spanish Rule.* Stanford: Stanford University Press, 1964.
─────. *Tlaxcala in the Sixteenth Century.* New Haven: Yale University Press, 1952.
Gillmor, Frances. "The Dance Dramas of Mexican Villages," *University of Arizona Bulletin.* XIV, No. 2. *Humanities Bulletin,* No. 5, Tucson.
─────. "Spanish Texts of Three Dance Dramas from Mexican Villages," *University of Arizona Bulletin.* Vol. XIII, No. 4. *Humanities Bulletin,* No. 4, Tucson.
Gonzalez de Esclava, Hernán. *Coloquios espirituales y sacramentales y poesías sagradas.* No. 3. Mexico: Antigua Librería, Portal de los Agustinos, 1877.
Icaza, Francisco A. "Orígines del teatro en México, *Boletín de la Real Academia Española,* II, (1915), 56-76.
Johnson, Harvey Leroy. *An Edition of "Triunfo de los santos."* Philadelphia: University of Pennsylvania Press, 1941.
León-Portilla, Miguel. *Aztec Thought and Culture.* Translated by Jack Emory Davis. Norman: University of Oklahoma Press, 1963.
─────. *Los maestros prehispanicos de la palabra.* Cuadernos Americanos. Mexico: Cuadernos Americanos, 1962.
─────. "Teatro nahuatl prehispanico," *La palabra y el hombre,* No. 9, Feb.-March, 1959, pp. 13-36.
─────. "Tres formas de pensamiento nahuatl," in *Cuadernos del seminario de problemas científicos y filosóficos,* No. 14, Second series. Mexico: Universidad Nacional Autónoma de México, 1959.
Lorenzana, Francisco. *Consilios provinciales.* Mexico, 1769.
McAfee, Byron and Barlow, R. H. (Translated and edited), "Un cuaderno de Marqueses," *El México Antiguo,* VI, Nos. 9-12 (March, 1947) 392-404.
Magaña Esquivel, Antonio, and Ruth S. Lamb. *Breve historia del teatro mexicano.* Manuales Studium No. 8, Mexico: Ediciones de Andrea, 1958.
María y Campos, Armando. *Guia de representaciónes teatrales en la Nueva España.* Mexico: Costa-Amic, 1959.
Marie, Sister Joseph. *The Role of the Church and the Folk in the Development of the Early Drama in New Mexico.* Philadelphia: University of Pennsylvania Press, 1948.

Martí, Samuel. *Canto, Danza y música precortesianos*. Mexico: Fondo de Cultura Económica, 1961.
Martinez Espinosa, Ignacio. "La estética y el significado de las pirámides." *Boletín bibliográfico de la Secretaría de Hacienda y Crédito Público*, No. 272, Year IX, June 1963, pp. 16-17.
Mendieta, Fray Gerónimo de. *Historia eclesiástica indiana*. Mexico: Editorial Salvador Chavez Hayhoe, 1945.
——. *Vidas Franciscanos*. Mexico: Imprenta Universitaria, 1945.
Molina, Alonso de *Colección de incunables americanos, siglos XVI, vocabulario en lengua castellana y mexicana*, IV. Madrid: Ediciones Cultura Hispanica, 1944.
Monterde, Francisco. (ed.) *Teatro indígena prehispanico, Rabinal Achi*. Mexico: Imprenta Universitaria, 1955.
Motolinía, Fray Toribio de Benavente. *History of the Indians of New Spain*. Translated by Elizabeth Andros Foster. Berkeley: The Cortes Society, 1950.
——. *Memoriales*. Mexico: Luis García Pimentel, 1963.
Noguera, Eduardo. "Huitzilopochtli," *México prehispanico*. Mexico: Impreso por Rafael Loera y Chavez para la Editorial Emma Hurtado, 1946, pp. 454-457.
Oeste de Bopp, Marianne. "Autos mexicanos del siglo XVI," *Historia Mexicana*, III, No. 9 (July-August, 1953), 112-123.
——. *Influencia de los misterios y autos europeos en los de México*. Unpublished thesis in the Library of the Faculty of Philosophy and Letters, at the National Autonomous University of Mexico, 1952.
Orozco y Berra, Manuel. *Códice Ramirez*. Edited with commentary. Also entitled, *Relación de los indios que habitan esta Nueva España según sus historias*. Mexico: Editorial Leyenda, 1944.
Paso y Troncoso, Francisco del. *Adoración de los Reyes*. Translated, edited, and annotated. Florence: Salvador Landi, 1900.
——. *Destrucción de Jerusalén*. Translated, edited, and annotated Florence: Salvador Landi, 1907.
——. *Invención de la Santa Cruz por Santa Elena*. Translated, edited, and annotated. Mexico: Imprenta del Museo Nacional, 1890.
——. *Sacrificio de Isaác*. Translated, edited, and annotated. Florence: Salvador Landi, 1899.
Paz, Octavio. "Todos Santos, dia de muertos," *Evergreen Review* (1959), November, pp. 22-37.
Pazos, Manuel. "El teatro franciscano en México durante el siglo XVI," *Archivo Iberoamericana*, Madrid, XI, No. 42 (April-June, 1951), 129-189.
Pimentel, Fernando Horcasitas, "Piezas teatrales en lengua nahuatl: Bibliografía Descriptiva," *Boletín Bibliográfico de Antropología Americana*, XI (1949), 154-164. Mexico: Instituto Panamericano de Geografia e Historia.
Plancarte. Alfonso M. "Piezas teatrales en Nueva España del XVI," *Abside*, VI, No. 2, (April-June, 1942), 218-224.
Pomar y Zurita. *Relaciones de Tezcoco*. Mexico: Salvador Chavez Hayhoe, 1891.
Ravicz, Robert. "Compadrinazgo," *Handbook of Middle American Indians*. VI, 238-252. Austin: University of Texas Press, 1967.
——. "La Mixteca en el estudio comparativo del hongo alucinante," *Anales*, Instituto Nacional de Antropología e Historia, XIII, 73-92. Mexico: Secretaría de Educación Pública.
——. "The Washing of the Hands: A Structural Element in Indigenous Interpretation of Christian Baptism," *Summa Anthropologica en homenaje*

a Roberto J. Weitlaner. 281-290. Mexico: Instituto Nacional de Antropología e Historia, 1966.

Simeón, Rémi. *Annales de Domingo Francisco de San Anton Muñon [Chimalpahin Quauhtlehuanitzin.]* Sixième et septième relations. Translated and edited. Paris: Maisonneuve et C. Leclerc, 1889.

Rey, Agapito. *Cultura y costumbres del siglo XVI en la península ibérica y en la Nueva España*. Mexico: Ediciones Mensaje, 1944.

Reyes, Alfonso. "Los autos sacramentales en España y América," *Boletín de la Academia de letras*, pp. 349-360. Buenos Aires: 1937.

———. "Teatro misionero," *Letras de la Nueva España*, pp. 57-66. Mexico: Fondo de Cultura Económica, 1948.

Ricard, Robert. *La Conquête Spirituelle du Mexique*. Paris: Institut d'Ethnologie, 1933.

———. *The Spiritual Conquest of Mexico*. Translated by Lesley Byrd Simpson. Berkeley: University of California Press, 1966.

Robelo, Cecilio A. *Diccionario de aztequismos*. Mexico: Ediciones Fuente Cultural, 3rd ed., n. d.

Rojas Garcidueñas, José. *Autos y coloquios del siglo XVI*. Mexico: Ediciones de la Universidad Nacional Autónoma de México, 1939.

———. "Fiesta in México en 1578," *Anales del Instituto de Investigaciones Estéticas*, Mexico, IX (1942), 33-57.

———. "Los primeros misioneros y el teatro de evangelización," *Divulgación Historica*, I No. 11, (Sept. 15, 1940), 475-482.

———. El Teatro de Nueva España en el siglo XVI. Mexico: Published by the author, 1935.

Sahagún, Bernardino de, O. F. M. "Informantes de Sahagún," in "Paralipómenos de Sahagún," Translated by Angel M. Garibay. *Revista Tlalocan* (Azcatpotzalco, D.F.:), XI, No. 3 (1947).

———. *El libro de las pláticas o coloquios de los doce primeros misioneros de México. Miscellanea Francesco*, Ehrle III. Rome: Pou and Martí, 1924.

———. *Florentine Codex*. Translated and annotated by Arthur J. O. Anderson, and Charles E. Dibble. Santa Fe: The School of American Research and the University of Utah, dates by volume.

———. *Historia general de las cosas de Nueva España*. Edited and annotated by Angel María Garibay. Mexico: Editorial Porrua, 1956.

Sanchez de Aguilar, Pedro. *Informe contra idolorum cultores*. Merida: E. G. Triay y Hijos, 1937.

Santos y Salazar, Manuel de los. *Invención de la Santa Cruz por Santa Elena*. Translated and annotated by Francisco del Paso y Troncoso. Mexico: Imprenta del Museo Nacional, 1890.

Schilling, Hildburg. *Teatro profano en la Nueva España*. Mexico: Imprenta Universitaria, 1958.

Shoemaker, William Hutchinson. *The Multiple Stage in Spain during the Fifteenth and Sixteenth Centuries*. Princeton: Princeton University Press, 1935.

Smith, William. *Classical Dictionary of Biography, Mythology, and Geography*. New York: Harper and Brothers, 1884.

Soustelle, Jacques. *La pensée cosmologique des anciens mexicains*. Paris: Hermann et Cie, 1940.

Torquemada, Juan de. *Monarquía indiana*. Mexico: Editorial Salvador Chavez Hayhoe, 1944.

Wasson, V. P. and R. G. *Mushrooms Russia and History*. New York: Pantheon Books, 1957.

MISCELLANEA:

Actas de cabildo de Puebla. (various) In manuscript form in the Palafox Library in Puebla, Mexico.
New Catholic Encyclopedia. Prepared and edited by The Catholic University of America Staff. New York: The McGraw-Hill Co., 1967.
Cantares mexicanos. Archives of the National Library of Mexico.
Códice Franciscano, siglo XVI. Mexico: Editorial Salvador Chavez Hayhoe, 1941.
Poesía nahuatl. This is a long-playing record the songs of which are translated and edited by Miguel León-Portilla. Mexico: Universidad Nacional Autónoma de México, 1962.
"Comedia y drama precolombinos," lecture presented on August 22, 1961, by Miguel León-Portilla, under the auspices of Dirección Geneṙál de Difusión Cultural, and the Teatro Estudiantil de la Universidad Nacional Autónoma de México.

SUPPLEMENTAL BIBLIOGRAPHY OF RELATED WORKS:

Barrera y Leirado. *Catálogo bibliográfico del teatro antiguo español desde sus orígines hasta mediados del siglo XVIII.*
Campa, Arthur León. "The Churchmen and the Indian Languages of New Spain," *The Hispanic American Historical Review,* XI, (November, 1931), 542-550.
Charles, Pierre. "Le théâtre missionnaire après la conversion," *Les Dossiers de l'action missionnaire,* No. 140. Louvain, pp. 181-191.
Garate, Román Zulaica. *Los franciscanos y la imprenta en México en el siglo XVI.* Mexico: P. Robredo, 1939.
Jiménez Rueda, Julio. "Aspectos del teatro español de los siglos de oro," *Historia de la literatura mexicana.* Mexico: Ediciones Botas, 1934.
———. "Documentos para la historia del teatro en la Nueva España," *Boletín del Archivo Generál de la Nación.* Mexico, XV, No. 1 (1944), 101-144.
Magaña Esquivel, Antonio. "Formas dramáticas indígenas," *Revista mexicana de cultura,* Supplement of *El Nacional,* No. 317, April 26, 1953.
Monterde, Francisco. "Pastorals and Popular Performances, the Drama of Viceregal Mexico," *Theater Arts Monthly,* XXII, No. 8, (August, 1938), 597-602.
Paso y Troncoso, Francisco del. "Comédies en langue nahuatl," *Selected Papers of the XIIth International Congress of Americanists.* pp. 309-316. Paris: Ernest Leroux, 1902.
Torre, Revello. José. *Orígenes del teatro en hispano-américa.* Buenos Aires: Instituto Nacional de Estudios de Teatro, 1937.
Weckman, Luis. "The Middle Ages in the Conquest of America." *Speculum,* XXVI, No. 1 (January, 1951), 130-141.

Index

Acculturation, 1, 3, 31, 46, 82
Acosta, Jose de, 39
"Adoration of the Kings," 65-66, 119-140
Adultery, 141, 228, 230
Angels, 120, 123, 220
  guardian, 100-101, 114-116, 156-157, 213-220
Antichrist, 149, 151, 157
Anti-Semitism, 248 n. 9
Architecture, of Mexican churches, 79
Authority, obedience to religious 94-96, 97, 166-167, 172
  secular, 59, 91-93, 97, 156, 196-200, 208, 235-236
"Auto sacramentale," 28-30, 47, 63, 240 n. 54
Aztec Indians
  calendar, 5, 9, 10-11, 100
  gods, 8
  kings, 72-74
  language, see Nahuatl
  music and dance, 12-14, 20-24, 39-42
  prostitution, 17-19
  religiosity, 4, 41-42
  rituals, 9-11, 16, 32
  theaters, 23-24
  warfare, 4-5, 11, 41-42, 179, 250 n. 3

Baptism, 36, 72-73, 172-173, 188-189, 204, 252 n. 6
Bautista, Juan, 67-68
Bishop, role of, 166-167, 172

Cannibalism, 183, 250 n. 3
"Cantares Mexicanos," 12-13
"Carros," 63, 78
Catechism, 36-38, 41
Censorship, of drama, 74-78, 140
Christ. See Jesus Christ
Christmas, 43-44, 65-66
Church, Holy, 145-146
Church Council, First (1555), on music and dance, 40-41
Colleges, 33, 70
"Coloquios," 29, 66
Comedy
  Prehispanic, 19-20, 21, 23, 25
  secular, 39, 42, 62, 67
  colonial religious, 74-77, 168-169, 173, 178-179, 203

Commandments, the five of the Church, 229
Commandments, Ten, 212-213, 227-229
Communion, 229, 232
Confession, 100, 111-116, 117, 141, 147, 149, 229
"Conquest of Jerusalem," 54-55
Conquest, Spanish, 30, 40-42, 58
Constantine, Emperor, 160-179
"Conversion de San Pablo," 47-48
Cornyn, John, 57, 142, 211
"Corpus Christi," 25, 28, 29, 47, 51, 67, 160, 178
Cortes, quoted, 23, 30-31, 72
Costumes, 12-14, 20, 23, 55, 68 121
Cross Holy, 160, 165, 168, 171 173, 176-177
Crucifixion, 208

Dead, cult of, 59, 212-233, 253 n. 12
Death, 59-60, 61, 146-147
"Destruction of Jerusalem," 181-209, 235
Devil. See also Lucifer, 100, 114, 160-179
Devils, 143-156, 216-218, 220-222
Diaz, Bernal, 30
Dominicans, 36, 68
Drama, humanistic, 39, 62, 64, 99-100
Drama, missionary in sixteenth century, 38-39, 48-71
  didactic purpose of, 48, 58-59, 66-67, 69, 74, 141, 156, 183, 208, 212
  indigenous culture used, 47-48, 58, 73-74, 80, 84, 97, 100, 157, 182
  music and dance, 80, 120-121, 138, 160, 213
Drama, profane, 70, 74-77
Drama, Spanish liturgical, 27-29

Easter, 10
Education. See also schools. 40-41, 57-58, 67, 72-74, 86, 208, 235, 246 n. 1
Epiphany, 65-66, 83, 120, 139
Esclava, Gonzalez de, 71
Eucharist, 28, 73-74, 240 n. 54
Evil, 56, 160, 166-168
"Examples," 67

Farce. See comedy
"Fiestas," 10-11, 21, 63, 81

261

Index

"Final Judgment," 49-51, 100, 141-157, 233, 235
"Flor y canto," 236
Franciscans, 31, 34, 36, 43
Fuensalida, Luis de, 57
Gante, Pedro de, 34-36, 45, 47
Garibay, Angel Maria, 45, 47
Hallucination, 73-74
Hell, 144, 146, 148, 157, 253 n. 11
"Hongol," 72-74
"How the Blessed St. Helen Found the Holy Cross," 159-179, 235
Huitzilopochtli, 4, 22

Jesuits, 36, 61, 64, 69-70
Jesus Christ, 60-61, 86-87, 143-156, 184-209, 224-225, 230
Jews. See also Anti-Semitism. 123, 161, 174-176, 184
Jimenez, Martin, 68
Judas, 159-179

Latin, 35, 70, 181-183
Life, brevity of, 7, 160, 252 n. 5
Lucifer, 143-157, 214, 226

McAfee, Byron, 50, 142, 211
Marriage, 146, 148-149, 156
Mary, Virgin, 58-61, 123, 141, 224
Mass, 134, 139, 179
   for the dead, 212-214 216, 220-221, 228
Mayan Indians, 24-25
"Merchant, the," 99-118, 233, 235
Merchants, social status of, 117
Mexican Roman Catholicism, 3, 32, 82, 232, 236, 247 n. 1
Miracles, 170, 176, 201
Missionaries, 30-38
   and education, 32-36
   and poetry, 41-47
Montufar, Alonso de, 75
Motolinía, Toribio, 51-53, 208
Mushrooms, hallucenogenic, 73-74

Nahuatl Indians
   cosmology, 6-8
   language, 10, 30, 58, 81, 83-85, 182-183, 211-212, 238 n. 16
   poetry, 12-16
   priests, 10, 12
   "senores," 11-12
Necromancers, 160, 170, 179

Obedience, to authority. See Authority
Offerings, for souls of the dead, 222-224

Olmos, Andres de, 142
"Open chapel," 79

Passion of Christ, 64-65, 67, 69
Pilate, 184-209
Ponce, Alonso, 120, 138-139, 140
Prayers, for souls of the dead, 222-224
Prizes, for drama, 20, 62, 63, 76
Processions 48-49, 51-56, 65
Prostitution, 17-19
Puppeteers, 20
Purgatory. See also Hell. 212, 214, 217, 220-221, 224-225, 230, 232

Quetzalcoatl, 14, 15, 16, 21, 48, 238 n. 29, 250 n. 10

"Rabinal Achi," 24, 81
Ramirez, Juan Perez, 62
Relics, religious, 160, 178-179, 186-188, 207-208

Sacraments, 51-52, 59, 213, 218, 223, 233, 236
Sacrifice, human, 1 2, 5, 10-11, 17, 24, 30, 42, 95-97 179
"Sacrifice of Isaac The," 89-90, 235
Saints, 58, 64, 66, 235-236
   St. Christopher, 46
   St. Francis, 56
   St. Helen, 159-179
   St. Michael, 143-156, 225, 227-229, 231
   St. Paul, 48
   St. Sebastian, 48
   St. Sylvester, 166-167, 171-172
Salazar, Santos y, 159
Salvation, 176, 179, 214
"San José de Belén de los Naturales," 34, 47
Satan. See also Devil. 143-159
Schools. See also Colleges. 20-21, 34-36, 241 n. 61
Settings, dramatic, 23-25, 78-79, 101, 120, 138-139
Sin, 100, 144-147, 148, 213, 218-219, 224, 228-230
Skull-rack, 1-2, 236
"Souls and Testamentary Executors," 211-234
Spain, King of, as censor of drama, 74-76
Stage props, 80
Suffering, 214, 219, 225-226, 230-231
Supernatural personages, 59, 141, 160

"Tablado," 78, 246 n. 165
Temples, 23-24
Ten Commandments. See Commandments
"Teponaztli," 13, 238 n. 23
"Teuquiquixti," 20
Tezcatlipoca, 10
Theaters, Prehispanic, 23-25
"Tlacahuapahualiztli," 57-60
Tlaxcala, 72-74, 182, 208
Toltec Indians, 4-6
"Triumph of the Saints," 64, 70
Troubadours, Aztec, 17
Troncoso, Paso y, 119, 123, 159, 181-183
"Tzompantli," 1-2

Uixtociuatl, 11
Usury, 102-117

Vasquez, Bernabe, 83, 119
Virgin Mary. See Mary, Virgin
Visions, 162, 165, 170-171

Wealth, 100, 117, 160, 213-215, 219, 226, 228, 233, 236
Wizards 160-179
Women roles in drama, 233-234

Zumárraga, first Bishop of Mexico, 50, 74-75, 77